RENEWALS 458-4574

DATE DUE

GAYLORD			PRINTED IN U.S.A.

THE AMERICAN WILDERNESS

THOMAS R. VALE

ᵀᴴᴱ American Wilderness

Reflections on Nature Protection
in the United States

UNIVERSITY OF VIRGINIA PRESS

CHARLOTTESVILLE AND LONDON

University of Virginia Press
© 2005 by the Rector and Visitors of the University of Virginia
All rights reserved
Printed in the United States of America on acid-free paper
First published 2005

9 8 7 6 5 4 3 2 1

LIBRARY OF CONGRESS CATALOGING-IN-PUBLICATION DATA

Vale, Thomas R., 1943–
    The American wilderness : reflections on nature protection in
the United States / Thomas R. Vale.
        p.   cm.
    Includes bibliographical references and index.
    ISBN 0-8139-2336-0 (cloth : alk. paper)
    1. Nature conservation—United States. I. Title.
QH76.V25 2005
333.72′0973—dc22

2004026001

This book is published in association with the Center for American Places,
Santa Fe, New Mexico, and Staunton, Virginia (www.americanplaces.org).

For Gerry

CONTENTS

THE AMERICAN WILDERNESS

INTRODUCTION   Secure atop North Dome, 3,500 feet above Yosemite Valley, I scan an immense landscape that soars above my already elevated perch more than it arches off and falls away below my feet. Exfoliated domes and glacially steepened cliffs, sentineled Jeffrey pine and rock-hugging huckleberry oak, scampering yellow-pine chipmunks and darting white-throated swifts, sand grains partially filling linear rock joints and desiccated ovate leaves carpeting the rolls of rock beneath the oaks, towering cumulus rising over the higher Sierra peaks to the east and intense sun beating down on the convex dome of glaring gray granite where I stand—together they tell me where I am as much as the massive face of Half Dome rising immediately beyond Tenaya Canyon. But the identity of this landscape comes too from what humans have done and continue to do here. It was the first wild landscape protected by Congress, initially a singular action but then a beginning for systems of parks and wilderness and refuges. It reversed the intentions of a world wanderer, John Muir, who sat—the verb is correct, *sat*—long hours on this very dome during his first, rooting summer in the Sierra. It became the cause célèbre for the most influential and well-known conservation group today, the Sierra Club, and an annual destination for visitors, in the late nineteenth century in the hundreds, today in the millions. It has been a focus of recreation debates—fire fall and golf course (gone), automobile and horseback riding (questioned), rock climbing, tube riding, and bicycling (in need of questioning). It is a locale for modern programs of nature manipulation—meadow and black oak restoration, black bear management, peregrine falcon reintroduction, prescribed burning. It is a landscape of nature, protected by people, debated by people, enriched—because of that protection and that debate—by people, a landscape that binds the natural and human worlds together, a landscape made a place by that binding.

This book offers an overview—a descriptive synthesis—of nature protection in the United States. Its favored approach is typological, with the structured taxonomies encouraging the identification of similarities and differences among the various phenomena. Comparisons and dissections developed from these categorizations may be read as analyses, although the book's strength remains its broad sweep and sense of organization. This weaving together of disparate threads constructs a cloth that I hope will enhance appreciation of the extent and richness of sentiment and action for nature protection in this country. That intellectual appreciation—the sense that nature protection derives from multiple motivations and expresses itself in various ways—forms a primary purpose of the book. It is a purpose well served by description and unification.

Synthesis, however, offers more than mere awareness. By seeing the sweeping structure of nature protection, a reader should come to accept reserves of wild landscape as a legitimate natural resource. No less than farmland or energy sources or timber or water or minerals, the protected areas of parks and wilderness and refuges conform to the meaning of any natural resource—something in the natural world that serves a human need (an anthropocentric definition, yes, but nothing to apologize for). Any of us may disagree on what human needs should be served in American society, but only insensitive arrogance would casually dismiss the expressed needs of at least a substantial part of the population.

The diversity of both those perceived needs and their expression in policy, moreover, requires that the synthesis mingle new ideas with old. Whatever the virtues of contemporary interpretations of this resource—some of which express disapproval—they should not be seen as modern, truthful views supplanting older, false ones; intellectual progress, in this case, emerges from diverse enrichment rather than categorical replacement. The fertile overview recognizes, then, that the phenomenon of nature protection involves more than deconstruction of key words or expressions of power relations or applications of conservation biology or devolution of decision making to local communities, just as it encompasses more than romantic ideals about the natural world or heroic tales of conservation success or historical sagas of American policy. Nature protection in its full richness is all these things and more.

If to synthesize is the primary purpose of this book, a second goal is to demonstrate that—contrary to expressions in some recent literature—acts of nature protection represent a linking of people and the natural world. This linking results from the human deed of bounding and protecting a piece of wild landscape as a reserve. That deed necessarily involves a diverse array of human interactions with the reserved landscape's natural characteristics: the perceiving of symbolic meanings, the understanding of historical change, the questioning of land use policies, the identifying of appropriate recreation, the struggling with diverse human purposes, even the problem of deciding what "protection" and "natural" mean. "Connections" focus on protected and conserved nature no less than on harvested and converted nature. To say otherwise is to misunderstand the profoundly human act of nature protection.

The connections, in turn, transform protected landscapes into places. A concept continuously redefined, reevaluated, and reinvented, "place" enjoys a central spot within geography, an axillary position in many other disciplines. But even among geographers, the meaning of the concept varies enormously. Places may be defined as landscapes of people and nature, particularly involving blends of subjective and objective knowledge (Johnston 1991, Entrikin as discussed by Barnes and Gregory 1997, M. Smith 2001). Places are described as locales with specific, even unique characteristics (Meinig as quoted by Findlay and White 1999: x). They are said to be areas controlled by human institutions (Sack 1986), involved with human emotions (Tuan 1979), or defined by social interactions, particularly those expressing differential power relations (Massey 1994; Feld and Basso, eds., 1996; cf. Hoelscher 1998). In this book, the concept of place reflects elements of all these expressions, although I see the notion of linkages between the human and natural worlds as pivotal to the place-creation of protected landscapes. Such linkages create the site-specific characteristics of a myriad of nature reserves, bounded territories defended by devotees who express their wishes in the political arena.

The tone in this book appears in little of the written and published work on landscapes of protected nature. Most books and articles on parks, wilderness, and other wildland reserves rather easily fall into two distinct groups. The first simply celebrates, typically uncritically, either the elements of the protected natural world or the success of the nature protection activity. The writings in the second group, by contrast, share the tone of critique. Criticism appears as frustration with a presumed failure of the protection effort—too much attention to scenery, too much accommodation for recreation, too little scientific management. Or the critical interpretation expresses outright disdain for the protectionist enterprise as either a manifestation of social injustice or a misguided idealization of what is conceived to be "natural." In this book, a combination of these two characteristics—celebration and criticism—dominates the tone. I recognize and even applaud the success of the nature protection effort but question some of the specifics of attitude and policy, including a few specifics most cherished by wilderness enthusiasts. I take the stance of a celebratory critic.

This is a perspective that may please no one. Environmental activists may read too much celebration, too little doom and despair; development-minded promoters will find too strong an embrace of nature protection, too little accommodation of nature harvesting; academic social scientists may see too much recognition of the natural world as real and distinct, too little appreciation for the social construction of nature. The book's tone reflects not simply my position as an enthusiastic supporter of nature protection, my enthusiasm tempered by skepticism of some of the specific expressions of the protectionist sentiment; the tone also reflects my conviction that critique unbuffered by celebration can generate only ulcers of cynicism. I take some comfort in one of the final essays written by Stephen Jay Gould, who articulates the virtues of celebration combined with criticism, the "awe of reverence mix[ed] with the skepticism of learning" (Gould 2002: 57).

Beyond overall tone, five additional points help to position the discussions in this book. Although they appear in various places in the following chapters, they deserve specific attention here.

First, when I talk about "American" characteristics—such as American attitudes toward landscape or American traditions in outdoor recreation—I realize that I am vulnerable to the stigma of "essentialism." I am aware that not all citizens, much less all residents, hold similar feelings and values regarding the subjects I discuss, and that attributes I associate with Americans may equally characterize people in other countries. Yet between the extreme individualism that recognizes that no two individuals are identical and the extreme essentialism that sees national traits equally replicated in all who live here, some generalities can be applied to large numbers of Americans who involve themselves with the natural world and express concern for or against nature protection. These are the people I am referring to when I speak of "Americans," specifically those whose values and activities influence society's institutional embrace of parks, wilderness, and refuges.

Second, the focus on those Americans who support nature protection invites the criticism that the discussions derive from a particular (elite) class-based perspective. They, in fact, do so derive, as must treatments of a wide range of other admirable topics, from higher education to fine arts to much social criticism; consider the tiny elite who know the meaning of "essentialism," certainly an intellectual shibboleth. In fact, chapter 2 argues precisely the point that nature protection rests with those who are well fed ("full-stomach environmentalism") and well educated.

Third, I appreciate at least some of the difficulties with the word "nature" and its adjectival form, "natural." Although the book's purpose precludes prolonged focus on these difficulties, the text in many places involves itself with the vagueness and multiple meanings of the terms. Certainly I believe that an external nature exists and that the counterassertion, that nature is nothing more than a social construction, is "outlandish" (Castree 2001: 16). I also might gently observe that the situations often cited as evidence of such social construction—natural hazards affecting social groups unequally (Blaikie et al. 1994), famines differentially devastating peoples in low social classes (Watts 1983), vagaries of nature influencing humans unevenly because of political economic structures (Yapa 1996), and toxic pollutions harming less powerful groups (Heiman 1996)—express interactions between the human and natural worlds more than the nature of nature itself. Similarly, I appreciate that bounding a wild landscape and calling it "natural" is a humane act (that is, a social construction) but I suggest that features within the bounded landscape may nonetheless be produced by natural forces.

Fourth, in spite of recognizing the broad areas of overlap between the human and natural worlds and the confusion resulting from that overlap (for example, see Vale, ed., 2002: 2–9), I find the people–nature dichotomy useful as an initial position for intellectual development. Issues involving separations and connections between the two realms emerge strongly in the first chapter and less obviously (often implicitly) in subsequent discussions. This identification of the two worlds of the dichotomy does not negate the myriad of ways in which the human world is connected to the natural.

Finally, the meanings of "wilderness" and "wild" may vary with the context; in statutes, for instance, the meanings may be quite different from those invoked by a particular observer (Cronon 1995). Nonetheless, from the perspective of characterizing concern for the natural world and the manifestations of that concern, I often find no appreciable difference.

The book's ten chapters are structured in three groups. The first, comprising chapters 1 and 2, provides a context for nature protection—perceptually, with the various meanings that people see in wild landscapes, and politically, with the positioning of nature protection within the conservation or environmental movement in America. Chapters 3 through 6, the second cluster, describe and characterize the organization of protected landscape reserves in the United States, first overall—a discussion that serves to illustrate the ambiguity of what is meant by "protection"—then with individual treatments of the three federal land systems that collectively account for the bulk of protected acreage. Chapter 4, on particular systems, explores units of the National Park System, identifying common critiques of those most well-known nature reserves, and chapters 5 and 6 apply these critiques to the National Wilderness Preservation System and the National Wildlife Refuge System; these discussions become commentaries on wild nature enthusiasts and the inconsistencies with which they apply their rhetorical judgments. The final group, chapters 7 though 10, examine four major issues related to nature protection—outdoor recreation, as a human use of wild landscapes; conservation organizations, as the structure for nongovernmental concern for wild landscapes; biodiversity, as the contemporary focus of nature protectionists; and the "new" conservation, as the umbrella phrase for turn-of-the-century trends in preservationist efforts. A final reflection on the chapters and the arguments concludes the book.

The pages that follow, then, explore the American experience in nature protection. The view from North Dome might have stimulated a book using Yosemite as the exemplar for the themes that structure the discussions in this work. (Someone should write such a volume, not alone for Yosemite but for each of the myriad of nature reserves—famous and obscure, large and small—scattered across the country.) But for now the view lies elsewhere. It prods a man who has loved Yosemite for more than half a century to document and reflect more generally on the national success and the national problems of preserving wild landscapes.

CONTEXTS American Wilderness

"trees . . .

pandered in whispers to

. . . human dreams"

1 MEANINGS OF WILDERNESS, OF WILD LANDSCAPES, OF NATURE

F. Scott Fitzgerald, in his classic American novel *The Great Gatsby*, suggests how the east coast of the future state of New York may have appeared in the seventeenth century to the first colonists from across the Atlantic: "I became aware of the old island here that flowered once for Dutch sailors' eyes—a fresh, green breast of the new world. Its vanished trees . . . had once pandered in whispers to the last and greatest of all human dreams; for a transitory enchanted moment man must have held his breath in the presence of this continent" (Fitzgerald 1925/1995: 189). What those Dutch sailors saw along the shore was not just gentle waves lapping against a shadowy wall of trees; they saw in that expanse of greenery an opportunity, a promise, a future. They saw meaning in the landscape.

Their experience was hardly unique. It may not be possible for anyone to view any landscape without some sort of connotative sense (Meinig 1979). On a regional scale, for example, scenes of New England villages, midwestern farmsteads, southern antebellum mansions, or western mountains and deserts conjure up a variety of meanings, varying from person to person and from time to time (Vale and Vale 1984). Such abstract evaluations characterize generic landscapes as well, including the common, city-bordering commercial strip, which may give viewers a variety of impressions that extend along a continuum between polar dichotomies: at one end a wasteful and inefficient economic system, at the other a success of wealth-generating capitalism; farm-destroying short-sightedness or a parklike creation that blends people with nature; a land-squandering subsidy by the public sector or a success of tax-generating growth; an unrecognizable sameness or a familiar landscape of home. As individuals, as groups, as a society, we Americans, like all peoples, look upon our landscapes with eyes and minds that transcend the immediate and the tangible.

Wild landscapes, too, carry a richness of meanings. That diversity explains the differing responses to Michael Pollan's hypothetical tabernacle pines protected in a nature reserve but blown down in a windstorm and facing a questionable future (Pollan et al. 1990)—should the area to be left alone to allow nature to persist as a "continually evolving process" (p. 38), or replanted with pines as a re-creation of a "Pilgrim's forest" (p. 42), replaced with other locally native species in a "gardening [of] the forest and weeding out [of] the exotics" (p. 39), or reconceived by planners with other particular visions in mind, perhaps as "an environmental education site" or a commercial center of "limited development [but without] sprawl" (p. 45)? These different notions of what should be done reflect different meanings of nature and different views of the role of humans in the natural world. Such varying interpretations of wild nature, of wilderness, are particularly diverse in the American mind, given our history, our collective economic success, and our diverse social and cultural mix. The meanings embrace protected landscapes at all scales, from the wooded corners of a city park and the local reserve of wetland to the Adirondacks and the Anza-Borrego Desert to the vast wilderness of the Everglades and Okefenokee, the Bob Marshall and the Gray Ranch, the Yellowstone and the seemingly endless sweep of the Alaskan Arctic. It is the meanings of the natural landscape, of nature itself, that we identify and discuss in this chapter, although the enumerated connotations easily describe also the meanings of specific protected areas, whether small and local or vast and continental.

Caveats need articulation. As noted in the introduction, the references in these pages to "Americans" should not be read as essentialist characterizations of national traits; the Americans here are the segment of the population involved in the dialogues over protected nature. Moreover, the meanings cannot be pigeonholed easily; the discussion of one image often laps over onto others, and at times they swirl together in defiance of the comfort offered by rigidly bounded types. Similarly, the discussions can lead off into an endless array of connected phenomena and contexts, so varied and rich are the core meanings. Such diversity and openness, moreover, preclude completeness in the citations for and explorations of the ideas and people involved. No apology is being made; no postmodern comment about the impossibility of "truth" should be uttered. The chapter works toward something much more immediate and prosaic: the wild or natural landscape generates enthusiasm (and scorn) for reasons as bountiful as a Gulf Coast estuary or a northern plains prairie in spring.

Positive Images

WILDERNESS AS SACRED SPACE   Nature is, for some, an Eden, *the* Eden. In accord with this general conviction, the wild landscape unfolds as the purest form, the highest expression, the grandest manifestation of this Edenic natural world. The wilderness experience becomes, then, an opportunity for a parishioner to transcend the physical body and contact a Godly Nature, the "Wholly Other" (Graber 1976), a religious sensation in which one gains a "sense of overwhelming power beyond the self" (Otto 1925). No one better exemplifies the adherent of this wilderness meaning than John Muir, who saw in the wilderness of the Yosemite high country a religiously sacred landscape:

No wonder the hills and groves were God's first temples, and the more they are cut down and hewn into cathedrals and churches, the farther off and dimmer seems the Lord Himself. The same may be said of stone temples. Yonder, to the eastward of our camp grove, stands one of Nature's cathedrals, hewn from the living rock, almost conventional in form, about two thousand feet high, nobly adorned with spires and pinnacles, thrilling under floods of sunshine as if alive like a grove-temple, and well named "Cathedral Peak." (Muir 1911/1987: 146)

It is easy to think of this vision as a recent development in human attitudes toward nature (Olson and Cairns, eds., 1996; J. Smith 1997). This is the interpretation of Roderick Nash (1967/2001), who documents the shift in the American view of nature from a "howling and dreadful" wilderness to a beloved and cherished wilderness. Yet nature worship permeated both New World native peoples (Spencer et al. 1965) and Europeans of premodern times (e.g., J. Taylor 1979, Vest 1985); Tuan (1974: 34) suggests, in fact, that nature appreciation reveals a "cross-cultural character . . . across broad chasms of time and place." Nonetheless, a certain ambivalence has generally characterized human attitudes toward wild nature. In traditional Christian thought, for example, places of wilderness were at once the "haunts of demons" as well as the "realm of bliss in harmony," where monks could live in "small models of paradise" (Tuan 1974: 110). Nicolson (1959) suggests a similar ambivalence about mountains in seventeenth- and eighteenth-century Europe, when they increasingly became less "worts" and more "sacred." This historical perspective suggests that the Sierra Club's analogy between the bottom of the Grand Canyon and the top of the Sistine Chapel (D. Brower 1990: 368) and the characterization of the Colorado River as "the environmental Ganges" (Sides 1996) and of Mono Lake as "a holy place" (Gilbert 1983) articulate a sentiment not entirely contemporary.

In fact, for some people, a sense of the sacred is what the modern, Western world lacks in its destructively exploitive dealings with the natural world. Such critics look back to premodern times when sacredness impregnated nature, a worldview that produced a healthy bond between people and their environments, and bemoan the rise of modernity as humanity's fall from grace. This story line structures many more specific narratives, which string together a familiar logic. The hunting-and-gathering societies of prehistory were "Eden-like"; humans displayed "no evidence of attempts to dominate nature technologically"—the downfall came with agriculture, which began "humankind's turn upon the environment" (Oelschlaeger 1991: 17, 24, 31). Native Americans, whether agriculturalists or not, commonly generate a stereotype of ecological wisdom (Speth 1977, Nelson 1983, Sierra Club 1996; but see R. White 1985 or Callicott 1989). In contrast to the worldviews of these "noble" folks, the European Renaissance redefined nature as valueless, indifferent, and separated from humanity, thereby fueling the subsequent environmental crisis (Opie 1987). Born from the Renaissance, modern science defined nature as natural, which made possible technological transformations that may have eased our physical existence but simultaneously stripped nature of spirits and mystery, and has cost humanity in other ways (Duerr 1985, Opie 1987). Our modern abuse of nature, derived from a too-narrow view of scientific understanding, not only leads nature to lash back—an environment less healthy for people—but causes our own human natures to be transformed destructively: we, like the natural world, become objectified and devalued (Alford 1985). What we need, most of these critics would agree, is to infuse our worldview with a sense of the sacred in our science (Evernden 1985, Worster 1987), our environmental policy (Backes 1995), and our everyday lives (Krist 1993, Lopez 1995).

This declensionist narrative appeals widely among today's nature enthusiasts. Yet others argue that the scientific study of nature in the nineteenth century, whether by amateurs (C. Porter 1986) or by professionals such as Clarence Dutton (Stegner 1977: ix–x) and Charles Darwin himself (R. Young 1985), easily fused detached evaluation and emotive involvement. Such fusion even characterized the interpretations of nature by the protectionist icon himself, John Muir (Vale and Vale 1998).

From the perspective of contemporary nature-protectionist sentiment, the most thorough and intriguing assessment of wilderness as sacred space

Figure 1.1. Graber models the wilderness experience as a religious experience, with the wilderness landscape as sacred space. (Adapted from Graber 1976, p. 11)

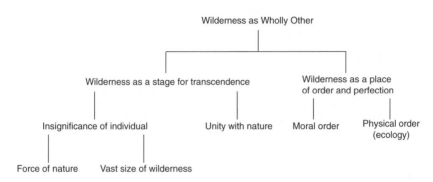

is that of Graber (1976). Her model of the wilderness enthusiast's encounter with wild nature suggests that it is an essentially religious experience (fig. 1.1). Reactions to Graber's characterization can be varied: the wilderness enthusiast may be pleased to read an affirmation of the fundamental sanctity of the natural world, while the critic of "wilderness sentimentality" could find in Graber an exposé of "the cult of wilderness," a baring of the shallow and misguided "religion of nature" (Lowenthal 1959–60, 1962; Chase 1986, 1995). Even a little reflection on the specifics of Graber's model, however, reveals that the reaction to *any* much-valued landscape or landscape feature is fundamentally "religious" (fig. 1.2). Such a revelation may bring discomfort to wilderness enthusiasts, who could resent the suggestion that their feelings toward nature may coincide with others' feelings about other landscapes, but it also disarms the critics of wilderness enthusiasts because it says that strong attraction to particular places or certain types of places, whether or not wilderness, is common, perhaps universal, among humans.

WILDERNESS AS PLEASURING GROUND Whether or not wilderness is seen as sacred, it may be viewed as a landscape for use by people. The wild mountains, deserts, and shores become human habitats, temporarily occupied during hourly excursions, weekend outings, or summer vacations. The activities that people seek in these wild landscapes exemplify many of those usually connoted by the term "outdoor recreation," and the purposes for such seeking express varied human motivations: learning about nature, bonding to natural forces, exercising the body; stress reduction, mettle test-

Figure 1.2. The old basketball arena on the University of Wisconsin campus (the "Field House") may be interpreted as a sacred landscape, in accordance with Graber's model of sacred space.

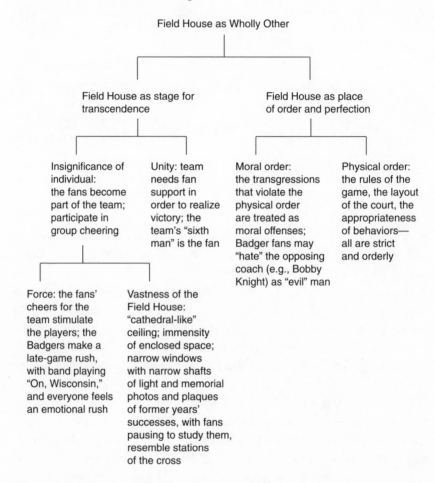

ing, skill enhancement; relaxation, invigoration, inspiration. John Muir, at the same time that he found the Yosemite high country a temple, urged people to explore the mountains and canyons, thereby legitimizing a human presence in the cathedral: "All of these excursions are sure to be made memorable with joyful health-giving experiences; but perhaps none of them will be remembered with keener delight than the days spent in sauntering on the broad velvet lawns by the river, sharing the sky with the mountains and trees, gaining something of their strength and peace" (Muir 1912/1962: 162).

The roots for the American appreciation of wild landscapes as pleasuring grounds extend deep into the past, at least as far back as the aristocratic European traditions of hunting and fishing. Nonetheless, changes in the nineteenth century—notably the improved opportunities for travel, the emergence of leisure time, the lessons of the Transcendentalist philosophers, the discovery of the spectacular landscapes of the American West, and the capitalist commodification of nature—contributed to making areas of protected nature a focus for recreation (Huth 1957). Moreover, this appreciation of wilderness, broadly conceived, as a temporary habitat for humans emerged primarily from urban populations, as Schmitt (1969/1990) so effectively argues. He suggests that such admiration differed from "agrarianism" or the "back-to-the-land" movement in that it represented an attempt to embrace "Arcadia,"

a place [that] lay somewhere on the urban fringe, easily accessible and mildly wild, the goal of a "nature movement" led by teachers and preachers, birdwatchers, socialites, scout leaders, city-planners, and inarticulate commuters, all of whom applauded William Smythe when he offered in *City Homes on Country Lanes* "the cream of the country and the cream of the city, leaving the skim-milk for those who like that sort of thing." (Schmitt 1969/1990: xvii)

This "Arcadian" movement, then, did not reject city life so much as it sought an addition to urban experiences and opportunities (cf. Harrison, Limb, and Burgess 1987); other than an exuberance for suburban homes, it did not embrace "country-living" as a permanent lifestyle except for short and nonsubsistence periods of time. Its sensitivity to nature parallels the historical development of appreciation for wild landscapes that Daniel Luten describes for American society, grown sufficiently "rich" to allow and encourage nonutilitarian uses of the natural world (Luten 1986). Its vision of the future is not the "Garden Earth," a realization of the agrarian ideal in which "fruit trees support songbirds" and "many [people] live on self-sufficient family farms," but an urbanized Earth, because "there are simply too many people on the planet to decentralize into garden environments and still have significant amounts of wilderness" (Nash 1967/2001: 380–81). Its contemporary expression continues among the urban members of those environmental groups that so vehemently defend parks and wilderness. The vision accepts the need for clear air and adequate food but articulates the equal necessity of an enduring wild Earth to accompany utilitarian survival (Quammen 1991, Botkin 2000).

WILDERNESS AS ECOSYSTEM More reductionist and analytical than the sacred space meaning but equally anthropocentric as the pleasuring-ground image, the vision of wilderness as ecosystem stresses conventionally scientific mechanisms in a nature that enhances the well-being of people. According to this perspective, nature everywhere may produce commodities for human use and services for human health (Myers 1984; Westmann and Gifford 1973; Baskin 1997; Costanza 1997; Daily, ed., 1997; Heal 2000), but the purest form of nature in unmodified wild landscapes best provides a secure base for those natural goods and services. Although little acknowledged by his admirers, Aldo Leopold emphasized this pragmatic, mechanistic, and human-focused basis for his land ethic:

Land . . . is not merely soil; it is a fountain of energy flowing through a circuit of soils, plants, and animals. Food chains are the living channels which conduct energy upward; death and decay return it to the soil. The circuit is not closed; some energy is dissipated in decay, some is added by absorption from the air, some is stored in soils, peats, and long-lived forests; but it is a sustained circuit, like a slowly augmented revolving fund of life. . . . Whatever may be the equation for men and land, it is improbable that we as yet know all its terms. . . . What of the vanishing species, the preservation of which we now regard as an esthetic luxury? They helped build the soil; in what unsuspected ways may they be essential to its maintenance? . . . [W]ho knows for what purpose cranes and condors, otters and grizzlies may some day be used? (Leopold 1949/1970: 220)

A key element in this vision is the sense that a natural system can be whole or complete, because protection of "entire ecosystems" is required to ensure continuation of natural functioning. To ensure this integral character of natural systems, a premium is placed on large areas of protected wild landscape; expansive wilderness comes to mean continuity of nature's systems. Conversely, protection fails when nature reserves are too small to encompass all of what is considered desirable, whether populations of grizzly bears (Clark and Harvey 1988), sources for water flow (M. Shelton 1990), or areas of forest large enough for natural fire regimes (but see W. Baker 1989). Yet a popular misconception arises here: "real" ecosystems, which have discrete boundaries and thus may be said to be either "whole" or "incomplete," do not exist in nature, as biologists have long recognized (Curtis 1959) and as Alston Chase (1986, 1995) exhorts us to appreciate when we design land policies. Ecosystems are abstractions—a volume of space at an instant in time—created by the human mind to focus on a particular biological species or on a certain sort of natural functioning, such as grizzly bears or water flow. Ecosystem thinking should prod us not to define what is a complete system but to seek connections, often unexpected, between components of the natural world (cf. Vale 1997).

In addition to the notion that ecosystems have some sort of discrete reality in the outside world, the image of wilderness as ecosystem is also linked to a sense that the natural world is fragile and easily disrupted, even destroyed, by human activities. This alarmist view not only underlies all conservationist thought, which stresses the limits of nature (Luten 1986), but also helps to explain the historical rise of the conservation movement (Lowenthal 2000: 404–31), and emerges in nineteenth-century humanistic as well as scientific writing (Bevis 1986). The concern sees nature as delicate, intricately balanced, and constantly on the verge of change and thus susceptible to destruction. It is a vision reminiscent of an older articulation, the "delicate balance of nature," still often expressed but now replaced by more contemporary phrases such as "sustainability of ecosystems."

More provocative than either completeness or delicacy, the concept of a living earth—including all that is alive and all that is inanimate—represents a sort of conceptual extremism of wilderness as ecosystem. Named Gaia— the Greek Earth Mother goddess—by its initial articulator, James Lovelock, the notion that the Earth functions as a living organism, with complex feedback loops linking everything into a single entity and its key processes derived from the activities of microorganisms, never fails to generate reaction (Lovelock 1988; West 1989; Schneider and Boston, eds., 1991; Kellert 1997). Many conventional scientists find fault with the imagery, even if they accept the mechanisms described as supporting the vision. Favorite Gaian processes include the control of atmospheric carbon dioxide by shell-forming marine organisms, temperature-limitation functions of phytoplankton in the oceans, and organism-induced atmospheric cooling as a catalyst for crustal cooling and initiation of lithosphere plate movements (Mann 1991). The botanist Lynn Margulis even suggests that evolution itself results from Gaian principles: symbiotic links between organisms, not mutations, generate novelty in the biological world, and mutual interactions between organisms and the environment, not competition among individuals, drives natural selection (Mann 1991). Whether hard science or metaphor, the Gaia hypothesis resonates with those who see interconnectedness— ecosystem—in the natural world (Goldsmith 1988).

In contrast to the self-regulating mechanisms of an intricately organized Gaia, the "new ecology" that emerged in the 1980s sees nature as highly variable and lacking in simple, singular balances (Botkin 1990, 2000, 2004; Vale 2002). The present condition of nature, and presumably the condition of nature at any given instant, according to this view, reflects not some optimum configuration but rather historical contingency. Change is constant; stable states of ecosystems are variable; chance events structure the natural world. This perspective seems to undermine a rigid interpretation of wilderness as ecosystem.

WILDERNESS AS COMMODITY As utilitarian as the ecosystem image, that of wilderness as commodity sees the natural world as recreated by capitalism into a product for mass consumption. Drawing upon an empirical study of the landscape imagery of the area of Bedford, New York, Duncan and Duncan find the nature-protectionist sentiment to be a creation of the local population's elite social position: "Wilderness . . . [is a] product of . . . financial-market-generated wealth" (Duncan and Duncan 2001: 406). It is an assertion made often in analyses of nature protection, usually with a negative connotation (see "Wilderness as Aristocratic Castle"). Nonetheless, examples also suggest favorable interpretations of wilderness as commodity (Harmon and Putney, eds., 2003). For example, Huth describes an 1857 tour by the Baltimore & Ohio Railroad that carried a special train of artists from Baltimore to Wheeling and back as a promotion for tourism (a "joint undertaking of artists and railway company to interest the public in American scenery" [Huth 1957: 86]). Similarly, Runte celebrates railroads as an early force favorable to the national parks ("the railroads engaged in a flurry of national park promotion" [Runte 1984: 49]). Sax suggests the virtues of returning to a Steven Mather strategy of appealing to private enterprise to bankroll recreational development in the national parks ("Mather's scheme of recruiting major enterprises to provide minimum profit, or even nonprofit showcases . . . [remains today] suitable to the crown jewels of America's landscape" [Sax 1982a: 24]). The Fish and Wildlife Service documents the substantial economic impact of visitation to national wildlife refuges (Laughland and Caudill 1997), and the National Parks Conservation Association (1996) argues that national parks generate even more such activity. Price, although urging us Americans to be more sensitive to the consequences of our nature-consuming activities, also recognizes that our purchase of products at The Nature Company in suburban malls might "mitigate the materialism and artifice of modern capitalist society" (Price 1995: 201). Even Cronon's story of landscape change in colonial New England, which focuses on the uses of commodity resources, might be extended to include landscapes of protected nature, giving a more literal meaning to a 1653 phrase that he employs, "Wilderness . . . turn[ing] a mart for Merchants" (Cronon 1983: 167). Finally, a legion of outdoor magazines, from *Field and Stream* to *Outside*, testify to the importance of nature-seeking recreationists, from hunters (Reiger 1986/2001) to Sierra Clubbers (Cohen 1988), who become defenders of wild landscapes that might otherwise remain vulnerable as "places no one knew" (E. Porter 1963).

Problems linked to the positive interpretation of wilderness as commodity range widely, from the negative impacts of ecotourism (Brandon 1996) to the adverse effects of recreationists on scientific management of nature (Dilsaver 1992) and the masking of a more real natural world behind the facade of the television screen (Siebert 1993). The most serious problem, of course, arises from the assertion that commodification of nature for recreation camouflages a destructive capitalistic system. Yet "Birds Mean Business" cries out a promotional slogan (Ducks Unlimited n.d.), and tourism linked to protected landscapes generates not only dollars but also sentiment for more protection. To argue that such positive effects only superficially mask sinister impacts is to simplify the complexity of the world.

WILDERNESS AS EVOLUTIONARY ARENA If wilderness as both ecosystem and commodity emphasize utilitarian motivations in contemporary times, the image of wilderness as evolutionary arena sees a practical necessity for maintaining the threads of biological evolution into the distant future. Wild landscapes become the theaters in which evolutionary change is allowed to continue in an otherwise human-dominated world where the processes of ongoing diversification are truncated: "The shore is an ancient world, . . . a world that keeps alive the sense of continuing creation and of the relentless drive of life. Each time that I enter it, I gain some new awareness of its beauty and its deeper meanings," wrote Rachel Carson (1955/1990: 520). Consistent with Carson, E. O. Wilson (1994) and others before him (Iltis 1966/1997) identify a human need for nature, a consequence of our species' long historical association with the natural world; commonly called "biophilia," this genetic coding makes us yearn for flowers and birds, mammals and trees, rocks and water. Similarly, Nabhan and Trimble (1994) proclaim that children "need wildness"; in their narratives children "spiral around" the idea "like moths coming to an open, nectar-laden flower." To devastate or dominate nature, then, is to invite psychological peril.

The view that people harm or even destroy natural biological diversity is a modern perspective (cf. Cartmill 1983). As recently as the middle of the twentieth century the prominent botanist Edgar Anderson comfortably argued that humans, by their disturbance of forests and grasslands, allowed for the survival of new genetic forms and as a consequence helped to create new plant diversity. Among his many examples, Anderson cited sages (*Salvia*) in California chaparral, sunflowers (*Helianthus*) on the Great Plains, and iris (*Iris*) in the Mississippi Delta as genera in which human-disturbed ground has permitted the survival of hybrid forms: "Nature is evidently capable of spawning such hybrids throughout [the lower Mississippi River Valley], but not until one farmer unconsciously created the new and more or less open habitat in which they could survive did any appear in this part of the delta" (Anderson 1956: 771).

At the same time, a leading ecologist, Marston Bates, could similarly describe without constant disparaging remarks the effects of people as "agent[s] in the spread of organisms." He even observed that these human alterations of biotas created opportunities for learning: "The experimental-like situations produced by man's alteration of environmental factors, and by his movement of organisms into different environments, offer possibilities for study . . . of ecology . . . [and] of key aspects of the behavior of organisms and of the possible mechanisms of organic evolution" (M. Bates 1956: 801). That such comments today would be considered old-fashioned, even heresy, testifies to change, not so much in the impacts of humans upon nature as in the meanings that people see in those impacts.

The antimodern sentiment that underlies the turn-of the-century interpretation of people as destroyers of nature also creates the underpinning for a view of traditional, precontemporary, non-Western human societies as more wise, more balanced, more noble than we. Such indigenous peoples, according to this perspective, lived closer to and in harmony with the natural world. Whether or not empirical facts support this characterization of a more moral past, the imagery supports the idea of modern society gone awry, increasingly threatening the natural processes of the evolutionary arena.

WILDERNESS AS A NATION'S ROOTS If in the view of wilderness as evolutionary arena the meaning of the present natural world is found in the long sweep of the geological past, the vision of wilderness as a nation's roots finds in wild landscapes the historical past of America's national beginnings. Here the image focuses on the primeval continent, a pristine land that was swept over by predominantly European peoples, who forged out of the wilderness our modern society. The natural world becomes, in this view, our collective past, and, as a country, we treasure reminders of these roots.

Eastern landscapes may have swelled the proud breasts of early Americans—Niagara Falls carried early connotations of the sublime (McKinsey 1985) and of national purpose (McGreevy 1987)—but western landscapes, western wilderness, would come to dominate this mental picture. With his stirring prose describing a people pulled westward across the new continent, Bernard DeVoto embraces wilderness as the nation's roots:

When Bill Bowen sold his house a national emotion welled in the secret places of his heart and he joined himself to a national myth. He believed with Henry Thoreau in the forest and in the meadow and in the night in which the corn grows. Eastward Thoreau went only by force, but westward, ever since Columbus dared the Ocean Sea, westward he had gone free. The lodestone of the West tugged deep in the blood, as deep as desire. . . . Toward that Western horizon all heroes of all peoples known to history have always traveled. . . . And, if either Freud or the Navajo speak true, westward we shall find the hole in the earth through which the soul may plunge to peace. (DeVoto 1943: 49)

DeVoto's is the vision of Frederick Jackson Turner (1920), who, in addition to arguing that the open and free lands of the westward-advancing frontier shaped the American character, saw a nation spreading its civilization across the North American wilderness.

Contemporary "new" or "revisionist" historians want to reject Turner's imagery, which they characterize as a romantic illusion of noble and independent people, mostly white males, forging a society into an ever-better state. In their minds, the westward spread of American society had a darker side. These historians argue that attention must be paid to the powerless and exploited peoples—Native Americans, African Americans, Asians, women; to the dominance of political and economic elites who for their narrow self-interest controlled much of what happened in the American past; and to the effects of civilization on the environment, mostly attacked and abused rather than forming the base of a harmonious society (Wolf 1990).

While it is healthy to explore the past with insight and honesty, the danger of the "New Western History" (White 1991a, Worster 1992) is that its negative perspective, instead of simply demythifying Turner, may come to be seen as the entire truth. Even Patricia Limerick's (1987) well-known identifying phrase for the new interpretation of the western past, "the legacy of conquest," is loaded with connotation: to conquer is to subjugate, usually bad dominating good. In these terms, American history becomes a saga of good nature and good native peoples being subjugated by bad Anglo society. Rather than exposing the limitations of the Turner myth, the more extreme versions of revisionist history contribute, if mostly in the popular mind, to old myths of noble savages, and it more generally creates a new myth, the myth of cynical realism.

WILDERNESS AS ETHICAL STAGE To protest against a rigid revisionist history is not to protest generally against the importance of myths, of vision, of metaphors in the interpretation of wild landscapes. In fact, wilderness as ethical stage, a vision based on moral philosophy, has become increasingly popular in recent years.

Two manifestations of the ethical stage can be identified. First, the more common, is the assertion that nature, whether a condor or a lady's slipper, a free-flowing stream or a rock of quiet quartzite, has the right to exist. Therefore, ethical considerations should extend "to include the living creatures that share the planet with us [and] to the nonliving, the inorganic, to the springs, streams, lakes, rivers and oceans, to the winds and clouds and the air, to the very rocks which form the foundation of the land" (Abbey 1979; cf. Hearne 1991). This vision is fundamental to movements and groups commonly associated with so-called radical environmentalism, with names like deep ecology and green politics, ecofeminism and bioregionalism (Devall and Sessions 1985, Parsons 1985, Biehl 1987). All share the common belief in a world ethics that recognizes the centrality of life's, not simply humanity's, inalienable rights. This is biocentrism.

Roderick Nash (1987), in his history of such ethical concerns, asserts that the contemporary growing recognition of nature's rights represents only the modern expression of what has been a long history of an expanding universe perceived to have such fundamental rights. The freeing of serfs, the emancipation of slaves, the granting of the vote to women, the civil rights movement, the rights of nature—all are one and the same, an unbroken expansion of rights from aristocratic males to other people to animals to all of the natural world. Biocentrism is simply a part of egalitarianism.

This rationale creates a massive but simple dichotomy. On one side are biocentrism, left-wing politics, and wise and thoughtful environmentalism; on the other side are anthropocentrism, everything but radical politics, and dangerously exploitive environmentalism. This structure is naive. Anthropocentric perspectives (such as the other images of wilderness in this book) need not be destructive; political labels may not identify, simply and un-equivocally, where concern for nature protection lies in American society. Witness, for example, the successes of groups such as the big capitalist-based Nature Conservancy. Just as environmentalism overall is a complex movement, often with contrasting and opposing purposes, so too does complexity characterize a major part of that movement, concern for nature protection. Rooting out evil in the world is simple only for those who can easily aggregate all of the devil's incarnations into monolithic simplicity and capture it in a moral dragnet. The danger with such ready reductionism is that some virtue may be snagged in the webbing and some evil may escape to swim free.

A second expression of the ethical stage is explicitly anthropocentric. Nature writers, from Aldo Leopold to Joseph Wood Krutch, have recognized that concern for the natural world is a uniquely human trait. Other species may act out of concern for their own species or their own well-being, but humans alone consciously worry about creatures other than themselves. To encourage and enhance this characteristic, to emphasize not the universal-ity of moral rights but the specifically human-centered character of moral-ity (and thus to deny the fundamental tenet of "deep ecology" [Fayter 1990]), is to expand the human condition.

Two examples suggest the breadth of this part of the ethical stage. The first stresses self-identity: after separating a snake from a pheasant, Loren Eiseley wonders why he engaged in an act that did not gain him anything tangible:

The bird had contended for birds against the oncoming future; the serpent writhing into the bunch grass had contended just as desperately for serpents. And I, the apparition in that valley—for what had I contended? . . . Slowly, as I sauntered dwarfed among overhanging pinnacles, . . . the answer came to me. Man could contain more than himself. Among these many appearances that flew, or swam in the waters, or wavered momentarily into being, man alone possessed that unique ability. . . . I had struggled, I am now convinced, for a greater, more comprehensive version of myself. (Eiseley 1960: 176)

Eiseley sees his biological self transcended by an act of unique humanity.

A second example of the anthropocentric ethical stage also involves self-identify but in addition embraces an active role for people in the trans-formation of nature. Frederick Turner's (1985) view of nature as a "garden in need of weeding" established a metaphor widely admired and embraced

(Steinhart 1990, Pollan 1991, Higgs 2003). To the degree that we humans become ethical gardeners, we improve (in human terms) the natural world, and because of this involvement, we become more ethical beings. Eiseley focuses on what might be characterized as sentimentality; Turner justifies restoration ecology. Although usually articulated in opposition to hands-off protection of nature, the garden metaphor could be expanded into a wide range of human interactions with the natural world, including various types of outdoor recreation, perhaps some sorts of commodity resource development and even inviolate nature preservation. In each of these situations, the stress is not on the sanctity of nature as saved by an extension of ethics but rather on the ethical nature of people as saved by being participants in the natural world (cf. Higgs 2003). The richness of the anthropocentric ethical stage exceeds that of narrow biocentrism.

WILDERNESS AS PEOPLE'S PARK The ethical imagery of wilderness is not restricted to the people–nature relationships of the ethical stage; it may also embrace the people–people relationships of the people's park. Nature protection in America enjoys a strong egalitarian tradition, as part of the more general tradition of conservation as equality. Parks and reserves, seen in this light, may become symbols of ennobling human societies.

J. Ronald Engel (1983) traces the ties between progressive ideals, centered in turn-of-the-century Chicago, and the efforts to save the Indiana Dunes along the southern shore of Lake Michigan. In this history, the ideals of human cooperation, rather than competition, motivated the participants, whether the concern was the creation of a desirable human society or the scientific interpretation of the workings of the natural world. The Indiana Dunes became symbolic of this progressive ideology,

as the shrine of midwestern Progressivism . . . as the birthplace of ecology . . . as an invitation to a shared, artistic way of life . . . as a battleground in the struggle for social justice and environmental preservation. In the closing decades of the twentieth century, the fragmented, vulnerable, yet ever-renewing Dunes landscape was an apt metaphor of the struggle for community in the midst of a divided society and a broken land. (Engel 1983: 294)

The imagery reminds us of similar progressive sentiment that motivated Frederick Law Olmsted in his public park projects, notably New York City's Central Park (Beverdige 1983, Rosenzweig and Blackmar 1992, Thompson 1994) but also the 1864 Yosemite Grant (Sax 1976). Even George Catlin's famous 1832 proposal for "a nation's park" on the western plains (Nash, ed., 1968) seems to picture a nature reserve that serves a collective human purpose. More recently, Williams (1996a) suggests that Utahans have told their congressional delegation—characteristically unsympathetic to protection of wild land—to save their state's redrock wilderness as a demonstration of "a bedrock democracy."

The same sentiment arises in other contexts of nature protection. By encouraging discussions over administrative policies, parks astride national boundaries can stimulate international cooperation, "part of a growing force for solidarity" (Thorsell 1990). In an analogous way, efforts to protect widely distributed animal species may be catalysts for collaborative programs among disparate political entities: the United States and the Soviet Union cooperated on behalf of wildlife across the Bering Strait (W. Brown 1988, Graham 1991); a number of countries in Western and Central Europe created and maintained nature reserves across their boundaries even before their borders became porous with the end of the Cold War (Thorsell 1990, Lucas 1990); countries in southern Africa cooperated in the creation of parklands along their common borders (Zbicz and Green 1997). A particularly bold invocation of people's park imagery comes from the International Crane Foundation (n.d.), which promotes efforts to save breeding populations of various species of cranes by asking, "Can these birds bring unity to man?"

Arguably the most conspicuous contemporary expression of the people's park imagery is the belief that, particularly in Third World situations, concern for protection of nature goes hand in hand with protection of traditional cultures (Clay 1985, Eilers 1985, Dasmann 1991). In fact, the most distinguishing characteristic of "biosphere reserves" is the inclusion of human uses, particularly those of "indigenous tribal populations," in areas dedicated to nature protection (Gregg 1991). More specifically, the Dalai Lama suggests that the Tibetan plateau "should become a free refuge where humanity and nature can live in peace and in harmonious balance" (Schell 1991). Nietschmann (1984) carries the theme further than most with his promotion of the self-determination of local ethnic groups, a political reorganization of the world that will create hundreds of new countries and simultaneously, in his view, enhance protection of nature. However appealing, such imagery encourages the interpretation of traditional peoples as ecologically noble, a factually naive position (Redford 1990), and it obscures the obvious difficulty of reconciling the incompatible goals of allowing people to decide their economic futures and protecting the status quo in the natural world.

WILDERNESS AS PLACE The previous meanings envision wild landscapes as generic spaces, whether, for example, sacred space or ecosystem or ethical stage. The particular details of situation loom less important than the sense that wilderness is a type or a sort of landscape that we can abstractly call "Eden" or "natural system" or "moral theater." In the view of wilderness as place, by contrast, any given wild landscape is a unique set of natural characteristics and, perhaps more important, a human history that is peculiar to that locale. Yellowstone, in this view, becomes more than merely another wild landscape; it is a particular place dissimilar to Yosemite National Park or the Goat Rocks Wilderness or the Kofa Mountains National Wildlife Refuge.

Yi-Fu Tuan has explored the human patterns of dealing with parts of the Earth's surface as either space or place:

What begins as undifferentiated space becomes place as we get to know it better and endow it with value. . . . [I]f we think of space as that which allows movement, then place is pause; each pause in movement makes it possible for location to be transformed into place. . . . [T]he "feel" of a place . . . is a unique blend of sights, sounds, and smells, a unique blend of natural and artificial rhythms such as times of sunrise and sunset, of work and play. The feel of a place is registered in one's muscles and bones. (Tuan 1977: 6)

The learning about "undifferentiated space" that allows it to become "concrete place, filled with meaning," Tuan argues, is mostly subconscious. Long periods of time (long "pauses") are often necessary to generate the sort of intense but informal familiarity with a locale that is the essence of the sensation of place, although the intensity of experience may be more important than mere duration of exposure. The effort to generate a "sense of place," by contrast, is usually "deliberate and conscious," perhaps reflecting a desire for self-identity in a world that is perceived as changing too rapidly (Tuan 1977).

The appreciation of a particular protected wild landscape as a place may be within the grasp of those individuals who have spent time and emotional energy in the locale, although perhaps not for first-time or casual travelers. To enrich the experiences of such visitors and to stabilize land policy currently dependent upon changing concepts of nature, Meyer (1996) suggests that "senses of place" or "spirits of place" for parks and wilderness be articulated and promoted. Human histories and uses of landscape become critical elements in such articulation, contributing to the resulting decisions about appropriateness of opportunities for recreational experiences. For Yellowstone, Meyer suggests that this kind of definition might support several land use policies. The maintenance of slow, curving roads would continue the pre-automobile Yellowstone experience typified by the once much-anticipated "corkscrew bridge," by which a stagecoach road curved back over itself on a steep grade. The contemporary prohibition against snowmobiles might be justified by invoking the image of early visitors who wrote with particularly strong feelings about the winter Yellowstone of solitude, stillness, and loneliness. Even the long-ago activity of wading in thermal waters, now strictly prohibited, might be resurrected today in controlled situations.

Other observers echo Meyer's general thinking. Also looking at the Yellowstone landscape and similarly stressing the centrality of human experience, Schullery suggests that we have never stopped establishing Yellowstone. Whether as "first-time visitors or as world-famous biologists we continue to discover and explore it, and we also continue to create it" (Schullery 1997: 1–2).

More generally, Marston (1995) has long asserted that local people in the interior West, even those engaged in resource extraction, must be incorporated into landscape protection designs because such peoples belong to western landscapes, a vision championed in the 1990s by Interior Secretary Bruce Babbitt (Marston 2001a; cf. Wuerthner 1991). In a parallel fashion, Barbara Brower (1982) wonders if flocks of domestic sheep might be an important element for the maintenance of the personality of alpine meadows in national forests of Wyoming because such use continues the long-established tradition of sheep transhumance in that part of the Rocky Mountains. In a stance less threatening to the conventional feelings of wilderness enthusiasts, Pyne (whose prose and insight elevate the discourse on wild places) demonstrates for the Grand Canyon "how the place and its poets came together . . . how the Canyon became Grand" (Pyne 1998: xv). Finally, Steinhart (1988) argues that the recreational traditions in California's Sierra Nevada continue to reflect John Muir's vision of a place for simple and independent connections with nature: the Sierra has few major resorts and much protected wilderness, while the users of its wild land show little interest in guided trips, campcraft skills, or endurance-testing recreation. Steinhart might say that the Sierra Nevada is more a sacred place than merely sacred space.

Negative Images

Each of the previous images of wilderness, of nature, celebrates the natural world. Yet any typology of wilderness meanings would be incomplete, deceptively so, without consideration of the richness of negative perceptions.

WILDERNESS AS SPOILED NATURE Even for many of those who burn with passion over nature protection, the wild landscapes in parks and wilderness present a negative vision: the natural scene has been too much modified by the actions of modern people. These disquieting alterations of nature reflect human activities of various sorts: commodity resource extraction, such as mining or logging, before the beginning of landscape protection (Ahlgren and Ahlgren 1984); continuation of such activity, such as livestock grazing in national forest wilderness, after establishment of legal protection (Kerr and Salvo 2000); recreational impacts within parks and wilderness (Whitson 1974); elimination of natural factors, such as fire (Leopold et al. 1963) and predators (Diamond 1992); alterations resulting from the fragmented character of protected landscapes (Soule and Orians 2001); and change produced by human activities outside nature reserves (Stottlemyer 1981). Although recognition of such human impacts depends upon knowledge (Vale 1977), for those who are able and inclined to see them, these deviations from a more pure natural scene may render the landscape a cultural artifact. The extreme expression of this wilderness image is represented by Bill McKibben, who, in seeing human impacts as ubiquitous in the world, has proclaimed the death of nature: "The idea of nature will not survive the new global pollution. . . . By changing the weather, we make every spot on earth man-made and artificial. We have deprived nature of its independence, and that is fatal to its meaning. Nature's independence *is* its meaning; without it there is nothing but us" (McKibben 1989: 58).

The policy response to this vision is landscape management designed to reestablish and maintain a prior natural condition. The so-called Leopold Report of 1963 (reprinted in Dilsaver, ed., 1994) is usually credited with introducing and legitimizing the concept of active human manipulation of environments in protected landscape reserves. Under the report's aegis, fire has been reintroduced as an ecological agent in many parks and wilderness areas over the last several decades (both as let-burn and prescribed-burn programs), although some observers feel that the scope of management envisioned in the Leopold Report has not been realized. The movement for ecological restoration, extending back at least into the mid-1960s (see Spurr 1966), reflects the idea of wilderness as spoiled nature. Such efforts assume that merely reintroducing past agents of landscape formation, such as fire, will not necessarily produce the preexisting natural state; rather, active management is necessary to break the inertia of the undesired, human-induced change (Bonnickson and Stone 1981, 1982; cf. Vale 1987). The task of undoing the effects of anthropogenic atmospheric change seems even more daunting.

WILDERNESS AS FALSE IDOL AND WILDERNESS AS GARDEN For some observers the identification of wilderness as a landscape distinct from the human world creates a false dichotomy between nature and people. The dualism, moreover, is more than something to be argued in scholarly discourse regarding the "naturalness" of a region's vegetation or an ecosystem's functioning. The stress on wilderness as a landscape apart from people cuts off positive inputs from humans in the workings of the natural world.

Frederick Turner is perhaps the most provocative of those who stress this connection between nature and people, the true naturalness of people and their activities. He even turns completely around the common metaphor that articulates people as a cancer mortally consuming the natural world: "When life first appeared, the crystals and chemical organisms must have thought, What is this thing that keeps reproducing itself? It keeps on changing. It's messing up the atmosphere. It keeps transforming itself. . . . For what is life but a cancer upon the purity of the inorganic? . . . The nervous system is a glorious cancer that has evolved, and I stand with it" (F. Turner 1990: 48). Earlier Turner (1985) had criticized the dichotomous separation of people and the natural world because such a vision reduces human interactions with nature to either "raping it or tying it up in a plastic bag to protect it from contamination." Others have commented more specifically on issues that are confounded by the sharp separation of people and nature. Alston Chase (1987) invokes Turner's plastic bag image to criticize the hands-off policies of the National Park Service, which he claims are destructive of the very nature that the agency is attempting to save. Martin Bowden (1992) suggests that the perpetuation of the myth of the pristine landscape in the Americas (Denevan 1992), a vision of a natural landscape free of human impacts, negates the fundamental humanness of Native Americans. Lowenthal (1962), indifferent to wilderness protection, and Cronon (1995a), supportive of the protectionist impulse, observe that the dichotomy tends to portray nature as available only in remote parks and reserves, thereby reducing the possibility of people–nature interactions in the everyday world. The most extreme stance that emerges from the false-idol critique advocates the elimination—completely and unequivocally—of the category of nature and anything described as natural (Egan and Howell 2001).

For many such critics, the ideal lies not in inviolate, statutory wilderness but in the middle ground of the human-manipulated, cared-for but still somewhat wild landscape. We might look less to the Bob Marshall or the Yellowstone for guidance in nature protection and more to the humanized landscapes of the French national parks (Sax 1982b); or the New Jersey pinelands reserve, which provides for continued commodity resource production (Collins and Russell 1988); or the model of the biosphere reserve in many non-Western countries (Man and the Biosphere Program 1990); or the "wildness in our own backyards," a view of farmland emerging from mist and fog (Cronon 1995b: 86). Might we, then, find hope in the "explosion of green"—the reforestation of the nonwilderness landscapes of the eastern United States (McKibben 1995)—rather than lament the building of roads in Utah's wild south (Greeno 1990) or the development of petroleum resources on Alaska's Arctic slope (Corn and Blodgett 1988)?

Several images merge to form a particularly popular contemporary conceptualization, one that criticizes the positive imagery of "natural" and "pristine" wilderness. The implications of wilderness as false idol should be recognized, according to this view. That recognition will permit the active landscape management needed to reverse the consequences of hands-off protection, which have created, ironically, wilderness as spoiled nature. The pursuit of such management, moreover, transforms not only the landscape but also the human spirit, which bonds to nature in the constructive ties of wilderness as ethical stage. This array of images underlies the vision of wilderness as garden (Jansen 2000).

WILDERNESS AS BOORISH AMERICANA Whether or not they forge a barrier between nature and culture, American wild lands strike some observers as simply too lacking in the refined character of the superior pastoral landscape of Western Europe. It is the physical evidence of people and their activities, visually revealed in their artifacts, that gives the European countryside a stronger aesthetic appeal than the American wilderness. The Englishman J. Walter preferred the stronger sense of a "balance" of elements in the European landscape to the simpler structure of "essence" in the American scene:

In Britain . . . a cottage nestles by a lake with a little coppice close by and maybe some flowers. Across the lake are walled fields with sheep grazing, above them a hillside. . . . The beauty of the Swiss alps is composed in the same way: peak and pasture, glacier and cowshed, mountain and meadow, forest and village, all in delicate balance. The finest American landscapes . . . are either a vivid contrast between only two elements—skyscraper and waterfront, rock spire and desert, ice-clad volcano and forest—or they are one element in pure essence—aspens in fall, the canyon, the desert, the forest, the mountain. (Walter 1983: 46)

Walter nonetheless recognized his cultural bias in these feelings, observing that Americans have as difficult a time understanding Britons' reverence for the queen as he does appreciating Americans' love of wilderness.

The comparative aesthetics of European and American landscapes, with the former seen as superior to the latter, leads to two lines of argument. First, the earliest appreciation of the landscapes of Yellowstone and Yosemite may have been prompted by their physical similarity to the pastoral scenes of Europe, an idea developed by Shepard (1967). In Yellowstone, natural features resembled the artifacts of the villa garden: rock formations were ruins of castles; geysers were fountains; terraced hot springs were statued ornamentations; the mix of meadows and groves were manicured lawns and specimen trees; grazing elk and bison were flocks of cattle and sheep. The scene was not only "an image of paradise" but also a scene of "civilization's most ornamental achievement—the estate park" (Shepard 1967: 252).

Unlike Shepard (who strongly supports wild land protection), others report the historical importance of the pastoral scene to early park establishment in advancing a second argument, one presented in the spirit of a tabloid exposé of the unenlightened thinking of contemporary wilderness enthusiasts. "By and large, men find lived-in landscapes more attractive than wild ones," David Lowenthal (1962: 20) writes with cavalier simplification of variable human sensibilities. Elsewhere he argues both that the American landscape is characterized by "wildness," an element that "appalled [and presumably continues to appall] viewers" (Lowenthal 1968a: 66), and that a lack of human artifacts was not even what N. P. Langford envisioned in 1870 for the lands that would become Yellowstone National Park: "The march of civil improvement will reclaim this delightful solitude, and garnish it with all the attractions of cultivated taste and refinement" (quoted in Lowenthal 1968b:

29). These discourses are meant to stigmatize the value some people see in wild landscapes and to justify a culturally more "correct" perspective.

WILDERNESS AS ARISTOCRATIC CASTLE Culture is not the only basis for seeing ideological incorrectness in wild landscapes. Such lands also incite some egalitarians to argue that nature preserves restrict, directly and indirectly, economic opportunities for the poor: protected wild landscapes— a concern of the rich, powerful upper middle class in the United States— represent a nonegalitarian, regressive society. William Tucker (1982) argues that preservation of wilderness ("essentially parks for the upper-middle class") is a central concern of environmentalists ("a privileged minority") who face a "neo-Populist revolt against environmentalism . . . , literally a quarrel between the 'haves' and the 'have-nots,' between the urban and sub-urban liberal establishment intent on protecting its position of privilege and the broad reaches of lower-middle-class and poor people, who feel that they do not yet have enough" (Tucker 1982: 38).

The extension of this concept of parks and wilderness into the Third World raises even stronger cries of elitism. With strident assertion, Guha encapsulates both the logic and the emotion of the view:

Increasingly, the international conservation elite is using the philosophical, moral, and scientific arguments used by deep ecologists in advancing their wilderness crusade. . . . [David] Jansen exhorts his colleagues to advance their territorial claims on the tropical world more forcefully, warning that the very existence of these areas is at stake. . . . This frankly imperialist manifesto . . . provides an impetus to the imperialist yearning of Western biologists and their financial sponsors, organizations such as the WWF and IUCN. (Guha 1989: 76)

Similarly, whether in Africa (Neumann 1998) or Indonesia (Peluso 1993), the American model of state control and state coercion leads only to the loss of local rights and access to resources (Zimmerer 2000). Even in the United States, disempowered local peoples—typically Native Americans but also the rural poor in general—suffer a loss of livelihood when wild landscapes are protected behind inviolate boundaries (Spence 1996, Catton 1997, Keller and Turek 1998).

The vision of protected wild landscapes as aristocratic castles leads into radical interpretations of the underlying political economy, interpretations that typically critique the conventional concept of wilderness and park. A political-economic system that creates fundamentally exploitive human behaviors cannot successfully protect nature; in such societies, the creation of nature reserves deflects attention from the destructive activities that the system more generally encourages, and transforms protected nature into a commodity that becomes part of the market (see "Wilderness as Commodity").

The vision of reserves of wild landscapes as aristocratic castles is supported by many commentators on symbolic meanings of landscapes. Kenneth Olwig (1984), for example, documents the transformation of the Western concept of "nature" from "what . . . social and environment development ought to be" in classical times ("a process of change") to "landscape type" today (an "object"). This attempt to "freeze" landscape condition is incongruous not only because the world is naturally and socially changing but also because social symbolism is falsified: wilderness cannot preserve human individuality if society generally is based on integration of effort and specialization of labor, and Edenic qualities of wild landscapes are hardly ideal if preservation denies local peoples opportunities for human dignity. Denis Cosgrove is no less critical: the sense of the sublime in the natural scene, a strong motivating force for early (and presumably contemporary) nature protection, "avoid[s] analysis of capitalist relations while criticizing their consequences" (Cosgrove 1984: 234). Neither are the Duncans cautious: attempts by wealthy New Yorkers to protect the wild openness of their suburban landscape, although "seemingly innocent," actually masks a "highly effective mechanism of social exclusion and the reaffirmation of elite class identities" (Duncan and Duncan 2001: 387). The rhetoric of wilderness and parks becomes, in these views, not simply a childish and naive incantation but a sinister support of a fundamentally destructive, racist, and exclusionary political, economic, and social system.

The aristocratic castle becomes, in its extreme form, the postmodern critique of wild landscape protection, of nature protection: the categories of "wild" and "nature" are merely linguistic creations, suiting the purposes of the social elite. William Cronon, in concluding the published work of the scholarly group that explored the human "reinvention" of "nature," asserts the ambiguity of the terms: "The non-human world is not (just) our creation, but nature is. Nature is far less natural than we think" (Cronon 1995a: 458). His words intend to prod us to reflect on the meanings of the categories, on the temporal and spatial variabilities in these meanings, on the indefinite boundaries that enclose the categories, and on the interplay between the meanings of the categories and the workings of the human mind. Nonetheless, the discourse easily slips into the nihilistic quagmire where obfuscating cleverness replaces constructive enlightenment. Although Cronon did not intend such profound (and silly) skepticism, the negative reactions to his words (cf. Soule and Lease, eds., 1995; Worster 1997; Waller 1998) suggest that deconstructionists themselves may sway unsteadily on boggy ground, a ground created by their own use of the language.

WILDERNESS AS CORNUCOPIA Far more simple than the perspectives based on culture or economics, that of wilderness as cornucopia sees in wild landscapes an untapped natural bounty, a treasure box of wood, minerals, water, or energy resources. Looking out over a park or wilderness, a person with this vision would see the potential for commercial development: forests to be logged, metallic ores to be mined, reservoirs to be built, petroleum and coal deposits to be harvested. The mineral geologist Charles Park represents this perspective:

Minerals are where you find them. The quantities are finite. It's criminal to waste minerals when the standard of living of your people depends upon them. A mine cannot move. It is fixed by nature. So it has to take precedence over any other use. If there were a copper deposit in Yellowstone Park, I'd recommend mining it. . . . While I love the out-of-doors, I have no use for wilderness. We need to lumber. We need to mine. . . . You can't live without industry. But that is what preservationists will say. Sawmills, mines, and forests *can* live together. The forests are beautiful here. They really are. The Black Hills are an example of where industry has not ruined an environment. (McPhee 1971: 21, 67)

Such a view of a potential cornucopia of developable resources "locked up" in parks and wilderness is characteristically exaggerated. For example, the petroleum that might be produced on all of the wilderness lands of the eleven western states—all established wilderness plus all potential wilderness—represents between one-quarter and one-half of 1 percent of the ultimate production in the United States; at current rates of usage, this "locked-up" petroleum would supply the country for only two to four months (data from Dolton et al. 1981 and Miller 1983; see also Rice 1984). Similarly, the commercial forestland on the panhandle of Alaska constitutes but 1 percent of the total commercial forestland in the country, and the acreage within wild landscape reserves in southeast Alaska—much coveted by wood products interests—embraces a still smaller percentage and thus a trivial proportion of the nation's total (data from *Statistical Abstract of the United States*). An identical story can be told about livestock forage on the public domain—utterly inconsequential for the nation's need for animal feed (Vale 1974b). The repetition of such patterns suggests that resources in parks and wilderness typically remain of little consequence to the nation's resource base. In fact, Alfred Runte (1979) has argued that national parks (and by extension, protected landscapes generally) have been so compromised by utilitarian concerns that they lack economically useful resources and are thus "worthless." The failure to recognize the falsity of the vision of wilderness as cornucopia reveals a dominance of attitude over fact in natural resource controversy (Vale 1970).

The appeal of the image may lie deep in the American mind (and more generally in the human mind), a result of two centuries of economic growth and material expansion. Empirically, it seems logical to assume that more resources are only waiting to be discovered—after all, they have been found in the past for as long as anyone can remember. This is a vision of an infinite world (Luten 1986). The argument that the United States needs the resources that are "locked up" in parks and wilderness, moreover, entails an unsettling assumption: the country is so poor, so close to the edge of natural resource exhaustion, so poorly guided by its political leaders, that we need to extract what little the wild landscapes can offer.

At a scale regional or local rather than national or planetary, however, landscapes unavailable for development may have more serious economic consequences. For example, timber protected in a wilderness or park may mean little to the country's wood supplies, but it could contribute to a slowdown at a town's mill. This reality explains the opposition to nature protection that has nearly always characterized the local perspective. Still, factors other than creation of nature reserves characteristically influence the economies of towns dependent upon extractive activities, as exemplified by the example of wood production: the structure of the timber industry, the efficiency of mills, the cost of labor, the demand for wood products, and the availability of logs (quite apart from timber in parks) all influence corporate decisions about operating any particular timber town's mill (Vale 1970).

WILDERNESS AS THE HAUNT OF DEMONS Perhaps the most extreme negative vision of wild landscapes is that which sees wilderness as a space of dread and fear, a landscape of demons. The common assertion by wilderness enthusiasts is that such negative sentiments are those of the past and that modern peoples, if enlightened, embrace wildness in the landscape. But contemporary peoples hardly see wilderness, universally and unequivocally, in such a benign light. John Short, after describing the rationality of premodern fears of wilderness, suggests that today we are still frightened of the wilderness. In part it may be a reasonable response to the still obvious dangers of truly wild places. It may also be an element of our collective unconscious; there is a part of us still huddling together round camp fires, keeping our spirits up in the face of the great blackness beyond. . . . The wilderness represents the uncivilized, the untamed. It represents the underside of the individual soul and the collective unconscious. (Short 1991: 9)

The wilderness may have become sacred space, but the resident gods are not always benevolent.

The imagery of the demon-haunted wilderness lurks even in the minds, if not the hearts, of at least some wilderness enthusiasts. As a ploy to discourage recreational visitors, Edward Abbey (1977) not only accepts but actually promotes the sense that wild places are dangerous. The National Park Service, fearing personal injury and subsequent bad publicity or lawsuits, commonly issues a litany of cautions: wild animals threaten humans; water in lakes and streams needs purification; hiking alone invites trouble; violent weather suddenly arises; rock falls maim or kill; rushing waters may sweep visitors away; summer heat desiccates; overexertion leads to sickness or death. Joseph Sax (1980), by contrast, urges that such "threats" be seen as parts of wild land experiences, and that the parks continue to be "mountains without handrails."

The dangers present in the natural world are not simply imagined or created to serve some ulterior purpose. People occasionally do suffer serious harm and even die from encounters with wildness in the landscape, from grizzly bears or rock slides, from cold and exposure or untamed rivers, from drownings, even from murderers and other violent criminals (Shore 1994, C. Smith 1995, Clifford 1997, Sullivan 1997, Daley and Sohn 2003). Those who look upon wilderness as a landscape of kind and gentle Nature may, as in the Yellowstone country (Whittlesey 1995) or the taiga of Alaska (Krakauer 1996) or the barrier beaches of the Gulf Coast (Larson 1999) or the high peaks of the Himalayas (Krakauer 1997), find themselves unable to avoid the consequences of being excessively immersed in the natural world. Lyme disease and the West Nile virus, moreover, remind us that even the nature in the everyday world presents potentially mortal threats. Human survival depends, in fact, upon some separation from nature.

Reflections

Think of wilderness not only as vast, roadless landscape but also as the natural scene, however vague its precise definition. The 12 million acres of Wrangell–St. Elias National Park/Preserve and the 24,000 acres of Pinnacles National Monument, the 700,000 acres of the Washakie Wilderness and the 10,000 acres of the Brasstown Wilderness, the 200,000 acres of the Sevilleta National Wildlife Refuge and the 40 acres of the Nantucket National Wildlife Refuge, the 42,000 acres of the Afton Canyon Natural Area, the 1,600 acres of the Silver Lake Research Natural Area, the 3,000 acres of the Table Rock State Park, the 140,000 acres of the Red Lake Game Refuge and Wildlife Management Area, the 150 acres of Bringham County Park, the 30 acres of the Santa Cruz Long-Toed Salamander Ecological Reserve, the 2,000 acres of the Ridges Sanctuary—all protect the natural world, all "save the wilderness," all reflect the American impulse to preserve nature.

That impulse, however widespread, hardly permeates all of the national scene. The variety of negative landscape meanings explored in this chapter implies that sentiment unsympathetic to nature protection derives from a range of motivations, not easily subsumed under such common images as "greedy robber baron" and "insensitive materialist." Moreover, only one of the negative meanings—wilderness as cornucopia—might be readily analyzed from the perspective of detached inquiry in an effort to ferret out the truth and from that enlightenment decide whether or not wilderness incurs a practical cost. Otherwise, the negative imagery builds from various foundations and thus may not be readily susceptible to modification by direct and conscious "education," as in "environmental education" that promises "environmental sensitivity." An exploration of wilderness meanings, both positive and negative, in the context of the importance of myth and narrative in American (or, more generally, human) society might be more honest and ultimately more constructive than mere dogmatic assertions.

The variety of positive wilderness meanings discussed in these pages, too, suggests the diverse motivations for the protectionist impulse. Reflecting more than a vague tree-hugging sentimentality, these meanings may nonetheless emanate most strongly, although not exclusively, from those segments of the American population considered wealthy, educated, and powerful. Whether this observation generates critique—the stigma of elite, class-based preference (Tucker 1982)—or defense—the embrace of "everything that makes life graceful and civilized" (Stegner quoted in Vale 1998: 21)—might be argued endlessly.

This diversity of positive imagery more generally leads to the general point of the discussion: to see all of the protectionist impulse as a response to a single motivation, a single ideal, a single meaning of wilderness, a single meaning of nature, is to misread American motivation to protect nature. There is no single explanation, one right way to achieve the goal of preserving nature or interacting with nature in the American scene. This moderating comment seems as applicable to advocates of the false-idol view who cast aspersions on sacred-space idealists as to sacred-space enthusiasts who regret expressions of the wild pleasuring ground. Ironically, moreover, the diversity of positive and constructive meanings may suggest an endless cacophony, but a unifying note binds most of them together: the uniting music, however diffuse its tones, comes from the natural world, from wildness, from wilderness.

2 NATURE PROTECTION, CONSERVATION, AND THE CONSERVATION MOVEMENT

Variations in the ways people frame environmental problems contribute to a seemingly eternal debate on how to deal with those issues. The geographer Daniel B. Luten, in assessing the unremitting dialogue over the limits of the Earth—is it a plundered planet or a cornucopia with enough and to spare?—suggests that the discussion defies objective resolution because positions reflect opposing assumptions and purposes: "No wonder they disagreed so endlessly; conflicting faiths hid different premises—they were talking about different things" (Luten 1986: 314).

"Different things"—not only are the meanings of wild landscapes diverse, but so too are the larger contextual frameworks into which we place these meanings. Those contexts are the conservation movement or the environmental movement, the societal effort to deal with natural resources and relationships between people and nature. As with the wilderness imagery, this movement encompasses greater diversity than is sometimes recognized.

Ubiquity of Concern for Nature Protection, Ubiquity of Contradictions in Nature Relations

Positive meanings of wild landscapes do not reside uniquely in any particular society. For every expression of wilderness as sacred space that can be found in the books of John Muir or of the Sierra Club, for example, we find, especially within the animist religions of tribal peoples, divine beings dwelling among the world's wild places (Jordan and Rowntree 1986). Mountains commonly house the gods because they are places where Earth and sky meet, "where the human spirit could pass from one cosmic level to another" (Tuan 1974). Examples abound: Mount Olympus for the ancient Greeks, Mount Fuji for followers of Japanese Shinto, the San Francisco Peaks for the Hopi and Navajo. But the sacred lies not only on the peaks; Indo-Europeans worshiped oaks as the residences of sacred beings (Taylor 1979), and Celtic shamans went into forest groves in order to develop their wisdom (Vest 1985). The river Ganges remains sacred to the Hindus of India, and even the vast emptiness of the desert called Moses to meet God.

Other specific wilderness meanings expressed or implied by environmentalist America, as explored in chapter 1, appear in the idea flows of different societies. The sense of historical roots in nature is ubiquitous, as evidenced by the creation myths that see humans emerging from trees (Vest 1985) or created by Coyote (Lopez 1977). Similarly, the tendency of nonliterate peoples to value themselves and their home landscapes as superior to all others (Tuan 1974) resembles the American nationalistic tradition of valuing the American wilderness. In like fashion, the contemporary expression of wilderness as a scientific ecosystem shares similarities with the connectedness that typifies animist religions, such as that of the Zuñi: "If man, who is conceived as an integral part of the animate universe, is to receive the blessings of the supernaturals, the parts of the universe must be maintained as a harmonious whole, by prayers, offerings, magical practices, and above all by ceremonies" (Spencer et al. 1965). Today ecology-minded scientists promise continuation of the "blessings" of nature only if nature's "harmonious whole" is maintained, not with "magical practices" but with application of science. Perhaps, too, the contemporary urgings for an ethically based human gentleness toward nature to allow a continuation of evolutionary processes seems analogous to the worldviews of so many subsistence peoples who "respect other life forms" as part of "ideological systems that enforce sustainable use of resources" (N. Turner 1997: 277–78), or who as "wise environmental managers [are] nearly universal in their understanding of a sustainable land/culture relationship" (Martinez 1996: 50–51). Taken together, then, the positive meanings that emanate from nature-enthusiastic segments of American society are but modern manifestations of sentiments widespread in the human experience; so widespread, in fact, that those Americans who defend the natural world cannot be characterized as either a special people with unusual insights or aberrant folks who, because of their idealization of nature, have lost their sense of humanity.

Coherence in perspectives from one human group to another, moreover, also extends to destructive interactions with nature. Premodern societies were never peopled by noble savages who lived in romantic bliss with nature (Redford 1990). Prehistoric folks who embraced a sense of harmony with animals, for example, may have helped push large Pleistocene mammals into extinction (a still-disputed suggestion made long ago by Martin and Wright [1967]), and more recent North American native peoples were apparently carelessly wasteful in their killings of herds of buffalo and pronghorn (Frison 1978/1991, C. Kay 1994; but see Yochim 2001b). Similarly, the Indians who cooperated with European fur traders in the apparent depletion of North American fur-bearing mammals did so without contradiction to at least some of their environmental beliefs (J. Kay 1985). Moreover, Stone Age peoples may have deforested Western Europe (Iverson 1956), and premodern humans generally may have maintained large areas of the Americas in a perpetual deforested condition by the use of fire; we now regard burning to maintain grasslands as good, but it was nonetheless deforestation (Pyne 1982; cf. Vale, ed., 2002). The popularity of seeing animist societies as ecologically wise is intellectually naive and even patronizing:

At its worst, the tendency to define Indians as environmentalists verges on "noble savagery." Once more Indians have become merely a device for criticizing white society. . . . [Indians are] complex people rather than . . . the simple symbols they have become in popular culture. [Even] cultural ecology . . . [reduces] Indian social systems and practices to hidden and convoluted adaptations to various natural processes. In their own way these just-so-stories are often as simplistic as popular images of the Indian. (White 1985)

In other words, a premodern subsistence people may have treated, or today may continue to treat, the natural environment with the same contradictions as does a modern industrial country. Societies certainly vary—some modify nature more destructively than others—but all transform the natural world: "All of us must consume [nature] to live" (Tuan 1970: 249).

The United States as a Leader in Nature Protection

Strong sentiment favorable to nature need not result in behavior or policy that reflects protection of nature. In spite of attitude surveys that demonstrate popular environmental concern in all types of contemporary countries (Dunlap, Gallup, and Gallup 1993), in today's world of nations rich and poor, Western and non-Western, Marxist and capitalist, industrial and peasant, egalitarian and autocratic, democratic and despotic, the force for wild nature protection strongly resides in countries of one type, wealthy Western societies, and in one country in particular, the United States. In no other society is the concern for nature protection so strong, and nowhere else does that concern so permeate both the formal and informal parts of society. It may not be hyperbolic to claim that no society in the history of humanity, as a response to nature protection sentiment, has deliberately and consciously restrained itself more from commodity resource development in parts of its landscape than the United States. The institutionalized American concern expresses itself in systems of land reserves such as parks, wilderness, and wildlife refuges; in regulations for the protection of wild species; in nature protection organizations, from the National Wildlife Federation to Earth First! All of this activity simultaneously reflects a commitment to the strongest and most secure nature protection on Earth. The future of that protection elsewhere in the world, moreover, may similarly depend upon the Western industrial societies and especially the United States. Even the radical critics of Western industrial capitalism argue this very point: nature protection as it is known in the United States hangs as an imperialistic chain on the necks of disempowered Americans specifically (Beasley 1991) and the developing world generally (Guha 1989).

Such a vaunted characterization of the United States as preeminent in nature protection—can it possibly be true? The reverse portrayal seems far more common: Western industrial societies generally and the United States specifically are responsible for a disproportionate share of commodity resource use and environmental degradation, and thus are threats to the natural world rather than its saviors. Moreover, this reasoning continues, industrial societies, whether capitalist or not, are inherently destructive of nature, so that nature protection in such countries at best is futile and at worst distracts from the fundamental political/economic/cultural reform necessary to realize lasting nature protection (Walker 1989, Bahro 1984). Whatever truth may lie in these disparaging generalities, it does not negate the proposition that another contrary feature of such countries, and of the United States in particular, is concern for nature protection. Such contradictions and paradoxes in value systems and actions, as noted earlier, seem as characteristic of prehistoric animist societies as of modern industrial countries and may be characteristic of humans generally (Tuan 1974).

TEMPORAL PATTERNS The preeminence of the United States in contemporary nature protection sentiment and action is suggested by its conservation history. The recognition of an initial emergence of laws and groups for the protection of wild landscapes and wild species in the United States during the late nineteenth and early twentieth centuries appears commonly in environmental histories. The transformation of American views of wilderness, from "howling" to "sacred," structures Roderick Nash's (1967/2001) much-cited book, although the changes he describes in detail were recognized earlier (e.g., Leopold 1949/1970; Huth 1957) and might be traced back for several centuries (Nicolson 1959). In addition, histories of particular topics, including national parks (Runte 1979, Dilsaver and Tweed 1990, Pyne 1998), conservation organizations (H. Jones 1965, Graham 1990, Miles 1995), wild animals (Matthiessen 1959, Doughty 1975, Wilcove 1994), and prominent personalities (Cohen 1984, Lowenthal 2000), focus on the decades around the turn of the twentieth century for this transformation in attitudes and policies. In a broad evaluation of American natural resource policies, Luten (1986) characterizes the institutionalization of nature protection as an indication of the maturation of attitudes in the United States, a land of a "rich folk," a wealthy society no longer bound to solely utilitarian decisions about the appearance of landscapes.

The factors responsible for this development are complex. Reformulation of what constitutes natural beauty in eighteenth-century Europe (Nicolson 1959) preceded and allowed the subsequent North American transformation. Specifically, the pre-1700 ideal of an orderly natural perfection of the God-created Earth—a perfection taken to be beauty—seemed inconsistent with the aberrant irregularities on the planet's surface, especially high rugged mountains, deep extensive caverns, and vast ocean basins, the commonness of which became apparent with scientific discovery and increased world travel. This reconciliation interpreted the irregular world as the result of the wrath of God after the Fall. So seen, the monumental forms of nature inspired awe of the divine, though not initially a sense of beauty, simultaneously generating the human emotions of dread and wonder (the "sublime"). With this change in intellectual thought, several trends in the nineteenth-century United States elevated the sense of worth in wild nature: blossoming of the romantic vision of the natural world (Huth 1957, Pyne 1998), questioning of the course of civilization and the success of city life (Nash 1968), closing of the American frontier with the associated sense of loss of the nation's dominant myth (F. J. Turner 1920), and seeking of a national identity to contrast with European countries (Runte 1979). These beliefs fostered an increasing interest in spending leisure time in natural settings (Huth 1957), subsequently generating the economic forces that promoted nature reserves (Runte 1979). The latter point is favored by Walker (1989), who criticizes what he describes as "uncritical" and "apologetic" the suggestion that either rising affluence or historical association with wilderness plays a role in the recognition of wild nature as a resource, instead favoring a narrative of regressive suppression of "popular democracy" (Walker and Heiman 1981); perhaps simple, single-factor political/economic determinism is itself "uncritical." Overall, then, the end of the nineteenth century was a time when, for reasons political, economic, and cultural, Americans saw with increasingly clarity the various positive meanings in their wild landscapes. From these beginnings grew the institutionalized efforts on behalf of nature protection that exist in today's world.

SPATIAL PATTERNS Spatial patterns of reserved land in the contemporary world also suggest the preeminence of industrial countries, and especially the United States, in nature protection. Although the industrial nations represent but 39 percent of the area of the world's countries, they contain 46 percent of the Earth's protected landscapes and 67 percent of the world's reserves (fig. 2.1). If we omit the former Soviet Union and consider only the industrial societies that have long been capitalist, the percentage of the world's land decreases to one-fifth but the percentage of the world's protected land is still one-third. The figures for the United States alone are even more skewed: the area of the United States is only 6 percent of the area of the world's countries, but within its boundaries is 15 percent of the Earth's protected natural landscape. Whether or not these figures indicate that the nature protection effort in industrial countries is adequate is another question, and clearly no one committed to parks, wilderness, and wildlife will say that the job is finished. Rather, the numbers indicate simply that in today's world the Western industrial countries are leaders in nature protection.

To dichotomize humans into tree-hugging preservationists from Western societies and ax-wielding destroyers from the developing world would be to err as egregiously as to characterize Americans as nothing more than evil nature killers. Examples of nature protection sentiment abound in non-Western societies, whether as government policy in individual countries (Cahn and Cahn 1992, Simonian 1995, B. Taylor 1995), as part of national pride (Dunlap et al. 1993, Lipske 1994), or—the most common contemporary articulation—as an expression of cultural survival (Clay 1991, S. Stevens 1997). Nature preserves occur in societies throughout the non-Western world (World Resources Institute 1998) and reveal rich narrative histories that rival those told in the United States (Simonian 1995, Evans 1999). Indigenous peoples may have much to teach the Westerner in regard to the maintenance of ecosystems, and they play a major role in the ideal of the biosphere reserve for protected landscapes (Nietschmann 1984, Clay 1985, Gregg

Figure 2.1. Wild landscapes protected by countries of various sorts

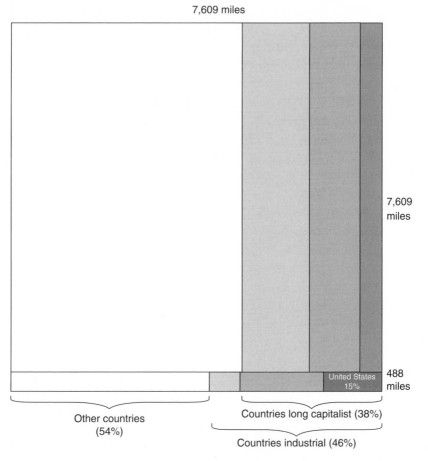

Square is area of continents; vertical bars are areas of unprotected landscapes; horizontal bar is area of protected landscapes.

1991, S. Stevens 1997). An international environmental opinion survey (Dunlap et al. 1993) even revealed that loss of biological species seemed more important to citizens of several Latin American countries than to those living in North America or Europe.

Still, in spite of these positive impulses in the developing world, both the opportunities to influence decisions for nature protection and the coercive abilities to exert that influence rest in powerful Western countries. Nature protection cannot be enhanced by dedication to anachronistic practices or to nostalgic and romantic interpretations of nonindustrial peoples.

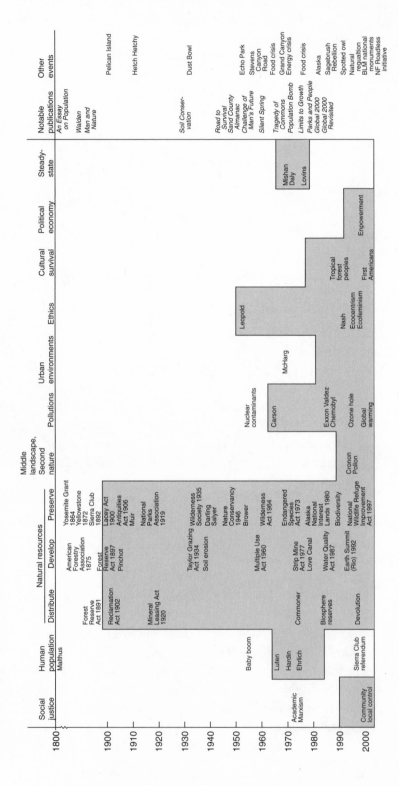

Figure 2.2. Issues embraced by U.S. environmental movement and salient events of concern to environmentalists, 1900–2000. (Simplified and updated from Luten 1986)

Its future success can be expressed only through the political will of modern societies such as the United States.

Conservation and Environmentalism

The concern for nature protection, increasingly institutionalized within American society over the last century, has been part of a still larger social movement focused on natural resources, also strengthening within the United States since the late nineteenth century, commonly called the conservation movement or the environmental movement (Kline 2000). Some observers would distinguish earlier conservation from contemporary environmentalism (e.g., Macinko 1968, Hays 1987), but the temporal distinction misleads more than it clarifies—the dichotomy might even be described as wrong. The same fundamental concerns that characterized the beginnings of the conservation movement typify those of the modern environmental movement. Specifics may have changed, but the threads that connect issue to issue backward in time are stronger than the imaginary lines that divide one period from the next.

In spite of continuity in broad concerns, the American conservation movement has become increasingly diversified in issues it embraces as environmentalism (Luten 1986; fig. 2.2). From an initial focus on forest protection and creation of national parks, conservation or environmentalism today touches on a wide range of issues, from human population growth to radioactive wastes, from cultural survival to electric utility profits, from Marxism to biodiversity. It is hard to see the limits to matters that the contemporary environmentalist would consider appropriate to address.

The broadening may suggest, in fact, that what we call conservation has become too diffuse to have any meaning, but that judgment would be unduly harsh. Whether called conservation or environmentalism, the movement has remained true to certain basic tenets. First, assumptions or faiths (Luten 1986) about the fundamental characters of the natural and human worlds underlie most conservation positions: the natural world is finite; the human capacity to manipulate nature is limited; and the two spheres of nature and people—themselves distinctive and separate—are necessarily and intricately linked. Second, conservation is concerned with the future, often the distant future, and with the welfare of humanity vis-à-vis its ties to the natural world. Third, conservation goals are collective goals, involving groups or society generally, and the successes of conservation perspectives have involved an expansion of government involvements, typically at the federal level, at the expense of unlimited individual freedoms. More generally, the conservation or environmental movement can be seen as a social effort to prod society into changing attitudes and policies from those that focus on immediate individual utility to those that focus on collective, distant, and diverse human purposes (Luten 1986).

Conservation Impulses

Between diversification that has characterized conservation at the level of particular issues and continuity that has typified conservation at the scale of fundamental tenets, the conservation movement, at intermediate levels of generality, reveals stability in purposes. Three arenas of concern may be identified, varying in expression with the particular issues existent at different time periods but continuing more generally from the beginning of institutionalized conservation policy into the modern day (cf. Koppes 1987). These arenas might be called schools of conservation or conservation impulses.

THE UTILITARIAN IMPULSE The utilitarian impulse expresses concern for the wise development of nature for human purposes. Historically, according to this perspective, conservation, as a social movement, was based on the late nineteenth-century worries of scientists and politicians over such utilitarian issues as deforestation, watershed protection, and soil erosion. Conservation policies, then, developed from the top down, from influential individuals in powerful positions who advocated more efficient use of resources; Hays (1959) has called this original motivation "conservation as efficiency." Early successes include the 1875 formation of the American Forestry Association, a group organized to monitor forest policy, and the passage of the Forest Reserve Act of 1897, which identified logging and grazing policies for the then new federal forest reserves. The concern continued through time, with such legislation as the 1934 Taylor Grazing Act, which provided for the management of the public domain lands for utilitarian purposes; the 1960 Multiple Use Act, which reaffirmed the varied management goals of the national forests; and the 1987 Water Quality Act, which extended federal control over national water standards. In all of these efforts, the conservation concern is for utility in the development of natural resources.

A multitude of issues characterize this concern in more recent years. Most come readily to mind: soil erosion as a threat to continued world agricultural production (Pimentel et al. 1995); loss of global forests as a risk to water cycling, energy budgets, and present climate patterns (Myers 1995); shortages and development of mineral deposits as influences on human well-being (Hodges 1995); pollutions of modern technologies as hazards to people's health (Hall et al. 1992; Wolkomir 1994; Wheelwright 1995; Colborn, Dumanoski, and Myers, 1996). In addition, this concern for utility underlies seemingly distant environmental issues. In some expressions of ecofeminism, for example, the "enlightenment idea of a female Nature (one that could be probed and penetrated by a masculinist science) legitimized the unrestrained exploitation of natural resources" (Sturgeon 1997: 366); and in most economic evaluations of biodiversity, "ecosystem services . . . are to a significant extent provided by natural and semi-natural ecosystems" (Edwards and Abivardi 1999: 239). The cautions about facile invocations of economic assets of biodiversity (Bulte and Van Kooten 2000, Nunes and Van den Bergh 2001) attempt to extend arguments beyond narrow utilitarian rationales, but in this issue humanistic narratives remain secondary to the more common articulations about human well-being. Rational utility, human health, and human survival—these epitomize the utilitarian school of conservation.

THE PROGRESSIVE IMPULSE The progressive impulse expresses concern for the American people's equal access to its natural resources. Historically, according to this thinking, the institutionalization of conservation began as a part of the turn-of-the-century Populist movement, with major motivation coming not simply from powerful elites worried about resource adequacy but also from political leaders who fretted over equity in resource allocation. A corollary, moreover, sees "common people" as the prod for institutionalized conservation, as the "spiritual source of the American commons" (Judd 1997: 266). Bates (1957) has termed this impulse "conservation as democracy." Early legislation reflecting this concern includes the Forest Reserve Act of 1891, which, by authorizing the federal forest reserves, first established a strong public presence in the future of the nation's forestlands, and the Reclamation Act of 1902, which initiated federal development of water resources in the American West as a stimulus to extend across the continent the ideal of the yeoman farmer and the small agricultural community (Smythe 1900/1969). The vision of the impulse continued with such laws as the 1920 Mineral Leasing Act, which retained federal (and thus public) ownership of nonmetallic minerals (i.e., most important, fossil fuels) on the federal lands, and such issues as the fight against the "sagebrush rebellion" of the 1980s, in which state and private interests unsuccessfully attempted to gain ownership of large acreages of the federal lands (Graf 1990). In all these situations, the concern is for egalitarian distribution of the natural resource base, for equity.

As is true of the utilitarian school, the progressive tradition remains strong in contemporary American and global conservation. Its expressions vary: antagonism toward corporate bodies (Sierra Club 1995); declarations of the common goals of environmental protection and human rights (Gottlieb 1993, Hurley 1995); advocacy for minorities, particularly Native Americans, as a conservation issue (Strickland 1981; Gmelch 1990; Beasley 1991; Baird 1992; Gabriel 1994; Spence 1996); concern for urban pollutions that disproportionately threaten minority groups, a part of the rationale for equating environmentalism with social justice (Hurley 1995); the popularity of "cultural survival" as an environmental concern (S. Stevens 1997); political alignment with the Democratic rather than the Republican party (T. Williams 1991); the view of powerful political entities as regressively evil (O'Riordan 1981, Worster 1986); and the appeal—especially among academics—of Marxist interpretations of natural resource matters (Walker 1989, Worster 1994). Perhaps the popularity of equating ecological wisdom with local initiative rather than with decisions handed down from remote political authorities (Kuzmiak 1991, Ladd and Bowman 1996) and even postmodern views of the undesirable consequences of contemporary policies (Morehouse 1996) might express the progressive, antiestablishment tradition in American conservation.

THE AESTHETIC IMPULSE The aesthetic impulse focuses on the protection of nature from development activities. Nash (1968) has labeled this concern "conservation as anxiety," because it emerged, according to Nash, as part of turn-of-the-century questioning of the benefits of the nation's physical/economic development. Historically, the authorization of the Yosemite Grant in 1864, the formation of Yellowstone National Park in 1872, and the creation of the Sierra Club in 1892 are particularly well-known early examples of this impulse, although other successes of those years are also noteworthy: the passage of the 1900 Lacey Act, which extended federal jurisdiction over wild birds killed in violation of state laws and transported across state lines; the creation of the first national wildlife refuge on Florida's Pelican Island in 1903; and the 1906 Antiquities Act, which authorized presidential proclamation of national monuments on the federal lands. Continuing through the century, the concerns of the aesthetic school were manifested in the formation of such groups as the National Parks and Conservation Association in 1919, the Wilderness Society in 1935, and the Nature Conservancy in 1946. Legislation representing this concern in more recent years includes the 1964 Wilderness Act, by which Congress assumed respon- sibility for creation (and dissolution) of formal wilderness areas on the federal lands, and the 1973 Endangered Species Act, which extended federal authority over biological species facing extinction. The focus of this perspective is based on the belief that "the world is more to be admired than to be used" (Thoreau, as quoted by Luten 1986), and thus this conservation impulse might be said to be a concern for preservation of the admirable beauty in the natural world, or, in short, for beauty. It is, of course, the subject matter of this book.

Continuing as a part of contemporary conservation, causes of the aesthetic impulse come easily to mind—the reintroduction of wolves to Yellowstone, the return of water inflows to Mono Lake, the establishment of Escalante–Grand Staircase National Monument, Forest Service protection against gas drilling on Montana's Rocky Mountain Front, an "organic act" for the National Wildlife Refuges, restoration of the Everglades. In these issues, whether or not rhetorically justified in utilitarian terms, whether or not recognized as advances of progressive sentiment, the focus is on preserving what is seen as beauty in the natural world.

MULTIPLE MOTIVATIONS OR IMPULSES Particular laws, organized groups, or natural resource issues may reflect more than one motivation, and thus be representative of more than one conservation impulse. In fact, most conservation events manifest multiple motivations. For example, the Forest Reserve Act was intended not only to protect utilitarian resources of the federal forests but also to enhance the public interest in the management of those forestlands, and thus their progressive purposes. The Reclamation Act grew not only from an egalitarian vision of the family farm but also from a utilitarian sense of making the deserts bloom. The acts that created Yosemite and Yellowstone as reserves for protection of nature also embraced a vision of the new parks as places for the general American public to engage in recreation. So, too, with contemporary issues: the loss of global forests threatens not only the utilitarian uses of forests as wood-producing systems but also the function of forests as habitat for wild animals and plants, which are part of the aesthetic resource; enhancing Native Americans' control over parts of the landscape seems to many to serve both the progressive cause of human rights and the utilitarian cause of conservative consumptive use of nature; prohibiting gas development on the Rocky Mountain Front saves wild landscape and constrains energy conglomerates. In sum, then, complexity, rather than simplicity, characterizes the motivations of those involved with the conservation movement.

Nonetheless, in spite of the overlapping causes, the multiple purposes that prod conservation-minded folks to action, the distinctive goals of conservationists remain distinct and separate: they are not the same. An appreciation of the differences in conservation traditions is vital both to the historical understanding of why particular actions occurred in the past and to the contemporary strategic planning for present and future policies. Because the motivations not only differ from one another but often are in direct conflict, satisfying the purposes of one impulse may not achieve the purposes of another, and if fact may jeopardize them. The universality of this simple observation seems to be too rarely appreciated.

Illustrations of the lack of simple concordance among the conservation impulses vary from the obvious to the subtle. For example, the fundamental disagreement between conservationists who are associated with the utilitarian and aesthetic schools is legendary in environmental history. Early in the twentieth century, Gifford Pinchot and other adherents of utility argued on behalf of wise development of natural resources, such as the damming of Hetch Hetchy Valley in Yosemite National Park, but were opposed by John Muir and followers of the aesthetic impulse, who argued for protecting the natural beauty of such places. Hawkes (1960) interpreted these types of arguments as issues of opposing forces—not of selfish and destructive development interests against altruistic and creative preservation interests, but rather of two opposing schools of conservation. The issues become, in this perspective, not noble conservationists against vile developers but conservationists against conservationists. Luten (1986; see also Cohen 1988), moreover, suggests that the third impulse, the concern for equity, was also involved in the battle over Hetch Hetchy in that progressive thinking favored the building of the dam because it was seen as a boost to public power development. Wallach adds further complexity to the story by suggesting that even Pinchot revealed feelings consistent with the aesthetic tradition in his defense of fallen trees in Yosemite National Park: utilitarians wanted to harvest them but Pinchot saw them as "among the greatest of the beauties. . . . I would not touch one of them" (quoted by Wallach 1991: 49). Allegiance to the principles of utility or equity or beauty is rarely free of qualification, compromise, or contradiction.

Other examples, more subtle, link utilitarian and progressive sentiments against aesthetic purposes. Historically, wildlife conservation efforts at the turn of the twentieth century antagonized rural poor and native peoples and favored urban, sport-hunting elites (Warren 1997). More recently, the efforts to protect large areas of the wild Alaskan landscape, cause célèbre of the aesthetic school and strongly opposed by development interests, became entangled in Native Alaskan rights when the Reagan administration proposed transferring the rights to drill for petroleum in the Arctic National Wildlife Refuge to Inuit companies, a move designed to facilitate the development of the fossil fuel resource. "It's a way to divide natives from environmentalists," commented a regional director of the Audubon Society (Zielenziger 1987). Divisive it was, but it also demonstrates that enhancing the economic opportunities of Native Americans, a traditional part of progressive politics, may not advance the goals of protecting wild landscapes. An analogous situation, but one that attracted little attention among aesthetic impulse groups (at least publicly), occurred in 1975 when about 185,000 acres of Grand Canyon National Park were eliminated from the park and added to the Havasupai Indian Reservation (and still other park land was opened to Havasupai "traditional uses") (Keller and Turek 1998). In addition, the suggestion during the mid-1980s to remove the dam in Hetch Hetchy Valley was opposed by the normally progressive politicians in San Francisco, who looked upon the system of dams and reservoirs not only as their water supply but also, through the sale of hydroelectric power, as a money-generating facility. The issue of population growth—and particularly American immigration policy—reveals how distinct the aesthetic (or utilitarian) tradition is from the progressive in American conservation: in spite of an earlier critical position on both immigration and population growth more generally (Luten 1986), the Sierra Club board of directors in 1996 formally took no position on immigration policy, prompted by a concern that any explicit opposition would detract from efforts to counter "the root social problems of population growth" (Sierra Club 1997, 1998), a decidedly progressive articulation. At the turn of the twenty-first century, efforts to continue the protection of the Arctic National Wildlife Refuge from petroleum development were opposed by organized labor—one of the foundations of traditional progressive politics—who saw in the oil drilling an opportunity for jobs. Concern for equity may compromise concern for beauty.

Nonetheless, many more issues than not bind concerns for beauty and equality against those for utility, the common association of the two reflecting late twentieth-century conventional wisdom. For example, the halting

of below-cost timber sales on the national forests and the reducing of livestock grazing on the public lands both express positions of conservationists
of the aesthetic school, but progressive sentiment also typically favors these
goals because large corporations and big landholding ranchers benefit disproportionately from the production of commodities on the federal lands.
More generally, restrictions against commodity resource development, the
major thrust of those concerned with nature protection, may be seen as
restrictions against corporate America, an archfoe in progressive political
matters. Regardless of such overlaps, however, the egalitarian tradition remains distinctive, apart from other environmental concerns (Lewis 1992a).

Occasionally issues seem to generate unanimity among the three conservation impulses. The early development of nuclear power in the 1950s
was simultaneously favored by those who saw fission fuels as a utilitarian
resource, by others who hoped that it would become a public power source
and thus a boon to a more progressive society (Luten 1986), and by still
others who envisioned that it would eliminate the need for dams and thus
reduce pressure for hydroelectric power development in wild landscapes
(D. Brower 1990). It is no wonder that for a time nuclear power seemed a
panacea, although the simultaneous satisfaction of varied purposes was
probably always illusory: strings of nuclear power plants along the nation's
coastlines, whether built by government agencies or private utilities, might
mute the cries for hydroelectric dams, but they would intrude into still
other wild landscapes.

More recently the opposition to deforestation in the tropics appeals to
a broad spectrum within the conservation community (Denevan 1973, Myers
and Tucker 1987, Fernside 1989, Murray 1990), as protection of the Adirondack forests probably did in the nineteenth century (Schneider 1997, Terrie
1997). In today's concern for the clearing of low-latitude forests, utilitarian
concerns focus on the deterioration of the exposed soil or the modified climate; progressives defend the rights of indigenous peoples and the survival
of their cultures; aesthetic concerns stress the loss of biological diversity
(perhaps useful for human utility) or of wildness in the landscape. But, as
in the early years of nuclear power, when everyone also seemed to be on the
same side, the purposes of the different strains of conservationists remain
different, and solutions that satisfy one perspective may not further the purposes of another. For example, agroforestry or sustainable agricultural systems might serve as wise use of the tropical environments from a utilitarian
perspective, but they will not necessarily preserve wild nature (see McRae

1997) or enhance human rights. Similarly, land reform associated with more intensive human use of tropical latitudes might satisfy progressive purposes but not necessarily aesthetic or utilitarian sentiments. Finally, protection of nature, "saving the tropical forests," might not further the goals of either utilitarian or progressive groups. Multiple human purposes remain distinctive threads even if they are at times woven together.

Besides contributing to the unraveling of entwined purposes in the general political arena, the articulation of the distinctive impulses of conservation often requires groups and individuals to choose among conflicting purposes in particular situations. In the late 1970s, for example, the proposal to build the New Melones dam on California's Stanislaus River generated support from unlikely people: a former president of the Sierra Club, the archetype organization of the aesthetic school, and a former student eco-activist from the University of California on the Berkeley campus who had once argued for a revamping of "the guts of our entire culture." From their perspectives, these two found that the enhanced agriculture promised by the new dam seemed more important than the preservation of a wild river (Mitchell 1980). Similarly, Congressman Mo Udall, a champion of parks and wilderness and a member of a family beloved by environmentalists, also advocated dam construction in the Grand Canyon, in Grand Canyon National Park, and it would be too simple to say that his position was simply a reflection of his pro-dam Arizona constituency: the Udalls were a Western farming family dependent on irrigation, and Mo's outlook on dams was not one of blanket condemnation (Gendlin 1982). More recently the green movement in France, often considered a part of progressive sentiment, now seems to appeal as much to the right side of the political spectrum (including neo-Nazis) as to the left (Galtung 1986, Chase 1991). As a consequence, people who support the utilitarian or nature protection purposes of green politics may not be able to assume that their comrades will necessarily be progressive. Similarly, the efforts to protect nature in the countries of the developing world—a cause central to the purposes of the aesthetic conservation tradition—seem to progressive-minded observers to be exploitation of poor and powerless peoples, efforts by "authoritarian biologist[s]," through "the arrogance of anti-humanism," to act as "green missionaries" to extend "green imperialism" (Guha 1997).

In spite of these examples from both the past and the present, examples that illustrate the distinctiveness of the conservation traditions, a strong modern tendency sees the goals of the diverse conservation movement as complementary, even stemming from the same basic concern. Create a just society, the sense seems to be, and you will necessarily create a society that is both wise in resource use and noble in nature protection. The realities of diverse conservation impulses suggest that such a simplistic view is both intellectually naive and strategically unwise.

Reflections

A quarter of a century ago, Daniel B. Luten cautioned conservationists about the ease with which concern for beauty—for nature protection, for aesthetic impulse goals—drifted in the rhetoric of the political world into the arena of the utilitarian tradition. "The conservation battlefront is across the board. More and more, it begins on the preservation side and swings quickly across into utilitarian issues." He was afraid that the purposes of protectionist sentiment would be drowned in the ocean of utilitarian tides: "principles may be forgotten, entanglements may become unending, objectives may become confused" (Luten 1986). If Luten were commenting today, he might see as even more threatening the waves of the progressive school, which, in both the popular mind and the academic treatise, too often assumes that concern for beauty floats as but a passive raft in the fundamental current of egalitarian conservation. Ah, we should live in so simple, so monolithic a world.

Park and wilderness, refuge and reserve, healthy plant populations and robust animal numbers, preserved ecosystem and wild landscape—each expresses a nature protected, a focus for the aesthetic impulse of conservation. In the history of that impulse and in the contemporary expression of it, both the strength of conviction and the power to influence decisions emanate from Western industrial democratic countries. Such societies embrace other purposes, as does any individual who lives within their communities: nature protection cannot be, in either collective or personal decisions, the single issue that unites all human goals. But the future security of protected nature, the continued legitimization of wildness as a resource, seems to rest in those societies where its contemporary institutionalization arose and where it resides today.

American
Wilderness

3 WILDERNESS AREAS AND ACRES

In commenting on the spread of knowledge about places through word of mouth, Daniel B. Luten suggests that only the most well-known locales will dominate the dialogue: "If I ask one man where to seek a job, I can end up in any American city or town. . . . [I]f I wait until two men tell me to go to the same town, I will never end up in Poplar, Montana, and if I wait for a third confirmation, I can only end up in Los Angeles. . . . I can only go to the places I am told of and in the manner familiar to me" (Luten 1986: 172–73). If he were asking about places to encounter a wild American landscape and waited for multiple confirmations, Luten might only end up in Yellowstone.

The lesson applies to familiarity with and knowledge of wild landscape reserves. Anyone even peripherally interested in nature protection certainly knows of Yosemite and Yellowstone national parks, probably is familiar with the Boundary Waters Canoe Area Wilderness, and may have heard of the Wichita Mountains National Wildlife Refuge. But does that person recognize the names of the Signal Hill Research Natural Area in Nebraska, Cedarburg Bog Scientific Area in Wisconsin, Empire/Cienega Resource Conservation Area in Arizona, Ahjumawi Lava Springs State Park in California, Pond Pine Wilderness of North Carolina, or Missisquoi National Wildlife Refuge of Vermont? The dedicated enthusiast might know of one or two of these more obscure nature reserves, perhaps those close to home or within the realm of individual experience, but rarely more. To be honest, it would be naive to expect any individual to be familiar with more than a handful of the hundreds of thousands of named areas of protected natural landscape. To appreciate the vastness of this wilderness is to recognize the strength of the institutionalization of protected nature in American society.

An Inventory of Protected Landscape—What to Include?

In principle it may be easy to recognize the variety of protected landscape, but it is far more difficult to create a detailed list of preserved acreage: areas must be categorized as either protected, and thus included in the list, or vulnerable, and so omitted. This dichotomous classification simplifies the varying strengths of protection afforded various types of landscapes, which actually are arrayed along a continuum of degrees of preservation. Multiple-use national forests, for example, should be seen as less protected than national parks but more protected than midwestern farmland, which, with its mix of cropland, pastures, and woodlots, seems to preserve the natural world more than Chicago's Loop. Our problem is to decide where along the continuum to draw the line separating protected from unprotected landscape.

Even the identification of the two types of nature reserves that might represent the poles—the most protected and the least protected of wild landscapes—similarly invites dissension. In deciding on criteria to determine which nature reserves to include in our list and which to exclude, we might consider the 7.5-million-acre Gates of the Arctic National Park as most protected and the half-acre of oak woods in Westmorland Park (the small city park behind my home) as least protected. Four such criteria come to mind. First, the size of the reserve matters: the greater the acreage, the more appropriate for nature protection. The national park wins easily over the woodlot by this measure. Second, the landscape context of any reserved land influences its effectiveness; again, the Alaskan park, surrounded by vast wild lands, offers greater security for the nature within its boundaries than the city woodlot, set within a grid of streets and houses. Third, the character of the statutory protection distinguishes any reserve. The national park, protected by legislation prohibiting development of commodity resources and shielded from recreational roads and hotels, is clearly more secure than the oak woods, which might be transformed into a baseball diamond by the city parks board or paved over for a bus transfer station by the city council. Fourth, the types of human uses permitted within reserves also alter the perception of protection; subsistence hunting by Alaskan natives might compromise the Gates of the Arctic, but the dirt-bike tracks and Saturday-afternoon boom-box noise seem to render the city park more threatened, even though its wildlife enjoys protection from hunters.

The final point—human uses allowed within reserved lands—comes closest to the critical characteristic that justifies inclusion or exclusion from a list of protected acreage. If the primary purpose of a landscape reservation, even if compromised by other purposes, is to protect nature from conversion to commodities and services, it deserves to be counted as exemplifying at least the spirit of the aesthetic conservation impulse. This criterion accepts the reality of variable degrees of protection—whether associated with small size, unfavorable context, political vulnerability, or less than absolute regulatory rules—and recognizes that not all nature protectionists will be satisfied by the inclusion of certain areas among the protected.

With this standard of purpose in mind, an initial judgment can be made about the degree to which landscapes have been dedicated to nature protection in a given modern society. It is the criterion of permitted land uses, in fact, that prompts wilderness enthusiasts to praise or criticize the nature-protection efforts of entire societies, typically expressed by the percentages of country areas that fall within reserves with constraints on commodity resource uses. Such expressions commonly appear in the literature:

If [Costa Rica] manages to conserve 25 percent of its forests in parks . . . it may well become a "super power" of a new kind. (Wallace 1992: xvi)

The countries of the former U.S.S.R. protect the least amount of their land area; just over 1 percent. (World Resources Institute 1994: 315)

The World Conservation Union estimates that nearly 10 percent . . . of the Earth's land surface is now designated as protected. (Quammen 2003: 77)

The overall coverage of conservation areas worldwide . . . increase[d] from anestimated 3.48% to 8.82% [from 1985 to 1997]. (Zimmerer, Galt, and Buck, forthcoming)

However helpful as an initial assessment, a spotlight on the percentage of landscape that has been protected cannot replace a more careful and complete assessment of nature protection in societal settings. Some critics of the status quo, in fact, might argue that a focus on the successes merely builds complacency, camouflaging what needs to be done, whether strengthening existing efforts or restructuring the very foundation of political economies. Hiding reality behind masks of strategy or ideology, however, can only limit the understanding of wild nature as a resource in American society.

The data on nature reserves are problems in themselves. Acreage figures issued by government agencies vary much more than a casual observer might expect, reflecting both changes in sizes of reserves through time and differ-

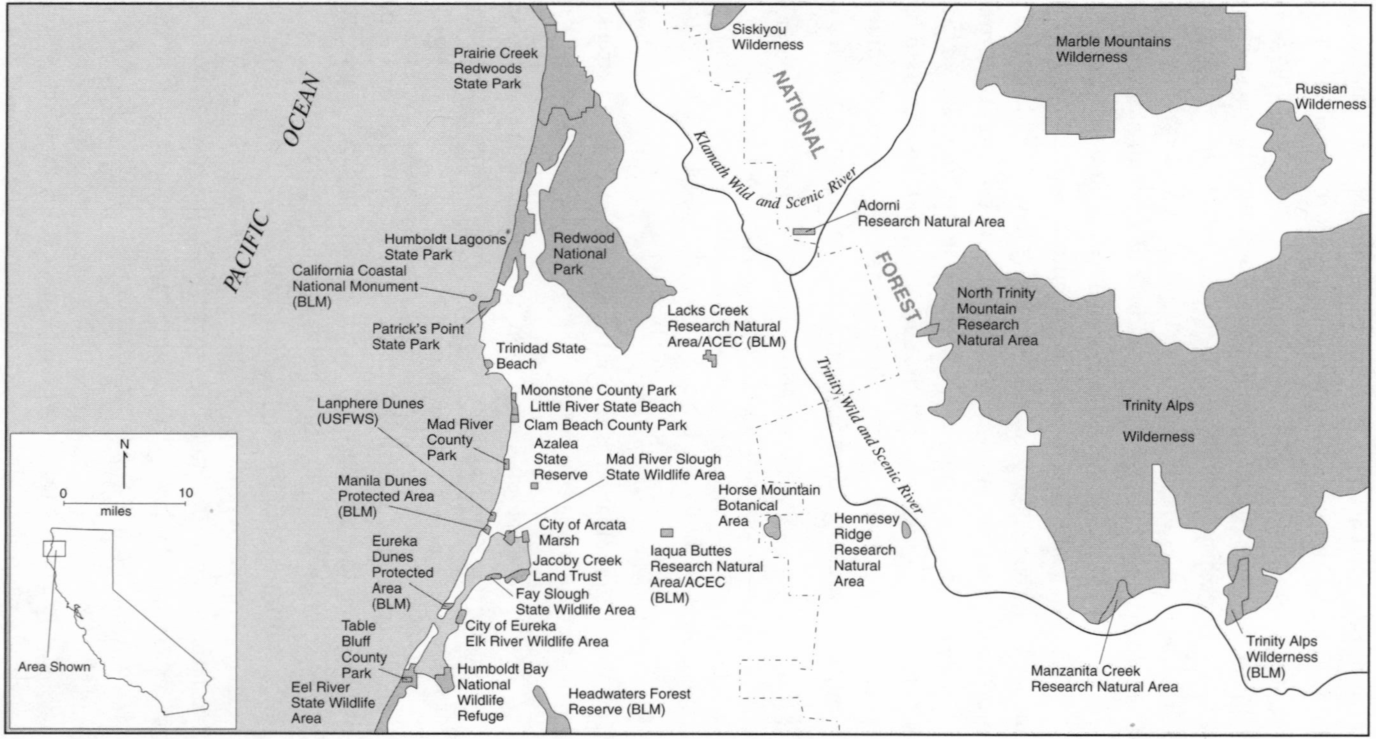

Figure 3.1. Protected landscapes of extreme northwestern California

ences in details of land administration. What numbers should be used to identify landscape area protected? For federal land reserves, for example, should the areas within authorized external boundaries be used, or only the acreage actually owned by the federal land agencies? Should land areas leased be grouped with land held in fee simple? What about state land within the exterior boundaries of federal reserves, lands over which some protective influence might be exerted, as opposed to private land, for which constraints on alternative land uses are much more problematic? These questions of land tenure become more critical when we consider landscapes protected by state wildlife agencies, where leased and cooperatively managed areas sometimes account for large proportions of the total areas of reserved land. Even more confusing are the patterns of overlapping designations, such as statutory wilderness within a national recreation area, or a research natural area within a national conservation area, or a state natural area within a state park. Consider the already existing protected landscape included within the exterior boundaries of Giant Sequoia National Monument, administered by the U.S. Forest Service, when that unit was established by presidential proclamation in 2001: portions of wild and scenic rivers, wilderness, botanical areas, research natural areas, and special areas designated for California condor nesting and golden trout habitat. Ambiguities and double counting appear not only in the less developed world but also in data-conscious Western societies.

Examples of Protected Landscapes: Northwestern California and Southern Wisconsin

The diversity of nature-protection preserves can be seen in many parts of the country. Two areas, a large area in extreme northwestern California and a smaller region of southern Wisconsin, illustrate that diversity, although questions might be raised about whether or not any particular preserve deserves to be labeled "protected nature."

NORTHWESTERN CALIFORNIA A region inland from the northern California coast near Eureka provides a broad array of nature reserves (fig. 3.1). This region, with its wetlands and forests, mountains and seacoasts, rivers and lowlands, exemplifies some of the landscape diversity in the country as a whole. The area's pattern of land tenure includes both privately owned and publicly administered lands, again paralleling the more general mix in America. Nonetheless, public lands are far more important here than in the country overall, a bias appropriate for the public sector's contribution to nature protection.

The largest acreage of protected landscape in northwestern California lies on the various systems of the federal lands, a local pattern echoing that of the United States generally. First, the charismatic and glamorous National Park System, administered by the National Park Service, includes, in northwestern California, Redwood National Park. Although the Wilderness Act, passed in 1964, provides for congressionally designated wilderness within units of the National Park System, no such wilderness has been established in Redwood National Park. (Should we listen to those critics who lament the roads and other recreational developments in the national parks and thus exclude these reserves from our list of protected nature acreage? I think not: national parks unambiguously deserve inclusion.)

Second, the national forests of the U.S. Forest Service protect congressionally established wilderness, several large units of which here embrace the high-elevation mountains well inland from the Pacific coast—the Marble Mountains Wilderness, the Russian Wilderness, and the Trinity Alps Wilderness. As with the national parks, statutory wilderness might constitute compromised protection because within national forest wilderness many nonconforming uses are permitted, including sport hunting and livestock grazing, although the prohibition against roads gives wilderness, even Forest Service wilderness, a privileged status in the eyes of most nature enthusiasts. Forest Service personnel categorize the landscape of each national forest into various types of management units, some of which protect natural values from commodity resource development, at least to varying degrees. In northwestern California such designations include the 650-acre Adorni Research Natural Area and the 1,077-acre Horse Mountain Botanical Area.

Third, the public domain lands of the Bureau of Land Management (BLM) contain congressionally established wilderness but also, like the Forest Service, administratively created landscape units that may protect natural values. Within the example area of northwestern California, only small and widely scattered tracts of land are administered by the BLM, but each includes landscape parcels protected as research natural areas/areas of critical environmental concern: 800 acres in the Lack's Creek drainage and 1,080 acres on the Iaqua Buttes reserve some old-growth forest, and 65 acres at Manila Dunes, on the Pacific Ocean, protect a dune environment, particularly from the incursions of off-road vehicles (but then, the cynic might say that the reserve is too small to be considered truly protected). In addition, a small area of BLM wilderness sits astride the Forest Service's Trinity Alps Wilderness. (As on national forest reserves, hunting and grazing is permitted within these BLM units.) Finally, the bureau administers the California Coastal National Monument, which protects offshore rocks and small islands along most of the state's coastline, including areas just off Patrick's Point.

Fourth, the National Wildlife Refuge System, managed by the Fish and Wildlife Service, appears within the example area with the Humboldt Bay National Wildlife Refuge, a relatively new unit for which land purchases are incomplete. (Wilderness might be designated on such refuges, although no such action has been taken on Humboldt Bay.)

Finally, the national wild and scenic rivers system—the units of which enjoy congressional protection against dams—includes the Klamath and Trinity rivers, which cross the representative area in northwestern California.

The federal lands may dominate the total statistics for protected natural landscape, but state land agencies administer reserves that may serve outdoor recreation or nature protection or both. State parks, for example, are maintained in most states. California's extensive system, administered with a strong preservation focus by the Division of Beaches and Parks (but also encouraging certain recreational uses), is well represented in the sample area by reserves in a variety of environments—Prairie Creek Redwoods and Humboldt Lagoons state parks protect forested slopes and coastal wetlands (and they are situated within the exterior boundary of Redwood National Park); Patrick's Point State Park, Trinidad State Beach, and Little River State Beach cling to the immediate Pacific shore; and Azalea State Reserve encloses thirty acres of spring-flowering western azaleas. In addition, the California State Department of Fish and Game oversees a network of wildlife habitat lands, particularly for wintering waterfowl and shorebirds, that are here exemplified by about 1,500 acres of tidal lands on the north side of Humboldt Bay. (Should small size, fragmented boundaries, and nonconforming recreation render some of these state lands vulnerable and thus unworthy of being considered protected?)

Local government bodies also protect wild landscapes. County and regional parks, which often serve primarily recreational purposes, nonetheless may contribute to nature protection efforts. Examples in northwestern California that do so include the Clam Beach and Mad River County parks along the coast. (Should we exclude these lands from our inventory of protected landscapes because of questionable uses—casual recreational vehicle camping on the back dunes, loose dogs and driftwood fires on the beach, absence of administrative personnel—or do we embrace the areas whose status as county parks precludes development of their ocean frontage?) In addition, the city of Arcata supports the Arcata Marsh and Wildlife Sanctuary, an innovative series of restored marshes and ponds that partially depend on treated wastewater from the city's sewage treatment plant, at the extreme north end of Humboldt Bay. The city's other major parks raise questions about suitability for inclusion on the list: Redwood Park protects a stand of coast redwood but includes playground equipment (but then, so do many states' parks), and the Arcata Community Forest encompasses more than 500 acres of wild lands, where motor vehicles are prohibited and recreationists are encouraged to "discover wonderful trails, wildlife, vegetation, and serenity," but some commercial logging is permitted.

Although the protection of wild landscapes primarily involves the public sector, private groups have become increasingly active in land purchases for nature protection. Most notable in this regard is the Nature Conservancy, whose national (and international) system of reserves is represented in northwestern California by the Lanphere-Christensen Dunes Preserve, in the belt of coastal dunes just north of Humboldt Bay (administration of the reserve has been transferred to the Fish and Wildlife Service). For almost a century the Save-the-Redwoods League has generated private monetary donations for the purchase of coast redwood forest for state parks. All of the redwood state parks in northwestern California, in fact, including the Prairie Creek Redwoods State Park, have benefited from the activity of this private conservation organization.

Quite apart from administering these named landscape reserves, government bodies at all levels also commit to nature protection through statutory regulations. For example, the federal government protects most bird species through the Migratory Bird Act and has claimed final authority for endangered species through the Rare and Endangered Species Act and for marine mammals through the Marine Mammal Protection Act. In northwestern California, then, the common Wilson's warblers that sing from roadside huckleberry thickets, the rare Clapper's rail that calls in nearby salt marshes, California sea lions that bellow from rocks off coastal waters, and gray whales that sing in distant depths far offshore—all are protected by federal law. The states retain primary responsibility for wildlife resources, however, and thus, in northwestern California, the California Department of

Fish and Game oversees mule deer in coastal brush, pine martens in inland forests, and salmon in the various rivers. Other state laws extend still further regulatory protection to nature: the 1970 California Environmental Quality Act, much like the federal National Environmental Protection Act, provides for impact assessment of public projects; the 1970 California Endangered Species Act provides for procedures to protect threatened and endangered animal species; and the 1977 Native Plant Protection Act extends the public interest to rare plants. California also has legislation that mimics the national laws for landscape protection of wild rivers and wilderness. In addition, the California Coastal Zone Conservation Commission (established by public referendum in 1972) oversees land uses along the coast; a permit from the commission is required for most development. This act has had a strong nature protection effect along the Pacific coastline.

Taken together, then, landscapes federal and state, local and private, reserved and regulated protect nature in our sample area of northwestern California. We might quarrel over what lands are most compromised, but we would have to agree that the mix of protected areas, whether or not adequate, presents an array varied and rich.

SOUTHERN WISCONSIN The lands of the American West include vast acreages administered by the federal land agencies, but elsewhere in the country, in varying degrees, other types of reserves loom larger in the picture of protected nature. A small area of western Dane County in southern Wisconsin serves to illustrate regions that lack major federal landholdings.

A dominating federal presence may be lacking in western Dane County, but that highest level of government nonetheless appears on the map of protected nature reserves in the form of small wetland purchases by the U.S. Fish and Wildlife Service (fig. 3.2). Categorized as waterfowl production areas, these parcels of marsh or pond-side grassland lack the size to be called national wildlife refuges but they serve much the same function. (Are they too small to be included in the list of protected landscapes? Does their accessibility to hunters render them questionable as nature reserves?) One such area in the sample landscape enjoys a designation—the Shoveler Sink—but most are too small to be given specific names; collectively these areas are designated the Aldo Leopold Wetland Management District. State lands include both state parks—the Blue Mounds and Governor Nelson (each has a small area of mowed lawn and playground equipment—should they not be included in the list?) and state wildlife areas, typically wetlands in marshy landscapes, such as the Lodi Marsh and the Brooklyn State Wildlife Area, and

Figure 3.2. Protected landscapes of Madison and western Dane County, Wisconsin

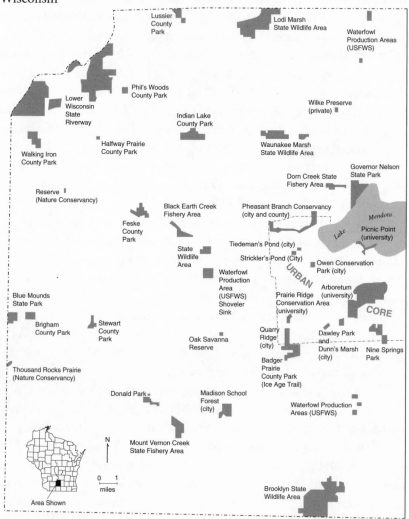

valley bottoms in stream-dissected terrain, such as the Mount Vernon Creek and Black Earth Creek state fishery areas. The state also administers lands within the Ice Age National Scenic Trail, nominally a part of the National Park System but administered by state and local land agencies in the southern part of the state; in our sample area plots of this reserve extend just north of the town of Verona. The Wisconsin State Riverway, in addition, represents a major project of state land purchases along Wisconsin's major stream. County parks are scattered across the map, from Walking Iron County Park in the northwest, at the edge of the bottomlands of the Wisconsin River, to Badger Prairie County Park, a former landfill being restored to tall-grass prairie vegetation in the southeast. (Does its genesis make it unsuitable for inclusion on our list?) The University of Wisconsin at Madison protects a major expanse of wild landscape in the Arboretum, whose major focus is the creation or restoration of native plant communities, and also campus areas of wetland, shoreline, and uplands as "natural areas." The cities of Madison and Middleton protect a number of "conservation parks," with prohibitions against many activities common to most urban parks and protections or restorations typical of nature reserves; Owen Conservation Park and Tiedeman's Pond serve here as examples. Moreover, the Madison School Forest, south of but owned and protected by the city, includes a fine stand of upland oak forest long free from cutting or grazing. Finally, private sector reserves in western Dane County include the Nature Conservancy's Thousand Rocks Prairie and the Wilke Foundation's Wilke Reserve.

Regulatory protections parallel the situation in California. Federal authority is the same in both states, and Wisconsin also has laws that provide for management of animal populations, protect rare and endangered species, require environmental assessments, and also constrain wetland drainage.

These snapshots of nature reserves and activities in northwestern California and southern Wisconsin testify to the diversity of nature protection. Are the preservation efforts adequate? Everyone probably has an opinion, and the responses are likely to vary widely. Moreover, it is difficult to know how broad the snapshot view should be, how far down the continuum toward areas with nonconforming uses the evaluation of nature protection should extend. The broad perspective, likely favored by those who wish to portray nature protection as adequate or even excessive, exaggerates the degree of protection, but the narrow view, characteristically adopted by wilderness enthusiasts, underrepresents American society's commitment to nature protection.

Table 3.1 identifies the number of acres of protected landscape under the jurisdiction of the various administrative bodies in the several states. Judgments led to inclusion or exclusion of acreage consistent with the criterion of protection as a primary land use purpose, as identified earlier, with further adjustments to the numbers as discussed in the following pages.

Table 3.1. Number of acres protected in landscape reserves of major federal and other land agencies, by state (thousands)

State	National Park System	National Forest System			Bureau of Land Management			NWRS†	State agencies		Regional & local agencies	Private groups	All agencies
		Wilderness	Other	Unassigned*	Wilderness	Other	Unassigned*		Park	Wildlife			
AL	2	41	9					56	50	627			785
AK	53,728	5,753	174			8,751		76,886	2,941	404			148,637
AZ	1,855	1,520	12		1,552	2,480		1,718	36	175			9,348
AR	105	117	35					316	45	325			943
CA	7,532	4,433	981		3,811	6,110		421	1,300	970			25,558
CO	648	3,148	15		152	874		84	337	390			5,648
CT	<1							<1	32	14			48
DE								27	15	50			92
FL	2,254	74						935	388	807			4,458
GA	40	115	38					479	63	973			1,708
HI	245							289	22	80			636
ID	422	3,962	681		<1	1,413		89	31	123			6,722
IL	<1	26						136	197	103			463
IN	10	13						9	59	80			171
IA	2							98	43	270			413
KS	<1							58	42	238			339
KY	72	17	3					2	26	41			161
LA	10	9	6					483	37	937			1,482
ME	141							48	259	28			476
MD	47							43	89	91			270
MA	28	12						13	69	100			222
MI	632	92	203					117	173	304			1,521
MN	133	810						518	231	1,100			2,792
MS	122	6	5					221	23	1,100			1,477
MO	63	63	14					65	131	127			463

MT	1,084	3,373	83	6	639	1,227	15	230		6,657
NE	6	8	7			171	30	102		324
NV	1,546	822	273	985	1,589	2,379	86	261		7,941
NH	<1	103	<1			6	70	17		198
NJ	2					64	294	263		623
NM	347	1,388	173	141	737	385	120	139		3,430
NY	30					27	2,657	200		2,914
NC	135	103	3			413	98	180		932
ND	71					1,401	13	128		1,613
OH	17					8	204	78		307
OK	10	15	59			163	69	282		598
OR	195	2,086	935	17	1,181	587	61	117		5,179
PA	66	9	47			10	271	1,366		1,769
RI	<1					2	8	30		41
SC	25	17	6			155	82	40		325
SD	264	10				961	154	285		1,674
TN	545	66				114	141	623		1,489
TX	1,159	38				461	467	750		2,875
UT	2,016	774	190	23	3,629	111	98	333		7,174
VT	<1	59	36			7	11	83		197
VA	224	87	116			124	13	171		755
WA	1,931	2,569	310	7		197	72	784		5,870
WI	77	42	62			232	129	467		1,009
WV	39	81				5	80	169		374
WY	2,562	3,111	10		696	90	112	109		6,690
All states	80,468	34,972	4,487	6,695	28,099	92,412	11,994	16,664	2,000	282,291
Reported by agency	83,600	34,868		1,000	500	93,600			3,000	

*Agency land protected but not assigned here to individual states   †National Wildlife Refuge System

Federal Lands

The examples of northwestern California and southern Wisconsin suggest the dominance of the federal land system in any overview of total area of protected wild landscape. Units of the National Park System, wilderness on the national forest and national resource lands, and areas of the national wildlife refuge system easily account for the bulk of the total protected acreage in the United States. But, in addition to dominating the summary totals, the federal lands include the largest areas of contiguous protected landscape, a key characteristic in light of today's concern over the inadequacy of small and fragmented reserves. The endless number of local reservations, frequently defended with great passion by activists who know them well, may function pivotally in both the preservation of rare biological species and the experience of common nature, but they contribute little to the total area of protected landscape. However crucial such small reserves may be, it is the total acreage of nature reserves, expressed as a percentage of a country's land area, that looms large in the assessment of nature protection efforts because such numbers are used to assess the political success of nature protection in a country and the society's dedication to the effort. For the United States, these summary numbers suggest considerable success and dedication.

THE NATIONAL PARK SYSTEM Units of the National Park System enjoy the strongest protection of any areas on the federal lands, in both the breadth of prohibitions against resource extraction and limitations to the power of executive branch administrators to permit nonconforming extractive activity (table 3.2). In general, logging, mining, commercial livestock grazing, and water developments are prohibited, as are sport hunting, trapping, grazing by recreational livestock, trail bicycles, and pets in off-road environments. Generally, congressional action is necessary to authorize most such uses in the National Park System. These strict protections typify the administration of major units of the system, notably the national parks and national monuments, but also largely characterize the policies for national historic sites and other historic units, national seashores, and national lakeshores; national recreation areas and national preserves enjoy somewhat lesser protection. All units are created by Congress, except that the president may proclaim national monuments on federal lands. Exceptions exist, such as certain mining in Death Valley National Monument, livestock grazing in Dinosaur National Monument, hunting of elk in a part of Grand Teton Na-

Table 3.2. Activities permitted in protected landscapes under various federal agencies

	Logging	Mining	Grazing	Water development	Recreational animals	Roads, hotels	Hunting, trapping	Fishing
NPS						x		x
NPS Wilderness								x
USFS, BLM	x	x	x	x	x	x	x	x
USFS, BLM Wilderness		x*	x	x†	x		x	x
FWS	x‡	x‡	x‡	x‡	x§		x	x
FWS Wilderness				x			x	x

NPS = National Park Service   BLM = Bureau of Land Management
USFS = U.S. Forest System   NWRS = National Wildlife Refuge System

* Mining in wilderness of the national forests and the public lands is prohibited, except for valid mining claims. Not all wilderness has been closed to mineral entry in the past, and thus such legitimate claims may exist. Exploration for mineral deposits in national forest wilderness was permitted by the Wilderness Act for a twenty-year period, 1964–84.

† The president may allow water development in national forest wilderness if he decides it to be in the national interest.

‡ Lands administered by the Fish and Wildlife Service may be utilized for commodity resource development if such use is compatible with and not detrimental to wildlife; this agency flexibility is the "compatibility" standard. Protections on refuges may or may not include rights to subsurface minerals.

§ Agency prerogatives determine the freedom of use of recreational animals (horses, dogs) on reserved lands. The use of recreational animals is far more constrained on national wildlife refuges than on wilderness administered by the Forest Service or the Bureau of Land Management, a consequence of the refuge focus on wild animals, which might suffer by interactions with recreational animals.

tional Park, and leashed pets on trails of Cayahoga Valley National Park; but in general, the policies are uniform. Facilities for recreational use, including roads, lodges, museums, stores, and campgrounds, are permitted, although such developments are limited in most units. Establishment of wilderness (44 million acres) within the National Park System does not enhance the fundamental protection against the extraction of commodity resources, although it does prevent the construction of roads and other recreational development otherwise allowable within the system.

Since Congress established the first national park, Yellowstone in 1872, and President Theodore Roosevelt proclaimed the first national monument, Devil's Tower in 1906, the National Park System has grown to more than 83.6 million acres, including about 500,000 in historical areas, many of which protect wild landscapes; the total also includes about 4.3 million acres in private ownership within the parks' exterior boundaries. Units appear in forty-nine of the fifty states and in territorial lands near and far from North America. Alaska's large acreage includes 19 million acres of national preserves in which hunting, whether subsistence or sport, and off-road vehicle use are permitted. Some national recreation areas include landscape flooded by reservoirs. Although the system includes a large number of historical and cultural sites (e.g., the monuments in Washington, D.C.), the total acreage is overwhelmingly dominated by areas of wild landscapes; all of this acreage is included in table 3.1.

THE NATIONAL FOREST SYSTEM The national forests and the national grasslands boast of areas designated for nature protection, although, in general, the barriers against development within these reserves are less than those enjoyed by units of the National Park System (table 3.2). Most notable of the national forest reserves are wilderness areas. These areas have allowances for commercial livestock grazing, entry for metallic mineral claims made prior to 1984, commercial trapping, and freedom for many recreational activities (e.g., sport hunting, use of private recreational livestock, and pets) not permitted in the National Park System. In addition, administrative fiat may circumvent certain protections, the most important of which is presidential authority to permit water developments. Permanent human artifacts, such as roads and buildings, are prohibited, except as they may be required by the legal nonconforming uses.

The initial wilderness-type areas on the national forests were declared in the 1920s, followed, after 1929, by a system created by executive order (proclamations by either the secretary of agriculture or the chief of the Forest Service). With passage of the Wilderness Act in 1964, the authority to designate or eliminate wilderness passed to Congress. Today 35 million acres, about one-seventh of the total area of the national forests, are within wilderness, with additions recurrently on the agenda of conservation groups and of Congress (table 3.1).

Other areas of the national forests also protect nature to varying degrees, as already encountered in the representative area of northwestern California. For example, Research natural areas, small reserves intended primarily for scientific investigations of natural systems and for baseline comparisons with the general forest landscapes, generally involve protections comparable to those of units of the National Park System; these areas total more than 550,000 acres. Also, administratively designated areas, collectively called special interest areas, protect small landscape regions of geologic ("geologic areas") or botanical ("botanical areas") interest, as well as historical or archaeological features; in addition, "late-successional reserves" in the forests of the Pacific Northwest, Native American contemporary use areas, and undeveloped dispersed recreation areas represent such agency-created protected areas.

The collective total acreage of all these types of areas is difficult to generate. Moreover, recreation areas provide some degree of enhanced protection; these may be created by administrative planning, such as the zoning that recognizes "undeveloped dispersed recreation areas," or by congressional mandate. The Smith River National Recreation Area in northwestern California, for example, includes prohibitions against new mineral entry and against the logging of large acreages of old-growth forest, and the Mount St. Helens Volcanic National Monument similarly offers landscape protection. For purposes of this tabulation, however, some areas were judged not to be "protected landscape," such as the Whiskeytown-Shasta-Trinity National Recreation Area of California and the Arapaho National Recreation Area of Colorado, both of which enclose major reservoirs and their shorelines but otherwise relatively little landscape. Finally, the 2001 Clinton administration decision, through formal action by the secretary of agriculture, to prohibit road construction on nearly 60 million acres (the so-called roadless initiative) reflects executive authority; the areas may remain roadless but otherwise receive no further formal protections, and they are also subject to executive reversal in the future. These lands seem sufficiently vulnerable to be omitted from our list of protected landscape. Altogether, between 5 and 6 million acres (ignoring the 60 million acres of the roadless initiative) are involved in these special use areas of the national forests.

BUREAU OF LAND MANAGEMENT LANDS The public domain lands of the Bureau of Land Management parallel closely the designations of the Forest Service. In 1976 Congress authorized wilderness designations on the public domain, although the bureau had begun administratively created wilderness-type areas in 1972. Regulations closely resemble those for the national forests (table 3.2). About 6.7 million acres of wilderness have been established on national resource lands, but acreage will be added on a state-by-state basis as the bureau implements its congressional mandate (table 3.1). Congress has also created fourteen national conservation areas, which provide protection—even if less than complete—of natural features; the 1.2-million-acre Steese National Conservation Area in Alaska and the 114,000-acre El Malpais National Conservation Area of New Mexico serve as examples. In addition, the public domain includes research natural areas (347,214 acres) and other administratively created areas zoned as "special management areas" for particular natural features (e.g., "outstanding natural areas" or "unique waters of exceptional significance") or for enhanced recreational uses; again, the protection is comparable to that of units on the national forests. Such reserves range in size from the 100-acre Walker Lake Relict Shoreline Natural Area in Nevada to the 4,480-acre Rainbow Basin Fossil Canyon Geological Natural Area in Wyoming; probably more than a million acres are involved in such administratively designated reserves.

Unique among the federal land agencies, the Bureau of Land Management has an extensive system of special management areas called "areas of critical environmental concern" (about 14 million acres), regions in which special management is identified to protect some natural, historical, or cultural feature. Also special to the bureau is its administration of the singular California Headwaters Forest Reserve, an area of old-growth forest in the coastal mountains. Finally, within the final years of the Clinton administration, the bureau became responsible for fifteen new national monuments, ranging in size from the 52,000-acre Siskiyou Region National Monument in Oregon to the 387,000-acre Upper Missouri River Breaks National Monument in Montana; collectively, these monuments total more than 5 million acres. But these reserves are not inviolate—livestock grazing and sport hunting, for example, make them less protected than, say, units of the National Park System.

Table 3.1 (which attempts to avoid overlapping designations) identifies about 35 million acres of protected landscape on the public lands. The bureau itself describes its major areas of protected landscape as the National Landscape Conservation System, which includes 820 units and 39 million acres, a total that differs from the calculations used to create table 3.1. Questions regarding the adequacy of protection permeate much of this acreage (including the large California Desert National Conservation Area), but in aggregate the total remains major.

NATIONAL WILDLIFE REFUGE SYSTEM The 93.6 million acres within the National Wildlife Refuge System fall mostly within formal refuges but also include more than 2 million acres of waterfowl production areas.

These lands seem to provide the least stringent restrictions against development in comparison with the other major federal land systems intended for nature protection, although the entire acreage of the refuges is included in table 3.1. Generally, commodity resource use may be permitted if the activity is deemed to aid, or at least not to hamper, the wildlife purposes of the refuges; these uses may include livestock grazing, timber cutting, and fossil fuel development. Recreational uses, in principle, are similarly broad— sport hunting and motorized boating are generally allowed, for example— although human entry to some refuge lands may be prohibited altogether if it is deemed a problem for particular animal species. Wilderness designation on the refuges (20.7 million acres) precludes most commodity and recreational resource development, although those uses not requiring permanent human structures, such as livestock grazing and sport hunting, may continue.

The purpose of the national wildlife refuges is to protect and develop, if necessary, wildlife habitat. This purpose justifies the inclusion of the entire acreage of the refuge system in the tabulation of protected landscape (table 3.1). The primacy of wildlife on refuge lands was reaffirmed in 1997 by Congress's passage of the National Wildlife Refuge Improvement Act, considered an "organic act" for the refuge system. Conservation groups often criticize nonconforming uses of refuge lands, but it would be incorrect to assume that the national wildlife refuges offer no protection to natural systems; in fact, the visual appearance of a typical refuge landscape is clearly wild, and the success of habitat protection seems hardly disputable. Perhaps more conspicuous than features associated with commodity resource development are the human artifacts built to enhance the environments for certain wildlife species; the most important of such artifacts are the water-control devices used to regulate water ponding and flowages in wetlands.

OTHER FEDERAL LANDS The National Park System, wilderness on the national forests, and national wildlife refuges may encompass the bulk of the protected acreage on the federal lands, but several other agencies warrant mention. The National Oceanic and Atmospheric Administration, under authority of the 1972 Coastal Zone Management Act, administers the national estuarine research reserve system—twenty-two coastal preserves of federal, state, and other public lands totaling 438,000 acres—for research and educational purposes. Most of these areas overlap with acreage totals of lands itemized in other categories. In addition, the national marine sanctuaries—twelve preserves totaling more than 10 million acres in offshore waters—protect ocean environments. The protection is not absolute; commercial fishing may continue, for example, but not drilling for petroleum. The marine location of these reserves renders them unique and thus important, although they are not included in the master list of protected acreage. The Department of Defense administers about 30 million acres, which, while obviously not intended to serve as protected landscapes, may sometimes remain surprisingly undeveloped (Vogel 1997, K. Brown 1998). The military abandonment of land suggests the preservation effects of Defense Department administration. Decommissioning of Fort Ord on California's Monterey Bay has released a wild area of dunes and shoreline suitable for parkland; the Rocky Mountain Arsenal near Denver has become an area noted for unplowed prairie and wildlife; the Hanford Reservation in Washington, infamous for its radioactive emissions over decades of plutonium production for nuclear weapons, now is eyed as a landscape for wildlife refuges and ecological research precisely because of its undeveloped state. The Bureau of Indian Affairs oversees almost 60 million acres, which include reserves set aside for protection by various tribal governments, but questions arise concerning not only the strength of governing regulations but also the political appropriateness of including such tribal lands in a compilation of federal nature reserves. The Corps of Engineers, the Bureau of Reclamation, and the Tennessee Valley Authority, in conjunction with reservoir projects, administer lands surrounding human-created lakes (themselves the classic "violations" of nature in the eye and mind of a nature protectionist) and may thus effectively preclude certain human uses, such as housing developments, although such lands probably cannot be counted in a total of lands of protected nature.

In sum, the area protected by the federal government in systems other than the national parks, national forests, and public lands seems large in the aggregate. Nonetheless, none of these areas is included in table 3.1 because of overlapping with other reserves and ambiguity regarding degrees of protection. Their omission makes the ultimate total conservative.

VARIABLE PROTECTIONS ON THE FEDERAL LANDS Wilderness enthusiasts, while recognizing the varying strengths of protection offered by the activities of the federal land agencies, do not respond consistently to those variations. For example, they frequently criticize the National Park Service as too interested in recreation and too responsive to concessionaires, thereby jeopardizing preservation goals, ignoring the fact that the National Park System provides the strongest of landscape protections. Less inviolate wilderness designation seems to enjoy greater enthusiasm among nature protectionists.

Two factors explain this paradox. First, wilderness enthusiasts wish to minimize interagency rivalries; that is, it is strategically advantageous for conservationists to avoid challenging the status quo among the federal land agencies, thus not alienating any of them, by encouraging every agency to duplicate preservation goals. Thus the conservation groups pursue wilderness designation on the national forests, on national resource lands, and in national wildlife refuges, rather than seek transfer of those agencies' lands to the National Park Service. But a second factor is probably even more important: the Park Service is suspect because it allows roads and hotels, whereas wilderness, administered by any agency, does not. Wilderness therefore appears visually to be free of human modification. It is ironic that in this modern day when scenery is deemed an inadequate measure of nature's worth, and when the justification for nature protection is typically expressed in terms of natural processes and functioning, the importance of the visual character of landscape is still vital, perhaps paramount.

State Lands

The states vary widely in their protection of wild landscapes (e.g., Cox 1988, J. Young 1989, Cupper 1993, Steely 1999). The ambiguities of the variable degrees of protection on different types of state lands in the fifty states and the problem of overlapping administration of lands make generalizations difficult. State parks often support developed recreation facilities, including such features as swimming pools and playgrounds, but the bulk of the total acreage probably may be considered wild, broadly defined. An annual compilation by the National Association of State Park Directors identifies 9 million acres of lands administered by the various state park agencies in 1997 as parks, natural areas, scientific areas, and environmental education areas. This total omits lands identified as state forests or recreation areas, which typically allow commodity resource uses and thus are excluded from this chapter's tabulations. Some lands in the state forests and recreation areas are protected (one of my favorite north woods walks, for example, circles a lake and several bogs on a state forest natural area in Wisconsin), but these omissions may be balanced by inclusion of inappropriate lands in parks. In addition, several states administer individual parks with independent park boards, the most conspicuous of which are the Adirondacks Park in New York (2.4 million acres of public land), Baxter State Park in Maine (200,000

acres), and Custer State Park in South Dakota (73,000 acres). Taken together, state park lands total about 12 million acres (table 3.1).

State wildlife land is sometimes administered by the same agency that
has authority over state parks but more frequently by separate executive
bodies whose responsibilities are focused on "fish and game." These lands
may be open to commodity resource development but presumably are
managed primarily for wildlife habitat. The meanings of state totals vary by
time of estimate and by types of land tenure; particularly confusing is
whether or not to include lands leased for wildlife purposes. Figures for 1960
from the Outdoor Recreation Resources Review Commission (ORRRC)
(1962b), for example, total 8.9 million acres for state fish and game lands in
the fifty states, but a 1977 survey by the Nature Conservancy (National Park
Service 1977) yielded a total of 18.8 million acres of state-administered wildlife land. The larger figure may reflect both lands purchased since 1960 and
lands leased rather than owned. Numbers for several individual states, moreover, illustrate the challenges of identifying numbers of protected acres.
First, Louisiana is said to have only 412,439 acres of state wildlife land in the
ORRRC report; the 1977 study identifies 1.1 million acres of "state-owned"
land for waterfowl and "state game and fish preserves"; in the late 1990s, the
state identified 1.2 million acres, but a disaggregation of this total identifies
one-tenth of the acreage as lying within Fort Polk Military Reservation,
which is leased as a wildlife management area. Second, Georgia is credited
with 433,610 acres by the ORRRC but with 1.1 million acres in "45 wildlife
management areas" by the Nature Conservancy study; a more recent tabulation identifies 77 areas but totaling only 973,278 acres. Third, Tennessee is
listed with 502,931 acres in the ORRRC report and 1.2 million acres "managed" by the state Wildlife Resources Agency in the 1977 compilation, although a late-1990s perspective reveals that 625,000 acres rest within the
Cherokee Wildlife Management Area, which is the Cherokee National Forest. Fourth, California is credited with 115,000 acres by the ORRRC, 112,000
by the Nature Conservancy, but 970,000 by the state Department of Fish
and Game in 2004. For our purposes, such differences in the acres recorded
in various studies and sources (including the state agencies themselves) are
probably less important than the compromised protection offered by most
of the lands involved. In table 3.1 the numbers offered by the Nature Conservancy form the base, with revisions made from more current sources; the
total for state wildlife land is about 16.6 million acres.

Regional and Local Levels of Government

Summary data reflecting natural landscapes protected by regional and local government agencies defy precise compilation, given the great number of both public bodies and protected areas involved, the lack of systematic surveys, and the constant problem of definition of appropriate landscapes to include. Data for areas used for recreation, although also problematic for the same reasons, are occasionally collected and can serve as the basis for estimates of protected landscapes.

Regionally or locally protected wild landscape—overseen by a dizzying number of governing bodies that care for an endless number of specific units—might total 1.3 to 6.2 million acres. In the early 1960s, the Outdoor Recreation Resources Review Commission (1962b) recognized about 10 million acres of recreational land administered by levels of government below that of the states. Within this total are such areas as city playgrounds, sports stadiums, town squares, and pedestrian malls, although it also includes wild lands such as forest preserves (e.g., the lands of the Cook County Forest Preserve District of Illinois) and natural areas (e.g., most of the units in the East Bay Regional Park District of California). About 8 million acres of the total might be considered wild (Chubb and Chubb 1981), but this number contains state forests, which, as noted earlier, are typically open to commodity resource extraction. Chubb and Chubb (1981) identify from the ORRRC data about 1.6 million acres of wilderness and nature reserves, and another 1.6 million acres of landscapes protected for wildlife habitat. A summary of individual units in the raw data that seem most clearly to protect wild landscapes yields a total of 1.2 million acres. As a general figure, then, about 3 million acres are tabulated for regionally and locally administered landscapes of protected nature (table 3.1).

Private Lands

Some conservation organizations purchase lands for nature reserves. The Nature Conservancy is the most notable example, having been involved in the acquiring of 7.5 million acres of landscape in the United States and Canada since the early 1950s. Because the organization often transfers or sells its purchased lands to a government agency or other group for administration, the system of preserves administered directly by the Nature Conservancy, numbering 1,300, covers much less area, about 0.5 million acres. The total acreage purchased or administered by the Nature Conservancy can vary dramatically over a short period of time. The 500-square-mile Gray Ranch in New Mexico, for example, was purchased in 1990 and donated to the Animas Foundation in 1993. Similarly, some of the 185,000 acres the conservancy acquired in Maine in the late 1990s has been sold to public agencies, and the organization retains development easements on other areas.

Other groups follow a parallel strategy. Most prominently, some hunting and fishing organizations actively purchase land for protection, including Ducks Unlimited, which cites more than 9 million acres of habitat conservation in its history, and Pheasants Forever, which has purchased more than 65,000 acres of grassland and wetland. The Conservation Fund has gained title to 296,000 forested acres in several northeastern states, with plans to maintain conservation easements on lands used for commercial forestry purposes and to sell other lands to state and federal land agencies. On a lesser scale but with comparable goals, the National Audubon Society and its affiliated local Audubon societies have purchased about 0.9 million acres for nature reserves, although it administers only about one-third of that total (J. Anderson 2000).

Any listing of groups similarly concerned with acquiring land for nature protection would be extensive; in 1981, for example, the Nature Conservancy recognized 277 private organizations involved in the purchase of natural landscape (National Park Service 1982). That report highlighted the Western Pennsylvania Conservancy, which had purchased more than 60,000 acres (but transferred most to public agencies), and Acres, Inc., which purchased small acreages for natural areas in northeastern Indiana. Still other examples would extend even that sizable list: the Committee for Green Foothills purchases open space on the urbanized peninsula south of San Francisco; the Ridges Sanctuary has acquired wild land in an area of old beach ridges—rich in acid bogs and pink orchids—in Door County, Wisconsin; the Sanibel-Captiva Conservation Foundation preserves an 1,100-acre natural area in coastal Florida; the Greenhills Foundation has an 800-acre environmental center near Dallas, Texas; the Nature Sanctuary Society of Western New York oversees the 130-acre William P. Alexander Sanctuary.

A complete accounting of such private parcels of protected natural landscape would be long. Although their extent is difficult to determine precisely, perhaps 2 million acres of nature reserves are administered by private groups (table 3.1).

Types of land tenure other than ownership in fee simple swell the total of private acreage protected. Land trusts (groups that may purchase areas for landscape protection) often buy and hold the development rights to pieces of land, and these easements might be considered nature protection. Certainly, many such areas accomplish such goals, as, for example, the 400 acres on the Cumberland River held by the Land Trust for Tennessee, and the 351 acres in California's Napa Valley protected by the Napa County Land Trust. The Land Trust Alliance, which coordinates at the national level the activities of more locally based land trust groups, reports that about 6.4 million acres have been protected through land trust activities, involving both outright purchases and conservation easements, with the lands sometimes held by the trusts, sometimes transferred to public land agencies. In addition, the lands protected under habitat conservation plans—agreements to permit the development of some landscape within project areas while maintaining a portion of it as wild (see chapter 10)—similarly involve millions of acres, held by a variety of land tenure arrangements. The Fish and Wildlife Service identifies 30 million acres within habitat conservation plans, only a fraction of which is in protected landscape. The total acreage involved in initiatives such as easements must be substantial, although the difficulty of identifying a meaningful number precludes including such lands in the table of nature reserves; again, this omission makes the final tabulation conservative.

Regional Patterns of Protected Lands

Lands privately and locally administered protect landscapes scattered widely across the country, but their large number and obscurity (at least to any particular detached individual) render difficult any attempt to generalize about their regional pattern. Whatever affection such reserves generate among a knowing and dedicated local public, and however strongly these lands suggest Americans' commitment to nature protection, they contribute relatively little to the aggregated acreage of protected landscape and consequently are swamped by the much larger areas of state and federal lands, even on a regional basis.

The 83.6 million acres of the National Park System sprawl disproportionately in the western states (table 3.3; cf. Dilsaver 2003). Alaska leads among the individual states, with more than 53 million acres of the total; among states in the lower forty-eight, California, with 7.5 million acres, includes about three times the acreage of the third-ranked state, Wyoming,

Table 3.3. Millions of acres of protected landscape in jurisdiction of various agencies, by region

	National Park System	National Forest System Wilderness	Other	Bureau of Land Management	Fish and Wildlife Service	State agencies
Alaska	53.7	5.8	0.1	8.8	76.9	3.3
	(67%)	(16%)	(2%)	(24%)	(83%)	(12%)
11 western states	20.1	27.2	3.7	27.4	7.9	5.1
	(25%)	(78%)	(82%)	(76%)	(8%)	(18%)
22 other states	6.7	2.0	0.7	<0.5	7.6	19.5
	(8%)	(6%)	(16%)	(<1%)	(8%)	(70%)
All states	80.5	35.0	4.5	36.2	92.4	27.9
	(100%)	(100%)	(100%)	(100%)	(99%)	(100%)

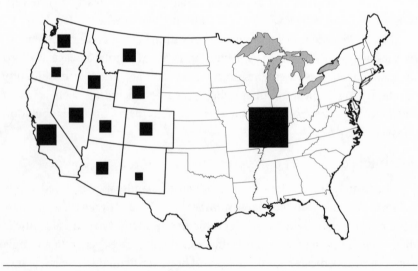

which has 2.6 million acres. Among the top ten states, those with more than a million acres each, the only eastern state is Florida, fourth among states overall, with 2.3 million acres.

Protected landscapes in the national forests—about 40 million acres total—similarly cluster in the American West (table 3.3). Alaska contains the largest total acreage of wilderness—5.8 million—and the next nine states in rank order are western, all with more than a million acres each. Among western states, only Utah and Nevada include fewer than a million acres of national forest wilderness. Minnesota is the single nonwestern state that comes close to the million-acre group, and it would qualify if the 277,000 acres of nonfederal land within the Boundary Waters Canoe Area Wilderness were included in the wilderness acreage total. Other national forest lands of protected nature—about 4.5 million acres—reveal a western bias, with California, Oregon, and Idaho claiming the bulk of the total, although less strongly than wilderness (table 3.3).

Reserves for landscape protection on the public lands of the Bureau of Land Management (over 35 million acres) are almost entirely in the western states (where most BLM lands are found), with California's 3.8 million acres of wilderness and 6.1 million acres of other areas making it the top-ranked state. Arizona's 1.6 million wilderness acres and Alaska's 8.7 million acres of other reserves represent major contributions to the total.

Alaska's 76.9 million acres dominate the total lands administered by the Fish and Wildlife Service (FWS), 92.4 million acres in all. The eight states with the next largest area totals suggest the breadth of regional representation of FWS lands in comparison with other federal land systems: four states—Nevada, Arizona, North Dakota, and Montana—contain more than one million acres each, and another four—South Dakota, Florida, Oregon, and Minnesota—have at least 0.5 million acres.

The national estuarine research reserve (NERR) system appears along all of the country's ocean shorelines— Wells NERR in Maine, Chesapeake NERR in Virginia, Sapelo Island NERR in Georgia, Elkhorn Slough NERR in California, Padilla Bay NERR in Washington. Similarly, the national marine sanctuaries are scattered along all the coasts, those of American Samoa and the Great Lakes as well as of the continental seacoasts.

Lands with a nature protection purpose administered by state agencies (28.7 million acres), not surprisingly, reveal less of a western bias than protected landscapes overseen by the federal agencies. Alaska tops the list at 3.34 million acres (in this game of lists, of course, large size is a distinct advantage), with New York (2.9 million, dominated by the Adirondacks Park) next. Seven other states protect between one and two million acres—Florida, Georgia, and Mississippi in the South, Pennsylvania in the Northeast, Minnesota in the upper Midwest, Texas in the Southwest, and California in the West. (Among these seven, wildlife lands dominate over parks in six; only California protects more parkland than wildlife acreage.)

Regionally and locally administered lands, as well as private reserves—together totaling about 3 million acres—are not assigned to particular states.

Their distributions suggest unevenness across the country, without the strong patterning revealed by the federal lands. As illustration, the East Bay Regional Park District in central California administers fifty-five park units and more than 85,000 acres; the Massachusetts Audubon Society, a local group with a long history and active program of land purchases, tends to about 27,000 acres in thirty-six sanctuaries; the Nature Conservancy in Florida manages about 40,000 acres of reserves.

Overall, the American West looms large in the aggregated picture of protected landscape, with 85 percent of the total acreage in the eleven western states, Alaska, and Hawaii. Not surprisingly, Alaska tops the list of individual states with 53 percent of all protected acreage; this disproportionate contribution even exceeds Alaska's share, 16 percent, of the total area of the country. More than a third, 39 percent, of the area of Alaska lies within nature reserves. California ranks second, accounting for 9 percent of the total (about 25 percent of the area of the state, including the entire California Desert Conservation Area, is within reserves), with Arizona contributing more than 3 percent of the total (about 13 percent of the state's area is protected). The next seven states, which round out the top ten, are all western, each with 2 to 3 percent of the nation's total. Even Hawaii, which ranks thirtieth in protected acreage, claims 15 percent of its area within nature reserves. Major nonwestern states include Florida (twelfth overall), New York (thirteenth), Texas (fourteenth), and Minnesota (fifteenth). As noted earlier, a state's size helps determine its position in the rank ordering.

Reflections

The protected acreage in the United States as a whole, about 283 million acres, represents 12 percent of the country's total area. The federal lands and the American West dominate the overall picture of nature protection in America. Simultaneously, however, that dominance may obfuscate the more widespread manifestation of concern for nature across the country, concern that leads to the protection of innumerable tracts of wild landscape, often small, typically obscure, tucked away in private reserves, local sanctuaries, state wildlife areas and parks, and even the lesser-known federally protected preserves. Just as people in Boston treasure the Massachusetts Audubon Society's Wellfleet Bay Wildlife Sanctuary, those in the Dallas–Fort Worth area value the Fort Worth Nature Center and Refuge; those in California's East Bay prize the Huckleberry Botanic Regional Preserve; those in Madison, Wisconsin, delight in the Greene Prairie on the university's Arboretum;

those in Georgia's Tattnall County praise the Big Hammock State Natural Area; those in eastern Idaho admire the Camus National Wildlife Refuge; those in West Virginia cherish the Laurel Fork Wilderness; and those in southern Arizona respect the Coronado National Memorial. The diversity of nature preserves, of wild landscape protected in a dizzying array of reserves, testifies to the commitment to nature protection in American society.

4   THE NATIONAL PARK SYSTEM

James Bryce, one-time British ambassador to the United States, once described the National Park System as "the best idea America ever had" (Pritchard 1991). This frequently cited quote (Wallace Stegner [1983] seemed especially fond of it) celebrates the nature protection purposes of the National
Park System, both historically and in the contemporary world. The exalta-
tion lacks equivocation: it does not say that national parks are *one* of the best
ideas, and lump them with wilderness areas, wildlife refuges, state parks, and
reserves of the Nature Conservancy. Moreover, it proclaims a common sentiment: the National Park System protects natural areas appropriately described
only in superlative terms—the finest, the grandest, the ultimate, the best. Such
an extravagant claim for the parks contrasts with characterizations by the system's critics, who find too little similarity between the promises of the parks
and the fulfillment of those promises. Yet despite its flaws, the National Park
System is the most successful landscape protection project ever attempted.

The National Parks

The 384 units of the National Park System are located in forty-nine of the
fifty states and in the territories of Puerto Rico, the Virgin Islands, Guam,
and American Samoa; Delaware holds the distinction of being the only state
without a system unit (fig. 4.1). Arizona, California, and Virginia have more
than twenty units each, although whether particular named units should
be counted is debatable. For example, should various national trails be included, even though they may involve no federal land? The largest unit is the
Wrangell–St. Elias National Park and Preserve in Alaska (13.2 million acres).
The largest in the lower forty-eight states is Death Valley, with 3.3 million
acres; the smallest is the Thaddeus Kosciuszko National Memorial in Penn-

Figure 4.1. Units of the National Park System

Shading indicates major natural areas of the National Park System; circles indicate small natural area units; numerals indicate additional units by state.

sylvania, an 0.02-acre memorial to the Polish-born military engineer who contributed to the American Revolution. The oldest unit that is today called a national park is usually identified as Yellowstone, established in 1872, but that status could be claimed by Yosemite, established in 1864 by Congress as a wild landscape reserve but administered by the state of California, or by Hot Springs, set aside by Congress as a national reservation in 1832. Hot Springs might also be identified as the most unlikely area to be called a national park, since it consists of fewer than 5,000 acres in urban Hot Springs, Arkansas. The city park landscape of the Cayahoga Valley National Park in Ohio, reclassified from its national recreation area status in 2000, may be close to Hot Springs as most improbable national park. Other than the Cayahoga Valley, the most recently established unit called a national park is the Gunnison National Park of Colorado, enlarged and renamed from its national monument status in 1999. The newest park not reclassified from an existing system unit is the Great Basin National Park of Nevada, authorized in 1986. The largest area called a national monument is Alaska's Cape Krusenstern (560,000 acres); in the lower forty-eight states, the largest monument is Arizona's Organ Pipe Cactus (about 330,000 acres). The aggregated

Figure 4.2. Millions of acres in the National Park System (natural areas), 1880–2000

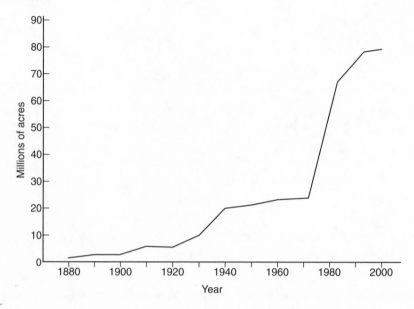

acreage of the National Park System has grown steadily but with major increases in the 1930s, reflecting the active additions of the Roosevelt administration, and in the 1970s, a consequence of the 1978 national monument proclamations for Alaska by Jimmy Carter (fig. 4.2).

The National Park as an Ideal

No words more clearly represent the ideal of the National Park System than those written in key congressional legislation. The phrases have become familiar parts of American environmental consciousness:

... that the said state shall accept this grant upon the express conditions that the premises shall be held for public use, resort and recreation; shall be inalienable for all time. (Yosemite Grant of 1864)

... a public park or pleasuring-ground for the benefit and enjoyment of the people ... shall provide for the preservation, from injury or spoliation, of all timber, mineral deposits, natural curiosities, or wonders within said park, and their retention in their natural condition. (Yellowstone Park Act of 1872)

... which purpose is to conserve the scenery and the natural and historic objects and the wild life therein, and to provide for the enjoyment of the same in such manner and by such means as will leave them unimpaired for the enjoyment of future generations. (National Park Act of 1916)

These articulations, which adorn articles in popular magazines, formal plaques at park visitor centers, and oral presentations on park issues, take on the aura of sacred text.

The sense of the words may ultimately originate with Frederick Law Olmsted, who influenced the authors of the Yosemite Grant legislation (H. Jones 1965). That 1864 reservation, in Olmsted's eyes, protected from commercial despoliation "the greatest glory of nature." Moreover, that "glory" for Olmsted served a human purpose. In his report defining policies for the Yosemite Grant, he argues that the preservation of nature and the recreation within that protected nature intimately intertwine: the Yosemite landscape should be protected "in its present condition as a museum of natural science" because such protected nature "gives [to visitors] the effect of refreshing rest and reinvigoration." In addition, Olmsted advocates an active role of government as necessary because the benefactor of this protection and recreation is "the whole body of the people forever" (Ranney, ed., 1990: 500, 504, 506). Olmsted's words and the legislation that derives from them identify three purposes: the protection of nature, recreation in these protected landscapes, and egalitarian access. Together they conform to an idealistic vision of what the national parks can and should be.

The growth of the National Park System suggests a fourth foundation for the ideal. From its initial reserve, Yellowstone, to the present expanse of more than 380 units, the history unfolds, for some observers, as a triumphant story of reason and vision forming an ever more connected and rational system. According to this perspective, individually created national parks and other reserves were combined into a cohesive whole with formation of the National Park Service in 1916. Subsequent growth and agency reorganizations have resulted in the modern family tree of the National Park System: the roots of individual units converge in the trunk of the National Park Service, which then branches out into the flowering of the integrated aggregation (fig. 4.3). The imagery is strong: a system structured organically into a whole that is discrete and logically connected. Huth (1948) echoes this metaphor of cohesion when he likens new park units to pearls added to a necklace.

Two additional considerations contribute to this vision of the parks as an organized and systematic array of units linked together. First, the long-

Figure 4.3. The family tree of the National Park System. (Adapted from R. Lee, 1972, Chart Illustrating Growth of the National Park System. Philadelphia: Eastern National Park and Monument Association.)

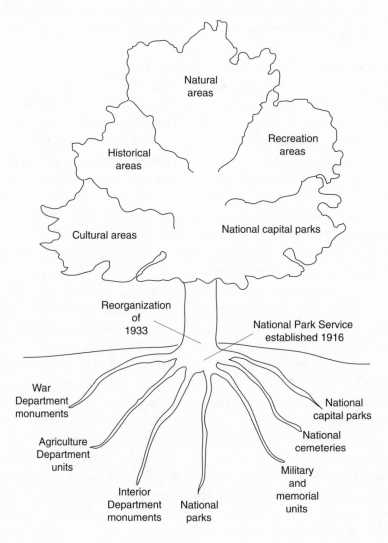

established concern for only units "worthy" of inclusion in the system suggests an ideal of quality. Throughout the twentieth century, this interest in standards for the parks permeated both the private and public sectors. It was the focus of the National Parks Association from the 1920s through the subsequent several decades, even prompting the conservation group to conclude by the 1930s that the system had already protected the most appropriate areas and was thus essentially complete (Miles 1995). The Park Service itself resisted proposals for "inferior" parks and readily worked for the disestablishment of those it considered undeserving of protection (Ise 1961). James Ridenour (1994), at one time director of the service, argued in favor of deauthorizing "unworthy" system units. A contrary opinion comes from Dwight Rettie (1995), who saw in each park a commentary on the culture and politics of the time it was established, thus imbuing all units with meaning and importance. Nonetheless, many people believe the family tree ought to shed the leaves that lack virtue.

Second, a National Park System plan in the early 1970s presented an ordered strategy for identifying what new units were necessary to make the system whole (National Park Service 1972, 1990; cf. Dilsaver 2003). Within each of forty-one "natural regions" of the United States the plan identifies thirty-three categories of natural phenomena (i.e., twelve types of "landforms of present," seven types of "geologic history," nine types of "land ecosystems," and five types of "aquatic ecosystems"). The evaluation then judges the "significance" of each of the resulting intersections of region and type of phenomenon (1,353 possibilities called "regional themes," not all of which actually exist; e.g., Precambrian geology does not occur in Hawaii) and assesses the degree to which each is already represented within the existing National Park System. The major gaps—called "regional themes" of "prime significance" with "little or no" representation in a unit of the system— number forty-seven and include such designations as Central Lowlands plains, Great Basin mountains, Wyoming Basin Eocene-Paleocene geology, New England estuaries, and Gulf Coastal Plain eastern deciduous forest. The gaps, surprisingly, include three "mountain systems" (Great Basin, Brooks Range, and New England–Adirondacks), one "desert" (Great Basin), and only one grassland (Central Lowlands). The most poorly represented "natural regions" cluster in the Pacific island territories and Alaska (recall that the date of the plan is 1972, before the Alaskan land act); the eastern states are generally less well represented than the western. Surprisingly, though, the northern Interior West—the Wyoming Basin, the Great Basin, and the

Columbia Plateau—is less well represented than the most poorly represented eastern regions, the Central Lowlands and the Coastal Plains.

The plan was intended to inform and influence additions to the National Park System, "to identify gaps . . . [and suggest] areas that would fill them . . . [in order that the national parks would come to] protect and exhibit the best examples of our great national landscapes" (National Park Service 1972). Additions over the years since 1972 have closed some of the gaps, notably in Alaska but also in the Great Basin mountains and the Columbia Plateau. The growing limbs of the family tree reach out to fill in gaps in the canopy.

Popular writing accentuates the vision of the national parks as the ultimate in nature protection. The perfection may reflect the character of the nature protected: "Each park is an expression in its own manner—a de luxe edition, so to speak—of some manifestation of natural forces" (Tilden 1951: 32). The ideal also may be associated with a sense of reasoned and careful thought to create a genuine "system of parks . . . with certain definite standards," and with a progressive political imagery of the parks springing "directly from the people" (D. Butcher 1969). In addition, the ideal is associated with a sense of inviolate protection: the parks "all embody our highest ideals for preservation" (Chase and Shore 1992: 54). The ideology of the parks extends to other celebratory characterizations, including the quality of recreation. Grossener (1979: 2), for example, proclaims that "as playgrounds for recreation and instruction our national parks are without rivals on any continent." In addition, the quality of the personnel of the National Park Service surpasses that of other government agencies: "The superintendents, naturalists and rangers have tremendous enthusiasm for the areas they protect, and highest devotion to the cause for which they work" (D. Butcher 1969). Finally, Schullery (1991: 19) suggests that the "parks . . . have always been laboratories of ideas, where we have studied our relationship with our world." Consistently, then, from laws and government reports to popular accounts, the national parks are seen as the finest expression of nature protection, judged by their landscape quality, coherence as a system, egalitarian purpose, and strength of protection. These four qualities underlie the national park ideal.

National Parks in Reality—Compromises to the Ideal?

The reality of the national parks, some people say, does not live up to the ideal. Compromises, according to this view, tarnish the promise in all four of the fundamental qualities.

LANDSCAPE QUALITY Critics sometimes identify the environments represented within the National Park System as inconsistent with an ideal array of protected landscapes. Historically, the patterns of landscape protection reflect the influences of monumentalism (a concern for spectacular scenery), nationalism (an American preoccupation with spectacular scenery as an expression of national identity), and tourism (a desire to generate profits from recreational travel, also an influence that favored spectacular scenery) (Runte 1979; see also Huth 1957). This interest in the monumental was not subconscious; rather, park proponents carefully advanced the goal of protecting spectacular landscapes and advocated that landscapes of "lesser" quality be eliminated from the system (Miles 1995). In more recent times, calls for "representative" environments, rather than spectacularly unusual scenery, have been consistently articulated, with particular reference to biologically based criteria for identifying what is "representative" (Steinbeck 1962, Curry-Lindahl 1974, Runte 1979; see also Vale 1988, Dilsaver 2003).

Unarguably, the National Park System disproportionately protects landscapes of high relief—the major characteristic of spectacular scenery—although still more specific patterns can be identified in the history of the system's expansion (fig. 4.4). First, high-elevation, rugged, and well-watered western mountains consistently remain the favored landscape for national parks, judging by the earliness (e.g., Yellowstone, Yosemite), the persistence (e.g., Great Basin, the only park established during the 1980s), and the frequency (e.g., Glacier, Rocky Mountain, Olympic, North Cascades) with which such environments have been protected. Such a landscape even adorns the official logo of the National Park Service, the familiar brown shield with snow-covered mountain and green conifer. Second, eastern mountainous terrain (e.g., Great Smoky Mountains), stream-dissected landscapes in arid environments (e.g., Zion) or in rocks that produce badland topography (e.g., Bryce Canyon), and areas of local rugged relief (e.g., Devil's Tower, Pinnacles) also contribute to the general emphasis placed on the spectacular. But many types of monumental landscapes seem to have attracted little attention: rugged coastlines, arid mountain ranges, western mountains apart from those with alpine crests, and some of the highest relief in the eastern states. The National Park System does not include units on the Big Sur coast of California or Cape Lookout in Oregon, the Aguirre Springs Range in New Mexico or Pilot Peak in Nevada, the Santa Ana Mountains or Mount Diablo in California, Mount Rogers in Virginia or the White Mountains of New Hampshire.

Figure 4.4. Units of various landscape types within the National Park System, 1880–2000, by dates of establishment

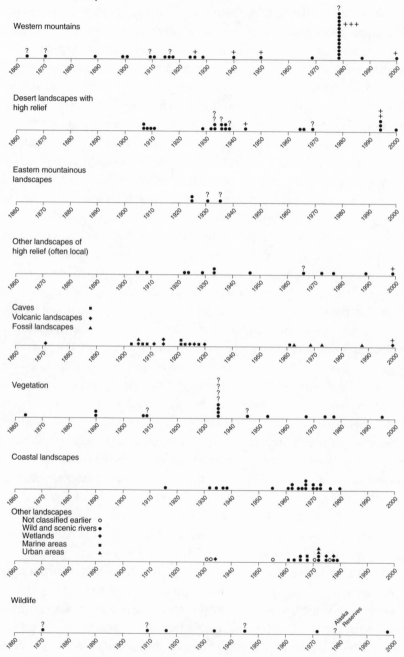

? = ambiguity in characterization of a particular landscape
+ = a major addition to an existing unit

The National Park System also protects caves and volcanic environments. The system embraced such landscapes with enthusiasm during the first three decades of the twentieth century (e.g., Wind Cave, Sunset Crater). Rothman (1986) suggests that caves, being geologic features, appealed as "monumental landscapes," although the focus on such natural features during those decades seems—inexplicably—to involve something more.

Even less conventionally scenic than cave or volcanic forms, landscapes of fossils periodically, but mostly in recent decades, have received protection (e.g., Florissant Fossil Beds, Fossil Butte). The exemplar of this tradition is Petrified Forest National Park, established early in the system's history and clearly a reserve for science more than scenery (Lubick 1996); otherwise, the creation of fossil-focused reserves characterizes the late decades of the twentieth century.

Plants have long prompted the establishment of parks, although not with great frequency and, in earlier years, only plants of monumental form (e.g., Sequoia, Saguaro). Vegetation could not generate major park units in the midwestern prairies, however, in spite of their historic symbolism to the nation, a deficiency only partly reversed today (see Stubbendieck and Willson 1987).

With a few exceptions, coastal landscapes generated little enthusiasm until after 1960, but over the next two decades more than a dozen coastal units joined the system (e.g., Cape Cod, Indiana Dunes). Aquatic environments, whether marine, riverine, or wetland, became a major focus for system expansion during the 1960s and 1970s (e.g., Biscayne, St. Croix, Congaree Swamp). Finally, a desire to protect animal populations—again, in the early years at least, mostly species of large mammals—contributed to the creation of several park system units (cf. Rothman 1989), including Yellowstone, Olympic, Everglades, Big Thicket, and those in Alaska. By contrast, biota often dominates contemporary assessments of park resources (e.g., Stohlgren and Quinn 1992).

Exceptions to these patterns abound. Yellowstone encompasses little rugged mountainous terrain. Isle Royale appeals as much for its wildness and insularity as for its topography. Acadia, established in 1916, is located on a rugged coast. Death Valley protects arid mountain ranges, though admittedly its claim to the lowest continental elevation in the western hemisphere and its extreme temperatures add to the area's allure. Santa Monica Mountains is centered on a range without high-elevation peaks.

The patterns need to be qualified in some instances. Some areas categorized as volcanic landscape might just as easily be classified as western mountains (e.g., Lassen Volcanic, Katmai), and some units associated with vegetation protect areas of major topographic relief (e.g., Organ Pipe Cactus, Joshua Tree). Historical importance or imagery may have contributed to the appeal of some areas (e.g., Death Valley, Voyageurs, City of Rocks). Too, recreational potential always looms large; this consideration is likely to have contributed to the early focus on well-watered western mountains (Vale 1995), to the somewhat later interest in arid environments, and to the contemporary interest in aquatic environments. Pyne (1998), moreover, suggests that Americans needed the development of an aesthetic sense for arid canyons before landscapes even as singularly monumental as the Grand Canyon, always of interest to the natural sciences, could be seen as scenic (see also Stegner 1977). Who knows the sources for the strong modern aesthetic valuation of wetlands and coasts—an extension of the well-established tradition of visits to urban beaches? a lesson learned from the Sierra Club, extending the virtues of wild rivers to other watered landscapes? a successful sales pitch by the manufacturers of pleasure boats or jet skis and the conveyors of white-water raft trips?

In sum, then, the critics say too much attention to the spectacular, too little focus on the representative; too much scenery, too little biology; too much recreation, too little nature protection. Rather than being "de luxe editions" of "natural forces," the units of the National Park System are glitzy picture books, devoid of serious text.

FACTORS IN THE ESTABLISHMENT OF PARKS   It could be argued that the family tree imagery of the National Park System is misleading: units of the National Park System have been created in response not to a plan for achieving some goal, even the goal of protecting the country's most spectacular landscapes, but rather to a set of fortuitous circumstances. Contingency, not rationality, has determined why we have the particular units that we do, why we have national parks in the Front Range of Colorado but not in the Sawtooth of Idaho, in the stands of Joshua trees in southern California but not in those of northwestern Arizona, on Mount Rainier but not on Mount Shasta, in the Great Smokies but not on Mount Marcy, on Isle Royale but not on Mount Washington. Even the word "system" inappropriately ascribes more organization than is warranted by this chance collection of individual parks and monuments.

The key to understanding why particular areas became units of the park system while others did not can be found in *promoters and promotion*. The history of any particular park typically includes a pivotal person, a patron saint, who spearheads a political movement for park authorization. Sometimes the advocate is an environmental activist, such as John Muir in Yosemite (H. Jones 1965), Enos Mills in Rocky Mountain (Buchholtz 1983), Marjory Stoneman Douglas in the Everglades (Douglas 1947), or Rosalie Barrow Edge for the expansion of Olympic (Kaufman 1996). It may be a politician, such as the state legislator E. E. Townsend for Big Bend (Ise 1961); a member of Congress—John Raker for Lassen (Ise 1961), Peter Norbeck for Badlands (Schuler 1989), Alan Bible for Great Basin (Elliott 1991a, 1991b); or a president who acts on behalf of a perceived national good at the risk of offending local or regional constituencies—Jimmy Carter for Alaska and Bill Clinton for a couple of Park Service monuments in the American West. Philanthropists have played their part, most notably members of the Rockefeller family for Grant Teton, Virgin Islands, and Arcadia (Ise 1961). Activist scientists may agitate for park creation, such as George Bird Grinnell for Glacier (Buchholtz 1976) and T. S. Palmer of the federal Biological Survey for a number of national monuments (Rothman 1989, Lubick 1996). Individual citizens often act as patron saints for reasons of their own: the socialite Minerva Hoyt for Joshua Tree (Cates 1984), the Mormon bishop Ephraim Pectol for Capitol Reef (Ise 1961), Judge William Gladstone Steel for Crater Lake (Ise 1961), and Lucy Peabody, at one time an office secretary, for Mesa Verde (Keller and Turek 1998). The park system's preeminent patron was Steven Mather, who acted in all of these roles (Ise 1961).

Promotion may also reflect the efforts of a formal group, whether in the public or private sector. Railroad companies, who envisioned profits by transporting tourists to and serving them within national parks, encouraged the establishment of parks, and their efforts contributed to the authorization of such parks as Yosemite, Grand Canyon, Glacier, and Yellowstone itself. Runte (1984), in fact, argues that Jay Cooke of the Northern Pacific Railroad, and not the members of the Washburn expedition of 1870, conceived the Yellowstone park idea and spearheaded its realization. State governments, foreseeing the same desirable increase in business activities as the railroads, also promoted national parks, and state purchases of land were critical to the formation of many eastern parks, including Big Bend, Everglades, Great Smoky Mountains, Shenandoah, and Isle Royale (Ise 1961, Boorstein 1992, Jameson 1996, Kirk 1999). Although not motivated by visions of profits, conservation organizations similarly have promoted park proposals by their selective political agitations, including the Boone and Crockett Club for Mount McKinley (Denali) (Ise 1961) and the Sierra Club for Redwoods (Vale 1974a, Schrepfer 1983). Neither a desire to generate revenue nor the call of the wild prompted the elite summer folk of Bar Harbor, Maine, to help create Acadia National Park: they thought it only prudent to preserve a bucolic landscape for themselves (Hornsby 1993). On occasion, even Congress, arguably acting in the long traditions of pork barrel politics, has added to the system units that the Park Service itself considered unworthy (Winks 1995).

Arguably even more influential than promoters in print (Harmon, ed., 1989; Herring 2004) were *painters and photographers.* The linkage between landscape art and the national park idea forms a mutually reinforcing relationship. The work of graphic artists prominently contributes to the success stories, including the earliest efforts to create Yosemite (the photographers Carleton Watkins and Edward Muybridge and the painter Albert Bierstadt) and Yellowstone (the photographer William Henry Jackson and the artist Thomas Moran). The visual portrayal of nature enhances the popular enthusiasm for nature protection, which stimulates the popularity of nature art (Cahn 1981, Ketchum 1981, Robertson 1984, Moore 2003). Goetzmann (1986), recognizing the importance of the American West in this history, articulates the reciprocating growth of art and public taste as a capturing of "the West of the imagination," by which he means the imagination of both the artists' work and the American mind. Moreover, artists helped to expand sensitivity to landscape. William Henry Holmes exposed the geological meanings of the Grand Canyon country in his powerful drawings of "a landscape whose emotive power derives from the scientific ideas behind it" (Pyne 1998: 100). Down through the years, photographers and painters have defined the natural world (Adams 1962, Porter 1962), thus promoting protection of it (Stegner 1955, Adams and Newhall 1960, Wilderness Society n.d.). Not even the challenges of revisionist artists (Avedon 1985) and historians (Truettner 1991) weaken Americans' desire for romanticized graphics of the natural world and for the landscapes that capture that desire.

Promotion of particular areas as national parks has been further facilitated by *federal ownership* of lands considered for addition to the system. Until 1961, when Congress authorized $16 million to purchase lands for the Cape Cod National Seashore, and 1968, when it allocated $148 million to create the Redwood National Park (Conservation Foundation 1985), major units of the National Park System were carved from areas already administered by federal land agencies (or donated by state governments), notably the U.S. Forest Service and the Bureau of Land Management. Interagency rivalries, particularly those between the Park Service and the Forest Service, create legendary stories in the history of American conservation (H. Hampton 1981, Twight 1983), even stimulating the precursors to the National Wilderness Preservation System (see chapter 5). The view that national monuments act as a sort of intermediate status for landscapes that eventually will earn designation as national parks (as suggested by both Ise, 1961, and Rothman, 1989) finds support in the histories of many parks, including the Grand Canyon, Olympic, Lassen, Petrified Forest, Joshua Tree, Death Valley, and many parks in Utah, only reinforcing the importance of prior federal ownership of park land. The power of presidential proclamation under the Antiquities Act, by which most national parks that once were monuments were created, extends only to federal lands.

Since the action that creates a national park is a political process, all successful park movements reflect a coincidence of *sympathetic political forces.* This point need not deteriorate into the disparagingly cynical view that approval of a new park merely reflects politics; the other factors should be seen as influencing political decision making. Nonetheless, political influences need to be aligned to allow a park to be created (cf. Dilsaver 2004). Moreover, they constitute a part of the story no less for Yosemite in 1864 than for Great Basin in 1986. No park history better illustrates the rich mix of public parlor pronouncements and smoky backroom deals than that of Olympic, as told by Lien (1991). All of the partygoers normally present and some that show up unexpectedly enliven the story: a Park Service sometimes defending forests from loggers but more often helping the timber industry; a Forest Service ineffectively working against park interests and aiding its tree-cutting allies; conservation groups, either duped by timber companies or, in the case of the Emergency Conservation Committee, saving the park; a powerful timber industry always effective in manipulation and dealmaking; local populations handled skillfully by corporate interests; members of Congress in bed with timber interests and willing to prostitute the public good; presidents of the United States, varying in leadership qualities, working either from some sense of societal good or to help corporate America. Similarly large casts populate the dramas of other parks. Dilsaver and Tweed's (1990) history of Sequoia–Kings Canyon is equally long and even more diverse, although told with a less cynical flavor than Lien's. Such narratives remind us of the political aspects of the effort to protect nature.

Finally, high levels of *stridency and dedication* may be necessary to over-

whelm the inevitable opposition interests. For example, the effort to establish a national park in the tall-grass prairie—endorsed by park enthusiasts
not only in the 1960s but also in the 1930s (National Park Service 1961, Ise
1961) and arguably as far back as George Catlin's famous proclamation in
1880 (Nash, ed., 1968)—never was taken up by any influential patron or any
conservation group and thus foundered until the compromise of the national preserve of 1997. Similarly, the Redwood National Park—envisioned,
endorsed, debated for much of the twentieth century (Ise 1961, National Park
Service 1964)—emerged into the national spotlight and received the ap-
plause needed for success only when the Sierra Club committed itself to the
proposal in the 1960s. Halfhearted campaigns may succeed when little opposition appears (a rare circumstance and itself perhaps crafted by park supporters [H. Hampton 1981]), but otherwise zealousness, even if not sufficient
alone, may be necessary to counter either outright opposition or congressional and bureaucratic apathy; indeed, Hampton (1981) identifies federal
indifference as responsible for the failure of a number of park proposals.

Imagine for a moment a counterfactual history to see how these factors
have influenced the establishment of parks. If John Muir had traveled to the
Sawtooth Range of Idaho instead of to the Yosemite Sierra in the 1860s, and
if the Union Pacific Railroad had decided to champion the tourist potential
of the Sawtooth (situated but a spur line north of its major route across the
Snake River plain), and if the railroad had hired prominent artists to promote that Idaho landscape (in geologic structure similar to the Teton range
and Jackson Hole), and if the interested parties had created a Sawtooth Club
instead of a Sierra Club, might we have had a Sawtooth National Park sweeping up from the Salmon River into the serrated peaks of that spectacular
mountain range? Even more plausibly, might we have had, with a less different history, a Mount Shasta National Park? Or a Big Sur Coast–Santa Lucia
Mountains National Park? But we do not have these parks. History unfolds
in certain directions rather than others, with outcomes caused by human
choices and human circumstances, and thus we have the National Park System that we do. It is a system that protects much of the most spectacular
scenery in the country but not all of it; many striking landscapes but hardly
all such terrain; hundreds of fascinating places worthy of protection but
scarcely all places that might generate a sense of fascination. It is a system
molded by contingency.

Several major park proposals that failed further illustrate the importance of historical circumstance. A plan to create a national park in the Lake

Tahoe basin, astride the California-Nevada border, was discussed repeatedly after its introduction in 1900 but foundered because timber cutting on privately owned land had reduced the watershed's forest cover and the politicians who advocated the plan were suspected of having a hidden agenda (Pisani 1977, Strong 1984). Might the cynicism have been overcome by effective champions, political and artistic? A proposal for an expansive Escalante national park in the Colorado River canyon lands along the Arizona-Utah border, first articulated in 1909 and considered into the 1930s, might have generated more enthusiasm if the Santa Fe Railroad had laid its tracks closer to the Escalante country (cf. Runte 1984); and the creation of the Escalante might have discouraged the subsequent construction of Glen Canyon Dam (Keller and Turek 1998). A plan to create an expansive park in the area of cliff dwellings centered on the present Bandelier National Monument of New Mexico, argued over the first two decades of the twentieth century, possessed several key elements that might have promised success: a patron in John Lacey, an influential congressman and shepherd of several key acts celebrated by conservationists; federal ownership of the land, although some of it was claimed by native peoples; and support by groups who envisioned increased tourism, including local business people, New Mexico newspapers, and the Santa Fe Railroad. Yet the proposal never generated the concentrated enthusiasm needed to overcome the hostility and indifference of interests both public and private (Altherr 1985). Finally, a proposal for a national park on the rugged landscape of Kauai in the 1960s failed to generate enthusiasm in part because Hawaii was already so saturated with tourists that the project was not high on the agenda of conservation groups (Schuh 1966).

Such stories suggest the political considerations that characterize the creation of individual parks and thus the nature of the National Park System as a whole. The interpretation of the parks as political footballs rather than an organized system, in fact, permeates Rettie's (1995) analysis. Even the 1972 *National Park System Plan* seems not to dictate conservationists' visions for new park units: the list of candidate parks drawn up by the National Parks Conservation Association (1988a) identifies eighty-six areas, many of which might fill gaps identified in the plan, but the largest proposals concern landscapes already well represented in the system—rugged western mountains (e.g., Kings Range of California, San Juan Mountains of Colorado, Sawtooth Mountains of Idaho, Ruby Mountains of Nevada, Jemez Mountains of New Mexico) and western deserts (e.g., Sonoran Desert of Arizona, Black Rock

Desert of Nevada, Owyhee Canyonlands of Oregon, Escalante Canyons and San Rafael Swell of Utah, and the Sweetwater Basin of Wyoming) (Simon 1988). The organization's more modest list of park proposals for 2001 continued the strong interest in the spectacular rather than in gaps. This description should not necessarily be read as a criticism; the point is simply that the park system has grown and continues to grow in response less to evaluative and detached planning than to aesthetic tradition, personal commitment, and perhaps whim.

Rather than reflecting a national plan, then, the National Park System, a critic might say, is revealed as a hodgepodge of parks and monuments, each created because of favorable historical circumstances and successful political maneuverings. If the system fails to preserve adequately the non-spectacular in the natural world, it also falls short of reflecting an organized effort to protect the nation's most vital scenery.

POLITICAL IDEOLOGY Denying the progressive component of the national park ideal, some observers see the National Park System as sinisterly reactionary, a government activity that runs "counter to American democratic traditions" (H. Hampton 1981: 40), a manifestation of the aristocratic playground. Two specific critiques structure this perspective.

First, social and economic elites promote, defend, and use units of the park system, whereas disadvantaged and powerless minorities do not or cannot (Tucker 1982). In the past (though not today), conservative Republicans were much more likely than liberal Democrats to promote the parks, whether among the leadership of the Sierra Club (Cohen 1988) and the Izaak Walton League (Fox 1981/1985) or presidents of the country. Contrast, for example, Theodore Roosevelt, a hero for nature protection but often identified as populist-conservative, with Woodrow Wilson, a progressive liberal who revealed little sympathy for parks (Rothman 1989). Labor unions often condemn park proposals as threats to opportunities for working persons (H. Hampton 1981); business interests proclaim that constraints on concessionaires amount to "stealing the national parks" from the people (Hummel 1987); political writers lament the growth of scientific considerations in park management as a force to deny human access, an expression of "selfish elitism" (Freemuth 1986). Even the conservationist celebration of the U.S. Army patrols in the parks early in their history, which saved them from trespassing commodity resource users (D. Hampton 1971), might be interpreted as a link between the most regressive federal agency and nature protection.

A second critique focuses on the social injustices suffered by local people, particularly Native Americans but others too, as a consequence of the
creation and functioning of parks (Lambert 1989, Boorstein 1992, Catton
1997, Jacoby 2001). Keller and Turek (1998) fill the pages of their book with
stories of historical abuse: in Yosemite the Miwok endured mistreatment
and were expelled from the earliest days of "discovery" deep into modern
times; the creators of Glacier National Park deprived the Blackfeet of their
rights by means of "fraud . . . confusing language, incorrect surveys, false
promises, and whiskey" (p. 63); in the Grand Canyon even the archdruid
David Brower engaged in "racial name-calling . . . poor taste . . . hypocrisy
and deception" (p. 181). The same stories echo in work by Spence (2000),
who draws parallels between the creation of reservations for native peoples
and for parks; by Burnham (2000), who calls park creation "the most recent, if least brutal, display of manifest destiny" (p. 308); and by Jacoby
(2001), who laments that "Americans have often pursued environmental
quality at the expense of social justice" (p. 198). Various efforts to redress
past wrongs have emerged in recent years (Keller and Turek 1998, Burnham
2000): joint management of park areas, as in Canyon de Chelly, where the
Navajo retain ownership of the land but the Park Service sets the rules, and
in Nez Perce, with its "partnership park" administration; land tenure shifts,
such as the transfer of 185,000 acres of Grand Canyon National Park to the
Havasupai and the more recent claims to Badlands National Park by the
Sioux (Ray 2003); Native Americans' access to and harvest of park resources,
as in the Grand Canyon and the parks of Alaska (Morehouse 1996, Catton
1997); and formation of "homelands" within national park boundaries,
such as the Timbisha Shoshone Tribal Homeland in Death Valley (www
.death-valley.us/contentid-14.html). Still, such efforts may only feebly allow
tribes "to remain politically and culturally distinct nations" (Spence 2000:
139), only nod toward a reconciliation between recreation pursued "at the
expense of people living in poverty" (Keller and Turek 1998: 239), only ges-
ture toward "social progress" (Burnham 2000: 310). Similarly, Native Americans' religious practices within parks arouse objections (T. Wilkinson
1993), and so do their interpretations of history (Turner 1997a). Such abuses
even more commonly structure debates over nature protection in the developing world (Hecht and Cockburn 1989, Peluso 1993, Neumann 1998, Redford and Sanderson 2000, Schwartzman et al. 2000, Terborgh 2000, Zimmerer 2000). Ultimately, this critique argues for social justice concerns to
assume preeminence over traditional nature protection (Keller and Turek

1998), and for "empty" wild landscapes to be redefined as "inhabited wilderness" (Catton 1997).

A rich and provocative interpretation of Virgin Islands National Park as contrary to American democratic traditions comes from Olwig and Olwig (1979). Wealthy mainland tourists come in large numbers to the one and only concessionaire, secured from competition by the Park Service, which "patrols the resort's beaches and tends its 'back yard'—the park itself" (p. 22). This lone resort originated on land purposefully withheld from federal ownership when the core of the park's land was donated to the Park Service by that icon of concentrated American wealth, the Rockefeller family. The resort, moreover, is called a plantation—Caneel Bay Plantation—and the major cultural landscape features preserved are "the ruins of the plantations, tangible symbols of the island's slave heritage" (p. 23). Locals who work for the concessionaire gain only "dead-end . . . low echelon unskilled jobs" (p. 22), and they are forbidden to engage in their traditional "small farming" on park land (p. 22). This "wild" land, finally, is nothing more than abandoned farmland, acres of "mixed pastoral human landscape created by the free farmers of the island" (p. 23). Overall, then, natural parks such as Virgin Islands—and the Olwigs intend to extend their characterization more generally—"may not be the simple, natural, democratic, cultural and civilizing enterprise which they may seem to be at first glance" (p. 23). Seen from this perspective, national parks become symbols of the regressive tendencies of American society.

STRENGTH OF PROTECTION In spite of the legal pronouncements, some observers argue, the National Park System offers anything but strong nature protection. Inadequacies, according to this view, abound. Administrative flexibility may allow nonconforming uses (Lien 1991, Yochim 2003b), but even congressional directives seem to many observers to be too lax. The critique revolves around three issues.

First, too often nature within the parks suffers from *commodity resource development and other nonconforming uses.* Hard-rock mining scars Death Valley. Livestock graze the grasses and herbs in Dinosaur National Monument. Dams mar the pristine landscapes in Yosemite, Rainbow Bridge, and Jackson Hole. Hunters invade the parks and reserves in Alaska. A commercial airport sprawls within the boundary of Grand Teton National Park. Off-road vehicles roar across the Mojave National Preserve and over much of the protected acreage of the Alaskan parks. Water diversions render protection for the Everglades only imaginary. Garbage, pollution, airplane overflights, jetties and other artificial structures—such problems plague the majority of coastal parks. Collectively, then, the classic conservation controversies, those stories that symbolize the tension between nature conserved and nature converted, all too often tip in favor of commodity resource development, even when the narratives celebrate the successful establishment of parks.

Taking an extreme position, Alfred Runte (1979) argues that the entire history of the National Park System is rife with exceptions to the ideal of nature protection, with boundaries drawn to exclude developable resources and allowances made to permit exploitation within the allegedly protected reserves. The exceptions are so commonplace, Runte suggests, that only economically worthless lands are included within the National Park System. The worthless-land thesis generates reaction both pro and con, with the discussions focusing on the meaning of "worthless" and even of "national park." As is so often the case in such disputes, the evasive truth depends on the meanings of such terms (Sellars 1983, Runte 1983, Utley 1983, Winks 1983, Cox 1983). If the thesis is interpreted to mean that the National Park System is not absolute in its nature protection, that compromises permit commodity resource development in some units, surely it cannot be denied. Similarly, if the thesis says that American society has not sacrificed its standard of living, that the nature protected is worthless in relation to the nature converted to commodity development outside the parks, again we must agree. If, on the other hand, the thesis is taken literally to mean that no potentially developable resources occur within park units, it clearly fails. The rain forests of Olympic stand unlogged. Sheep and cattle do not graze the meadows on Mount Rainier or Glacier. Dams do not flood the Grand Canyon, Yosemite Valley, or Yellowstone (Yochim 2003a). Dairy herds do not complete with moose in Isle Royale or with white-tailed deer at Acadia. Fields of corn do not replace the forested slopes of Shenandoah or Great Smoky Mountains.

The potential development of commodity resources within park boundaries—sometimes described as "internal threats"—less commonly concerns park enthusiasts today than the threats to the park system that originate from commodity resource development outside the protected landscapes. These external threats fill the pages of the conservationist literature: air pollution originating in distant urban areas threatens the purity of Sequoia–Kings Canyon's atmosphere, the vistas at Grand Canyon, the soil chemistry at Isle Royale, and the forests in Great Smoky Mountains. Upstream logging outside parkland imperils groves of protected coast redwoods in Redwood National Park. Water development for urban and agricultural uses in south Florida reduces water movement into the Everglades (Davis et al., eds., 1994). Tapping of steam and hot water jeopardizes thermal features within Yellowstone, perhaps Old Faithful itself. River flows—reduced by upstream diversions, modified by upstream dams—threaten Dinosaur and the Grand Canyon (Bassin 1985). Residential and even urban growth presses against park boundaries nearly everywhere. In 1980 park administrators identified 4,335 individual threats to 326 units of the system, half of them external (National Park Service 1980). By mid-decade, the Conservation Foundation (1985) judged internal threats to be far less critical than external threats, and the National Parks Conservation Association (1988b) urged biosphere reserve designations for all appropriate units as a means to surround parklands with semiprotected landscapes. O'Brien (1999) continues the call for attention to such threats. The rise of the "greater Yellowstone ecosystem" (or "area") similarly reflects the importance of external threats (Keiter and Boyce, eds., 1991). The Park Service nonetheless reveals a history of some timidity in addressing such problems (Foresta 1984, Sax 1987).

A second questioning of the adequacy of the protection offered nature within the National Park System focuses on the need for *active management* rather than passive protection of ecosystems and landscapes. Such human manipulation of the environments within parks is deemed necessary because protected nature reveals human influences: commodity resource development before the parks were established, elimination of natural processes under the aegis of protection, alterations associated with the small sizes of landscape reserves, and today's recreational uses of parks. These forces for change require active management. The 1963 report by a special committee appointed by Interior Secretary Stewart Udall and headed by A. Starker Leopold is usually identified as providing a mandate for more active management policies in the parks, not only for the specific subject of its inquiry, wildlife, but for nature more generally (Leopold et al. 1963). Echoing the Leopold Report, Stone (1965) called for the training of "vegetation-preservation specialists" (p. 242) to facilitate the needed ecosystem management in parks and other nature reserves. Over the following decades, the same message repeatedly articulated the need for the elevation of science in protectionist policy and the associated activity of hands-on management. P. White and Bratton (1980) challenged the park community to think "beyond preservation"; Agee and Johnson (eds., 1988), explored ecological management for parks and wilderness; Runte (1988) decried the Park Service's ignoring of biology; Dilsaver (1992) suggested that concerns for "anthro-pocentricism, autonomy, and automobile" too sharply constrain the role of science in park policy; Sellars (1997: 267) argued that "scientific research in the parks [is] the only real means of comprehending . . . the natural systems under the Service's care." No one generated more reaction over the issue than the journalist Alston Chase (1983, 1987), who argued that the Park Service and environmental groups together resist science and active management because they see in the natural world an expression of the divine, a condi-tion of perfection needing no human modification. Nuanced opinions ap-peared: Dilsaver (1987) identified varying degrees of hands-off protection and active management among land agencies, and Vale (1987) urged recog-nition of humanistic as well as scientific purposes for parks. For many observers the need for more human intervention in park ecosystems has become a call not to be denied (see chapter 10). For them the images of spoiled nature and false idol have merged to become the essential character of the national park landscape.

The critique focuses on biological nature: "management" means vege-tation and wild animal management, and "science" refers to ecological sci-ence. Ironically, however, the Park Service employs far more biological sci-entists than earth scientists (Applegate 1997) and probably more than all other natural scientists combined; moreover, it seems to take little interest in the earth sciences (Shaver and Wood 2001). Nonetheless, two specific bio-logical issues prominent in the Leopold Report continue to dominate the dialogue. First, the reintroduction of fire into landscapes where it was im-portant before America was colonized began in the parks in 1968, when Sequoia–Kings Canyon recognized areas where lightning-ignited fires would be allowed to burn. This policy of "prescribed natural fires" spread to other parks (Kilgore and Nichols 1995), and more than 388,000 acres in the park system were so burned from 1968 to 1988 (Botti and Nichols 1995). Over the 1970s and 1980s, the let-burn directive expanded to include "management-ignited prescribed fires," purposefully set burning "to restore area[s] to a nat-ural range of conditions before allowing use of prescribed natural fire" (Kil-gore and Nichols 1995: 24); between 1968 and 1988, more than 307,000 acres burned from such fires (Botti and Nichols 1995). After the Yellowstone fires of 1988, revisions to these policies constrained the number of fires and acre-age burned, a trend that concerned park scientists (Kilgore and Nichols 1995, Botti and Nichols 1995). Some criticism of fires in the parks springs from objections to "unsightly" charring on the bark of Giant Sequoias (Christensen et al. 1987) and traditional views of fire as destructive; the academic Harold Holt described the Yellowstone fires as "madness" (Holt 1988).

The most stinging critique, however, articulates, at least in part, a familiar narrative with a number of interconnected points. According to this view, the parks should be seen as landscapes with values that require active human management to be maintained; the fire regimes of precolonial times were the work of Native Americans, not lightning, and therefore were not "natural"; regardless of the characteristics of fire regimes in the precolonial era, fires today should serve the desired landscape values; modern humans, not lightning, are the only ignition sources for fires in parks consistent with the desired values; to depend on lightning fires is to bow to a policy of "letting nature take its course," a silly vision of the parks as "quasi religious temples" ruled by "mythical gods," rather than "the objectivity of science" and its "scientific management" (Bonnicksen 1989). The contrary perspective sees the same points differently: landscapes of "untrammeled" nature remain the primary value of the parks; precolonial fire regimes—most obviously in large areas of the American West—resulted from natural conditions of fuel, weather, and lightning, not ignitions by native peoples (Vale, ed., 2002); the history of fires should guide the identification of desirable contemporary fire regimes; lightning fires combined with human-set fires allow landscapes to continue as natural or to revert to prefire suppression conditions; science and management appropriately support and reinforce natural processes rather than substitute for them. It is an odd debate. Everyone involved embraces science, but the fundamental disagreement revolves around the existence of something called the "natural landscape."

The same biting criticism and the same rejoinders appear in a second management issue: the sizes of the populations of large ungulates in the parks. Although spurred by the Leopold Report, the controversy over populations of grazing animals—their "naturalness," their impact on vegetation—extends back into the early decades of the twentieth century. This drama unfolds particularly at Yellowstone, but not only there (Hess 1993, Baker et al. 1997). Should the numbers of elk be controlled by humans in order to protect park values threatened by their grazing, or should elk populations be allowed to fluctuate in response to weather, food supplies, disease, and predation ("natural regulation") (Robbins 1984, Chase 1986, Despain et al. 1986, C. Kay 1994, C. Kay and Simmons 2002, Meager and Houston 1998, Marston 1997)? Answers seem to depend on the presence or absence of large predators in precolonial times, the degree of hunting pressure by Native

Americans, the role of climate variability as an influence on elks' food supplies and their survival over the winter, and the importance of small grazers such as insects and pocket gophers on grassland vegetation. As with the issue of fire, however, underlying questions ask whether something called "nature" exists and whether what is "natural" is a desired goal for the parks. The advocates of more active management insist that they want to protect "natural" values in the parks, even "nature" itself, although their rhetoric sounds more like that of the utilitarian conservationist (nature needs to be molded to serve human needs), the technological optimist (applications of science will resolve resource problems), and the believer in human omnipotence (people can indeed control nature) than like that of the aesthetic conservationist, who is more likely to be cautious of simple technological solutions and human cleverness.

The most frequent contemporary criticism of the parks' management is its preoccupation with *recreation* at the expense of protection. This is the characterization that prompts wild landscape enthusiasts to regret the creation of new parks (Jackson 1987); it dominates the view that parks face a "dilemma" (Fitzsimmons 1976). Historians of the parks invariably point out that the parks have two purposes, protection of nature and provision for recreation, and that those purposes are incompatible (Sax 1976, Runte 1979, Mackintosh 1985, Frome 1992, Dilsaver 1992, Dilsaver and Strong 1990, Winks 1996, Watkins 1997, Margolis 1997). Just as frequently, these interpretations allege that recreation has received undue attention and that recreational development has so ruined the parks that the phrase "loving the parks to death" has become conventional wisdom, even a cliché (Kahler 1986, Stevens 1994). A comment from a cynic captures more imaginatively the degree and generality of the sentiment: NPS stands not for National Park Service but for National Parking Service.

Even a casual look at the national parks, however, suggests at least two vastly different models of recreational development. The first represents the older units, particularly the grand old parks established in the nineteenth century and the early decades of the twentieth (fig. 4.5a). These parks typically share a suite of characteristics: a road system (e.g., the loop drive in Yellowstone, Trail Ridge Road in Rocky Mountain, Rim Drive at Crater Lake), a focused site of development with some mix of lodging, campgrounds, stores, and visitor center at a major natural attraction (e.g., Yosemite Valley in Yosemite, South Rim at Grand Canyon, Paradise in Mount Rainier), a secondary area of development at another landscape feature (e.g., St. Mary

Figure 4.5. Two models of national parks, reflecting different perspectives on appropriate development

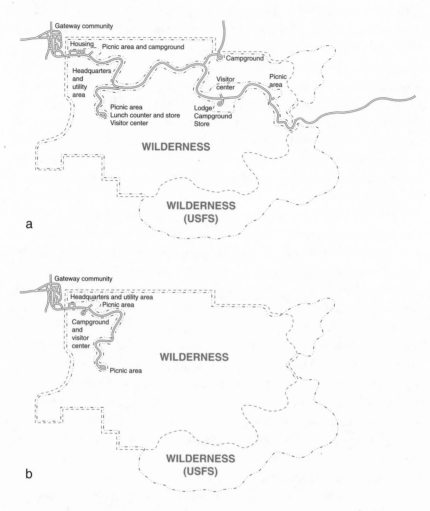

at Glacier, Tuolumne Meadows or Wawona in Yosemite, Roosevelt or Tower at Yellowstone), a "gateway community" just outside the park boundary at a major entrance (e.g., Estes Park at Rocky Mountain, Springdale at Zion, Gatlinburg at Great Smoky Mountains), a roadless and otherwise undeveloped landscape spreading over most of the park area (either statutory wilderness, as in Yosemite and Saguaro, or de facto wilderness, as in Yellowstone and Grand Canyon), and adjoining Forest Service (or sometimes

Bureau of Land Management) wilderness abutting park boundaries (e.g., Indian Peaks at Rocky Mountain, John Muir at Sequoia–Kings Canyon, Absaroka-Beartooth at Yellowstone). The repetition of these characteristics reveals what was considered appropriate development for parks in the first half of the twentieth century.

In the decades after the creation of Kings Canyon National Park in 1938, a second model for recreation development emerged (Dilsaver and Tweed 1990). Not only a proposed park-bisecting highway up the Kings River and across the Sierra Nevada was eliminated from further consideration but also a large complex of recreational facilities—both consistent with the older model—in the South Fork Canyon of the Kings River. Many factors contributed to this new style of development: small appropriations by Congress, reluctance of private investors, fears that a dam and reservoir might eventually invade the park, opposition by the Sierra Club, public indifference to a major resort complex, and growth in the general perceived virtues of roadless landscape. One modest lodge/store/coffee shop, several campgrounds, a corral, and a small visitor center are all that cluster beside the short road that barely penetrates the park boundary. Such restraint would come to characterize parks created in the second half of the century. Consider such units as Canyonlands, Guadalupe Mountains, the parks of Alaska, and the many national monuments that became national parks: access roads at most just inside the park border, minor recreational development at a site or two, virtually or literally the entire park area roadless, and a small gateway community (fig. 4.5b). Some parks created after mid-century inherited infrastructures (e.g., the road system at Great Basin), but otherwise the second model has become the rule.

In fact, the reduced emphasis on recreational development in newer parks expresses a more general trend appropriate for the entire National Park System. The Stevens Canyon Road in Mount Rainier, which opened in 1957, might be the last major road to penetrate previously unroaded landscape in the system, and as such deserves celebratory recognition. The lodging facility at Grant Village in Yellowstone, built in the 1980s as part of a plan to abandon the complex at Fishing Bridge, and the relocation of lodging from Giant Forest to a site near Lodgepole in Sequoia during the 1990s represent the newest lodging in the parks; note that both involve elimination of development elsewhere in the two parks. Downhill skiing facilities closed at Sequoia, Mount Lassen, and Rocky Mountain. Campgrounds closed at Yosemite, Mount Rainier, and Crater Lake. Nonconforming recreation comes under strong scrutiny, Yosemite's "fire fall" being the type example, and it was eliminated in 1968. Units such as the national seashores, which in many people's minds were to be mass recreation landscapes to serve nearby urban populations and thereby reduce pressures on the major parks, have instead become new wild landscape reserves with minimal development. Even Mission 66, a congressional program to modernize the parks over a ten-year period from 1956 to 1966, although criticized by most conservation groups for its emphasis on recreational development, focused much more on reconstruction of existing infrastructure than on creation of new facilities. Roads have been reconstructed, the Tioga Road project in Yosemite, completed in 1961, being particularly contentious. Some buildings were refurbished and other visitor-related installations were modernized, but in fact such facilities as sewage systems and water supplies in the parks require increased attention even today, not only for visitors' needs but also for nature's protection. The minimal development model dominates the recent history of the National Park System.

These trends away from the roads, lodging, and other recreational development that so characterized the National Park System in earlier years reflect the strength of protection sentiment among not only conservation groups but also the general American population. In a sense, the attitude that recreation development is antithetical to nature protection has been so successfully sold that it seems conventional wisdom. One reflective observer of the national parks, however, demurs. Ronald Foresta, in what remains one of the most thoughtful books on the national parks (1984), suggests that "the idea of the national park as a park should . . . be put back into System management"; by this he means simply that the parks should serve both "ecosystemic study" and "direct human appeal" (p. 269). Foresta calls for reasoning: "a visitor access road, even a paved one, on a tract of several hundred square miles is not on the same order of magnitude as clearcutting the tract"; to eliminate the opportunity to "sleep in a bed while in a national park" would be to deny the park tradition of "democratic, pluralistic accommodation"; "the impact of one thousand pairs of feet on a mountain is not the same as that of a chalet" (pp. 265, 270, 271). He argues for balance in identifying human purposes for the parks, for seeing both recreation and protection as linking people and nature.

Foresta's interpretation is persuasive. Perhaps his sense of compatibility between nature protection and recreation development, as existent in the National Park System, also emerges from questioning the logic of the opposing position: if the national parks have indeed been loved to death, why should we bother to worry about them any more?

Reflections

The assertion that the National Park System represents the finest in nature protection sounds like a romantic notion, strangely antiquarian. Over the early decades of the twentieth century, the dominant assumption was that the national parks could protect nature, while commodity resource development could continue outside park boundaries. The two uses of the land could be realized simultaneously as parts of the more general goal of human progress toward a grander America, a better world (Schrepfer 1976, Foresta 1984). Such a positive feeling probably persists among most of the millions who visit the parks today.

Among students of nature protection, whether independent writers or scholars, the vision of the park system as both an ideal in nature protection and a part of the ennobling development of human society has dimmed, even disappeared, replaced by a view of the parks as seriously flawed, even failures. The meanings so often perceived and articulated today by these observers, presumably the most thoughtful of park enthusiasts, reflect negativism, not about nature but about the modern human. The perspectives sound familiar: the vision of the National Park System as focused selectively and even arbitrarily on scenery means that superficial human desires may be satisfied but nature's need for functioning ecosystems is ignored, and thus the national park landscape fails as ecosystem. To recognize flawed nature protection in the parks is to see the protected landscapes as spoiled nature, and to perceive inadequate active management and restoration in the parks renders them as landscapes of a false idol. The critical emphasis on recreational impacts in the national parks reduces their landscapes to frivolous pleasuring grounds. Seeing suspicious political ideology in the parks reduces them to aristocratic castles. Overall, then, a common contemporary vision of the national parks sees humans as fundamentally destructive in their interactions with nature, even in their attempts to protect it, and fundamentally exploitive in their interactions with one another. The national parks reflect a vision of ourselves, and it is not a pretty picture.

General cynicism about the character of people and the course of human society is rampant in the modern world, but as a reaction to the American National Park System it is uncalled for. Particularly troubling, the portrait of the parks as manifestations of racist imperialism reflects a curious whitewash of the problems facing disenfranchised groups in American society. It might even be described as tokenism: social justice might more meaningfully demand that we return Times Square to the Manhattan Indians than advocate the gathering of pine nuts in Grand Canyon National Park. The rejoinder that taking pine nuts affects pinyon forests only trivially exposes the advocates of such a concession as less than serious supporters of protected wild landscapes as natural resources. It is defensible to argue that social justice trumps any concern for parks and wilderness, but it is illusionary to say that both can be served simultaneously.

The ideal of the national parks remains not simply alive but dynamically fluid: the system struggles with new concepts in protection and implements new policies in human use of its landscapes. Criticism generates reflection and change as the Park Service reaches out to a broad spectrum of visitors and struggles with honest interpretations of nature and American society. Celebration generates enthusiasm for continued wonderment about what types of landscapes should be added to the system, what the parks are for. Nowhere in the world, at no time in human history, has the conscious effort to protect nature seemed more likely to succeed.

People and nature coexist in the parks, and their coexistence transforms the parks into places. The interactions unfold as recreation and protection, stories of human history and studies of natural history, processes of nature continuing even where visitors congregate. Amid the crowds in Yosemite Valley, day walkers clamber among the boulders at Bridalveil Falls while spotted owls perch secretly in nearby trees. The LeConte Memorial offers exhibits on early Sierra Club activities, while in the nearby Merced River wind-downed trees lie where they fall, protruding from the quietly flowing green water. Peregrine falcons return to nest high on the cliff faces, where the bold rock remains untouched since losing its glacial ice. Rock slides thunder uncontrolled, even into recreational developments below. Yosemite is more the rule than the exception: the national parks, precisely because they combine people and nature, offer hope in their place-rich landscapes of plural purpose.

5 THE NATIONAL WILDERNESS PRESERVATION SYSTEM

The tarnish on the national parks—overcrowded, overused, overdeveloped—encouraged a different ideal at mid-century: the National Wilderness Preservation System. For many people the passage of the Wilderness Act in 1964, after a decade of debate in Congress, heralded salvation for the failed promise of the National Park System. In ensuing decades, conservationists widely proclaimed the law as a higher level of nature protection: "If the national park idea is, as Lord Bryce suggested, the best idea America ever had, wilderness preservation is the highest refinement of that idea" (Stegner 1990: 41). Roderick Nash, while recognizing the anthropocentric wording of the Wilderness Act, nonetheless articulated a common perception of that law as offering a new kind of nature preservation: "[Replacing the] very anthropocentrically defined national park ideal, [the Wilderness Act] seemed to some persons a legislative guarantee of freedom from human interference for wild creatures and ecosystems" (Nash 1989: 35, 171). The praise, gesturing to failures elsewhere on the federal lands, proclaims the triumph of the Wilderness Act: "No other statute aimed at protecting wildlands has proven as effective. National parks can be developed . . . wildlife refuges can be logged . . . wild-river designation protects only narrow bands. . . . But congressionally designated wilderness areas are diverse and inviolate" (Hamilton 1994: 46). When contrasting nature protection in the United States with that in other countries, writers commonly make comparisons not with America's national parks but with its wilderness system: "A biosphere reserve is the highest legal protection the Mexican government can offer, equal to wilderness status in the United States" (F. Williams 1994: 11). In support of their admiration for the Wilderness Act as "the climax of preservationist environmentalism" (Stegner 1990: 43) and "the holy grail of nature lovers"

Figure 5.1. Millions of acres of protected landscape in the National Wilderness Preservation System, 1964–2002, by administering agency. (Adapted from Landers and Meyer 1998, p. 8)

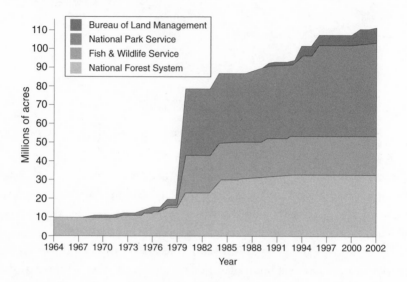

Figure 5.2. The National Wilderness Preservation System, 2002

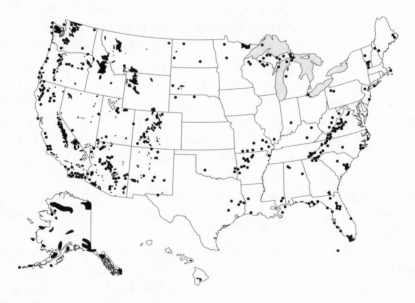

Dots indicate units too small to map by area.

(Mitchell 2004: 31), such commentators may quote the words in the law, invoking a new and modern sacred text:

A wilderness, in contrast with those areas where man and his own works dominate the landscape, is hereby recognized as an area where the earth and its community of life are untrammeled by man, where man himself is a visitor who does not remain . . . [where the wilderness landscape] retain[s] its primeval character and influence . . . preserve[s] its natural conditions . . . [and] appears to have been affected primarily by the forces of nature, with the imprint of man's work substantially unnoticeable. (Quoted in Dilsaver, ed., 1994: 278)

The commitment to nature protection, a vow broken by roads and hotels in the national parks, now seemed to have been enshrined in its genuine Magna Carta.

The National Wilderness Preservation System

Since its legislative inception in 1964, the wilderness system has grown from 9.1 million acres to 105.7 million acres, with a major increase marked by passage of the Alaskan National Interest Lands Conservation Act in 1980 (Figs. 5.1 and 5.2; see also Landers and Meyer 1998). Today the wilderness system protects 644 units on lands administered by four federal land agencies. Forty-four million acres (42 percent of the total in the system) lie within reserves of the National Park System, 35 million acres on the national forests (33 percent), 21 million acres (20 percent) on the national wildlife refuges, and 6.5 million acres (5 percent) on the public domain of the Bureau of Land Management. The Alaskan units fall mostly within the National Park System and the National Wildlife Refuge System; outside of Alaska, Forest Service wilderness accounts for nearly two-thirds of the protected acreage. Since 1980, however, Congress has authorized little increase in national forest wilderness.

Wilderness, National Forests, and Compromises to the Wilderness Ideal

The history of the National Wilderness Preservation System is strongly connected to the history of the national forests. In fact, a dichotomy honestly represents the related development of two federal land agencies and two manifestations of nature protection: the obvious linkage between the National Park Service and parks, the less apparent but no less real coupling of the U.S. Forest Service and wilderness. Other federal lands are included within the wilderness system, although, as discussed in chapter 3, the nature protection purposes of both the National Park Service and the Fish and Wildlife Service more strongly reflect their particular enabling and guiding legislation than they do the Wilderness Act; wilderness administered by the Bureau of Land Management closely parallels the situation of the national forests, but the BLM is a relative newcomer to wilderness protection and its contributions to the wilderness system are still minor. The historical story of wilderness, then, is a tale of the national forests.

THE DEVELOPMENT OF THE WILDERNESS SYSTEM   The successful efforts by Aldo Leopold to establish the first formally protected wilderness, on the Gila National Forest in 1924, are commonly cited as the beginning of the wilderness system, but the initial actions on behalf of wild landscape protection within the national forests involved other individuals and other places. The landscape architect Arthur Carhart is notable (Baldwin 1972, Roth 1988). Hired as the first recreation expert in the Forest Service (he had the title of "recreation engineer"), Carhart assumed the responsibility of surveying national forest land in District 2, which encompassed forests from the Colorado Rockies to the upper Midwest, for recreational development, including roads and summer home sites. His 1919 evaluation of the Trapper's Lake area on the White River National Forest, in northwestern Colorado, recommended that, instead of a looping east–west through road and several hundred summer home lots on the lake, the region not be developed at all. Carhart's suggestion was approved by his supervisor. A few years later, in 1922, Carhart recommended against the extensive recreational road system proposed for the Boundary Waters region of northern Minnesota, and this policy was subsequently accepted by both the district forester and the secretary of agriculture. Carhart and Leopold interacted during these years, probably enriching their respective concepts of wild landscape protection (Meine 1988: 177–79). Leopold's 1924 proposal for a Gila Wilderness Area in western New Mexico, as part of a more general recreation plan, was approved by the district forester, the first time that a specific region was formally demarcated as a protected area.

From this beginning the Forest Service crystallized its program for wilderness protection. During the 1920s, L. F. Kniepp, as chief of the Division of Lands and Recreation, identified 55 million acres of the national forests suitable for wilderness-type designations (Zaslowsky and Watkins 1994: 200). A centralized mechanism for wild landscape reserves was formalized in 1929 when the Forest Service issued an agency rule (the "L-20 regulation") that authorized the chief of the service to establish or abolish what were to be called primitive areas. By the mid-1930s, sixty-three such reserves had been approved. Still, great latitude was provided to local agency personnel regarding the permitted land uses in primitive areas: "logging activities were specifically permitted in twenty-three . . . grazing took place in fifty-three . . . in none of these areas were roads expressly prohibited" (Robinson 1975: 157). Moreover, primitive areas carried only temporary status; they were envisioned as protecting wild landscapes only until the Forest Service dictated ultimate uses (Robinson 1975: 158). In 1939 Robert Marshall (one of the great names in the history of wilderness protection in America), as head of the Forest Service Division of Recreation and Lands, initiated more stringent protection policies (Roth 1988). Issued as the "U regulations," this new designation scheme recognized "wilderness areas" of at least 100,000 acres and "wild areas" of between 5,000 and 100,000 acres. Road building and timber cutting were explicitly prohibited, but, perhaps more provocatively, wilderness and wild areas, unlike the primitive areas, were intended to be permanent. Authority to establish these reserves lay with the chief of the Forest Service and the secretary of agriculture. During the 1940s and 1950s, Forest Service personnel studied many of the primitive areas for reclassification as wild or wilderness areas. Over the following two decades, the agency engaged in more complete, system-wide inventories of possible protected areas. Specifically, under the authority of the 1960 Multiple Use and Sustained Yield Act, the Forest Service attempted to clarify what lands might be reserved and what might be freed from future consideration as wilderness—the "Roadless Area Review and Evaluations," the first (RARE I) begun in 1972, the second (RARE II) completed in 1978 (Roth 1988). The purely executive authority to create or abolish protected wild landscapes on the national forests is what the campaign for the Wilderness Bill in the 1950s and 1960s sought to overturn: the Wilderness Act shifted that responsibility to Congress, thought by conservationists to be more insulated from the pressures of commodity resource and recreational developers.

This brief account is not intended to replace the considerable descriptive and interpretive history of wilderness areas and the national forests (e.g., McArdle and Maunder 1975, Robinson 1975, Allin 1982, Baldwin 1972, Roth 1988, Runte 1991, Catton 1999, Sutter 2002). Rather, it is presented simply to provide background for the interpretation that the origins of national forest wilderness, like that of the national parks, developed from "impure" impulses, those sometimes haphazard human motivations focused on purposes other than protection of nature. Many of the issues involved in development of the national parks appear in the history of the Forest Service and its wild landscape protection. National forest wilderness, too, had its patron saints, in this case within the professional ranks of the Forest Service. The names of Carhart, Leopold, Kniepp, and Marshall are no less singular in their importance to national forest wilderness than Muir, Mather, Edge, and Palmer are to the national parks. Recreation loomed large in the minds of the patron saints of national forest wilderness, just as it did with the early framers of the national parks (Sutter 1998): Carhart's plans for roadless areas were part of recreation plans (Baldwin 1972: 57); Leopold's justification for the Gila Wilderness was "to preserve at least one place in the Southwest where pack trips shall be the dominant play" (quoted in Meine 1988: 205); Marshall was the consummate wilderness recreationist, concerned with recording peaks climbed and counting miles hiked (Glover 1986: 1–5). Even the Wilderness Act itself defines "wilderness" as having, among other attributes, "outstanding opportunities for solitude or a primitive and unconfined type of recreation." Finally, just as the national parks prospered by association with the railroads and recreational interests—an association often identified as inconsistent with pure nature protection sentiment—wilderness on the national forests grew and prospered because the Forest Service feared losing its lands to the rival National Park Service. The chief of the Forest Service in the 1920s, William Greeley, encouraged wild landscape protection on the national forests as a means of wooing wilderness enthusiasts, disillusioned by the penchant for recreation development of Steven Mather and his National Park Service, and thereby strengthened the position of the Forest Service in resisting land transfers from the national forests to the national parks (Allin 1982: 71–75). This rivalry between the two federal agencies flared into heated debate between Arthur Carhart and Steven Mather as early as 1921 and continues into contemporary times with disagreements over such landscapes as the Sawtooth Mountains of central Idaho and the Snake Range (now Great Basin National Park) of eastern Nevada (Ford, 1988, Elliott 1991a). The Forest Service–Park Service turmoil may have been helpful to nature protection interests, who could play one agency against the other (Allin 1982: 76), but neither can be seen as the white hat in this affair. An honest assessment would see both agencies as self-promoting.

This early history of wilderness protection on the national forests unfolds as a narrative of particular individuals, concerned with recreational opportunities and political motivations, who achieved a certain success at nature protection. But the parallels with the blemishes on the national parks continue. When the Wilderness Bill was debated in the 1950s, talk promised a change to a system, in the sense of a carefully planned, logically cohesive, integrated whole. Clearly the imagery of a true system for wilderness loomed large in the mind of the editor-author Howard Zahniser, father of the Wilderness Act and arguably the country's leading wilderness advocate of the time, particularly after the death of Aldo Leopold in 1949. The early versions of the Wilderness Bill, drafted by Zahniser, specifically used the word "system," presumably as a strategy to improve the overall effectiveness of wilderness protection. In a formally recognized structure, obscure and little-known units would be carried on the protective coattails of the widely recognized units (Roth 1988). Moreover, the initial versions provided for uniform and strong protections against commodity resource use and recreational developments, and they authorized oversight by a governing body— the National Wilderness Preservation Council, whose members would be citizens supportive of wilderness—even though the federal land agencies would continue to administer the wilderness areas under their respective jurisdictions. Overall, then, the early proposals for the wilderness system were highly structured, orderly, and consistent; that is, systematic.

The Wilderness Act as finally approved failed to realize this vision. Instead, the law created, in effect, a wilderness zoning authority in Congress for the federal lands. Gone were the uniform protection standards; eliminated was the unifying oversight by the Preservation Council. Congress would establish wilderness areas and only Congress could abolish them, but the policies of administering them would simply reflect the established traditions of each land agency. Do not misunderstand these comments: the Wilderness Act made a clear and unequivocal proclamation that preservation of landscape wildness should be a part of the management of the federal lands, and it set up mechanisms to ensure that goal; in this regard, the legislation deserves the accolades that the environmental community bestows upon it. But the conditions that describe what is "wilderness" also varies among the agencies. The National Wilderness Preservation System cobbles together wild landscape reserves overseen by different federal agencies with different administrative regulations. In spite of proclamations to the contrary (Wilderness Society 1984), it is no more coherent than the National Park System, and arguably less so.

The Forest Service can point to a long history of and elaborate mechanisms for natural resource planning (Office of Technology Assessment 1990,

1992a), which in turn has spurred environmentalists to generate plans in response to the government's procedures and recommendations (Wilderness Society 1983). Regardless, like the national parks, the wilderness system reflects the compromises of historical circumstance. The same characterization commonly invites criticism of the National Park System, but in the case of the wilderness system, we hear only platitudes about "highest refinement" and "Magna Carta." The double standard hardly seems warranted.

POLITICAL IDEOLOGY If accusations of elitism tarnish the glow of the national parks, the same shadow darkens wilderness on the national forests. Besides sharing with parks the imagery of natural resources "locked up" and of recreational playgrounds for the rich, national forest wilderness otherwise offers conflicting political ideological meanings. On the one hand, the historical importance of Forest Service personnel in early wild landscape protection encourages the notion that powerful elites create conservation policy. Arguing even more directly for the importance of persons other than egalitarian liberals in early wilderness efforts, in fact, Baldwin (1972: 202) observes that the foundation for national forest wilderness was laid during the Republican administration of Herbert Hoover and thus before the progressive New Deal programs of Franklin Delano Roosevelt. In addition, Forest Service personnel may always have seen their professional decisions as superior to those of ordinary citizens, however numerous (Roth 1988: 35). The users of wilderness areas, moreover, derive from highly educated and well-to-do segments of American society; more than a quarter of national forest wilderness users have attended graduate school, and more than a third have professional or technical occupations (Roggenbuck and Lucas 1987).

On the other hand, the history of wilderness protection mechanisms can be interpreted as increasingly democratic. The U regulations adopted in 1939, for example, required a public hearing before the decision to modify or eliminate any wilderness (Merriam 1989: 83). The Wilderness Act, because it shifts decisions from appointed administrators to elected members of Congress, has been said to allow more citizen participation, presumably to the benefit of wilderness protection (D. Scott 1984); so-called grass-roots wilderness groups gained access to the decision-making process in an unprecedented way (Cunningham 1991, Jenkins 2004). The environmentalist influences on the subsequent reviews of roadless areas on the national forests (the two RAREs)—blocking the initial evaluation as inadequate, initiating the second review, modifying its outcome—demonstrate the effectiveness of that participation (Roth 1988: 37–55). Finally, the costs of visiting wilderness actually may be modest; the elitist educational and occupational char-acteristics of wilderness users may reflect more their tastes and preferences than their affluence (Roggenbuck and Lucas 1987). Nonetheless, in sum, the processes of policy formation and characteristics of recreational users seem no less elitist in national forest wilderness than in the national parks.

Stories of contestations between nature enthusiasts who defend nature reserves and Native Americans and other local people who covet access to protected landscapes for nonpreservation purposes—narratives that are central to the critique of the national parks—hardly enter the discussions on national forest wilderness. The desire of Indian groups to continue cer-emonies on sacred mountains generates controversy, particularly in con-junction with recreation development, usually for skiing, outside wilderness boundaries; Mount Shasta in the Mount Shasta Wilderness of California and San Francisco Peaks in the Kachina Wilderness of Arizona come to mind. More generally, Native Americans have claimed rights to national forest land, sometimes successfully. In 1970 Congress transferred 48,000 acres of the Carson National Forest in New Mexico, including Blue Lake, to the Taos Pueblo (Shrake 1970, "New Era . . ." 1970). In the 1980s Congress consid-ered a bill to give the Lakota Sioux the 1.2 million acres of the Black Hills National Forest in South Dakota (Greider 1987, Naughton 1989); in the 1990s controversy continued over control of the Medicine Wheel area on the Bighorn National Forest of Wyoming (Rudner 1994). DeBuys (1985) fully ex-plores conflicts between local peoples and national forest authority in the Sangre de Cristo Mountains of New Mexico; local Hispanos resent the con-straining policies of the Forest Service and the aloof attitudes of outside recreationists, consider public lands rightly their own, and feel their appre-ciation of nature equals or exceeds that of outsiders. DeBuys recognizes that Hispanos' land uses have been and may continue to be abusive of the envi-ronment, but still he argues that "traditional cultures . . . are irreplaceable [and] society needs to conserve them" (DeBuys 1985: 319). In spite of such examples, however, the usual critique of the national forests and national forest wilderness, even among scholars, focuses on corporate power in com-modity resource extraction rather than social justice issues involving disen-franchised local peoples (C. Wilkinson 1992, Hirt 1999).

DEGREE OF PROTECTION   Though their statutory status has changed, wilderness areas on the national forests remain open to essentially the same land uses since passage of the Wilderness Act as they were before. Cutting of timber, construction of roads, and erection of buildings and other structures were already prohibited under Forest Service regulations. Hunting, trapping, and livestock grazing continue as legal uses of wilderness. Access to wilderness for water development remains the prerogative of its administrator (the secretary of agriculture before the Wilderness Act, the president of the United States thereafter). Instream water flows for wilderness remain insecure (T. Brown 1991). Only new claims for hard-rock minerals were prohibited with the Wilderness Act, and only after December 31, 1983, although legitimate claims can be developed. In addition, the act provided that only established wilderness and wild areas were to be parts of the initial wilderness system; primitive areas were to be reclassified, perhaps enlarged, maybe reduced, and then proposed to Congress for possible wilderness status. The Wilderness Act did not even require that the national forests be surveyed more generally for possible additions to the wilderness system.

Wilderness enthusiasts typically fail to recognize or articulate these compromised protections. More reflective and scholarly writers sometimes acknowledge the limitations of the Wilderness Act. Robinson (1975: 160), as a defender of Forest Service tradition and policy, does so explicitly, as do Zaslowsky and Watkins (1994: 211). Roth (1988: 11–12) describes the erosion of uniform and strong protection guidelines in early drafts of the bill. Roholt (1991: 7) sees the nonconforming uses as an asset, imparting a desirable "flexibility" to the Wilderness Act, which, as a consequence, has not been amended over the years since is passage. But more commonly the descriptions of the act imply more protection than actually exists. For example, D. Scott (1984: 6) states that in spite of individual agency administration of wilderness areas, "each agency must adhere to the strict requirements of . . . the Wilderness Act," whereas in fact existing agency policies mostly continued. Nash (1984: 5) proclaims the legislation "an environmental Magna Carta," an image philosophically assertable but in a tangible and practical sense questionable.

The point, again, is not to belittle the Wilderness Act, to declare it an environmental failure, or to suggest that it is anything but central to nature protection in the United States. Rather, it is to prod speculation about why the National Wilderness Preservation System, with its compromised protections, receives so little criticism in comparison with the National Park System, with its much more uniform and strong preservation purposes.

LANDSCAPE QUALITY Some observers celebrate the environmental diversity within the wilderness system. The Wilderness Society (1989b: 6), for example, characterizes this richness as "wetlands and deserts, forests and shorelines, mountains and valleys, glaciers and sand dunes." Regardless of the proclamations, however, the variety of landscapes protected on the national forests is modest in comparison with those of the National Park System. The Forest Service, according to mid-century environmental groups, has focused on wilderness areas of "rock and ice," a derisive comment on the agency's penchant for establishing wilderness in alpine environments. Although such landscapes may indeed lack marketable timber, they also, to be honest, appeal to recreation enthusiasts. This agency tendency continues into recent decades (Rothman 1992), thereby articulating a "worthless lands" narrative for national forest wilderness. More important, the landscapes of national forest wilderness can represent only the types of environments that the national forests, as a whole, contain. Disproportionately, then, national forest wilderness encompasses mountainous terrain in the western states. This bias toward high-relief landscapes reflects the historical importance of concern for watershed protection when the forest reserves were established from the public domain in the American West during the decades at the turn of the century (Vale 1995). When the National Park System's landscape classification scheme is applied to national forest wilderness, the lopsided representation of mountains becomes obvious: at least 84 percent of the 354 national forest wilderness areas are in mountains, 63 percent of them in western mountains. The numbers of acres rather than numbers of wilderness units are even more strongly skewed toward western mountainous terrain. These reserved lands include alpine environments, areas of brush and meadows, and some grasslands, but typically in association with forests in rugged landscapes. The remaining 16 percent of national forest wilderness areas are in forested environments of other sorts, either on floodplains and wetlands or rolling hills of modest relief; a particularly notable unit in this remainder group is the Boundary Waters Canoe Areas Wilderness of Minnesota.

The second survey of roadless areas suggests that ecosystem representation might be one criterion by which to evaluate possible additions to the wilderness system (U.S. Forest Service 1978). If we accept the technique used to delimit "ecosystems" (which creates arbitrary boundaries and overlapping types), we find that the numbers generated support the assertion that national forest wilderness cannot be truly representative of the environmental or ecological diversity within the United States: of 242 ecosystems in the country, more than half, 56 percent, were not present in the candidate wilderness areas, the roadless areas of the national forests. Vegetation covers other than forests dominate the unrepresented ecosystems. By contrast, virtually all of the forest ecosystems in the eleven western states, where most of the national forest acreage is located, appear in the candidate areas. Established national forest wilderness and possible national forest wilderness—even combined they cannot broaden the landscape limits imposed by the national forest boundaries.

By contrast, if we consider the more contemporary issue of biodiversity rather than landscape types, the importance of the national forests—evaluated for their potential for increased protection—swells immensely. The U.S. Geological Survey Gap Analysis (GAP) (J. Scott et al. 1993; updated in DellaSala et al. 2001 as "Protected Area Database," or PAD, and used by Ricketts et al. 1999) finds that the characteristics of vegetation best represented within the national forests—forest types—remain vulnerable, with "nearly three-fourths of all forest ecoregions in the United States and Canada . . . critical or endangered in terms of biodiversity loss and ecological integrity" (Ricketts et al. 1999: 102). Moreover, among all American forest types identified as "globally outstanding" for species richness, only Sierra Nevada forests meet the minimum protection level of 25 percent considered adequate, and they just barely so at 28 percent (DellaSala et al. 2001: 130). From the perspective of biodiversity values, then, the national forests may be strongly situated for major contributions to protection.

Through the years, environmentalists have argued for greater variety within national forest wilderness. Their rhetoric, however, has neither analyzed the landscapes within the national forests nor compared those landscapes with those in the national parks, and until relatively recently did not focus on biodiversity. Rather, the argument attempted to justify larger and more numerous wilderness areas on the basis of scenery and recreation. In the 1950s and 1960s, for example, they criticized the new boundaries of wilderness areas associated with reclassification from their status as primitive areas because the reserves omitted much lower-elevation forest in favor of high-elevation alpine terrain (Roth 1984, 1988); the Three Sisters Wilderness in Oregon and the Glacier Peak Wilderness in Washington (reclassified from a "limited area," not a "primitive area") remain the classic examples (Wilderness Society 1954, Hyde 1957). This defense of forests sounds contemporary—all it needs are the terms "ancient forest" and "biodiversity"—but the clamor was based on the visual appeal of large old trees in unlogged forests, particularly as a foreground for alpine peaks—landscapes for recreation—more than on species protection or ecosystem functioning.

The question of environmental variety also permeated, albeit indirectly, the purity issue, which was central to the debate over creation of wilderness in the eastern states during the 1970s. The Forest Service "rather doggedly insisted on a purist view of wilderness . . . [and thus was] reluctant to include lands where timber has been cut or roads or other still-visible structures have been built" (Robinson 1975: 169). Adherence to such standards seemed to preclude protected wilderness in the eastern states, where national forest land was mostly purchased either after and because of abusive logging or on abandoned and reforested farmland. Also, the relatively small areas of candidate wilderness in the East were less likely to be free of the sights and sounds of human activities. Conservationists saw the purity policy as simply a ploy to preclude expansion of the wilderness system, whether in the East or the West, although the Forest Service—which agreed to a separate classification of "wild area" for lands that contained the imprints of humans—may have wanted criteria that would have prevented all of its acreage from being "potential" wilderness (Robinson 1975: 172). The success of the protectionist position was realized when Congress passed the Eastern Wilderness Act in 1974, and as a result, the environmental variety protected within the National Wilderness Preservation System increased by the inclusion of additional eastern forest ecosystem types.

In sum, national forest wilderness, existing or potential, does not and cannot protect a representative sample of the natural world of the United States. Once again, do not misunderstand the comment: national forest wilderness contributes mightily to the protection of the total environmental variety of the country. The point of this discussion is to apply a criterion commonly used to criticize the National Park System in a similar evaluation of national forest wilderness, and such assessment concludes simply: If the national parks fail because they protect landscapes that are unrepresentative, disproportionately scenic, mostly rugged terrain, wilderness on the national forests seems even more deserving of that criticism.

The National Wilderness Preservation System on Other Federal Lands

The Wilderness Act required evaluations of all roadless areas of at least 5,000 acres both in the National Park System and on the national wildlife refuges for their possible inclusion within the wilderness system. The Bureau of Land Management was mandated by the 1976 Federal Land Policy and Management Act to conduct reviews of the public domain lands for possible wilderness designations. Still other parts of the federal lands have not been subject to wilderness reviews. The acreage administered by the Bureau of Indian Affairs was not included, even though it was evaluated by Robert Marshall in the 1930s (when he was head of the bureau, before he moved to the Forest Service). Marshall actually ushered through the administration a classification of sixteen areas totaling 4.8 million acres as "roadless" or "wild" on the Indian lands, an action carried out without consultation with the affected tribes and eventually reversed (Glover 1986: 209–12). The extensive areas administered by the Department of Defense are not being reviewed for possible wilderness, either, although, by the criteria of isolation, remoteness, and lack of development, some of these lands could be as wild as any of the federal lands. As military bases are decommissioned and the lands become available for other uses, they seem to present opportunities for nature protection purposes (Vogel 1997); perhaps in the future they may be seen as increasingly important for such uses.

THE BUREAU OF LAND MANAGEMENT AND THE PUBLIC DOMAIN
The history and issues of wilderness on the public domain resemble those of the Forest Service and the national forests. Begun as bureau zoning decisions in 1972, when the Arivaipa Canyon Primitive Area in Arizona was established, wilderness on BLM lands is now linked to the Wilderness Act and its congressional authority. The bureau has been evaluating its holdings and formulating proposals for wilderness designation on a state-by-state basis, although the agency seems not to be sympathetic to establishment of wilderness areas; in 1980 it found less than 24 million of its 175 million acres to be suitable for further evaluation. With more than 6 million acres subsequently reserved as statutory wilderness, the remaining 17.2 million acres remain as wilderness study areas, from which environmentalists fear only a few million additional acres may eventually be proposed as wilderness (J. Baker 1985, Voynick 1987, Hamilton 1989). Neither government bodies nor conservation groups—given the prospect of only minor success—seem eager to complete the state reviews and propose wilderness; as a consequence, only northern Arizona (in 1984) and southeastern California (in 1994, as part of the California Desert Protection Act, which was not an initiative of the bureau) have had completed surveys with wilderness areas established. Of the 133 wilderness areas on public domain lands, 70 are in the deserts of California and 49 are in Arizona; the other major contributing state is Nevada, with 10 BLM wilderness areas within the Black Rock Desert–High Rock Canyon Emigrant Trails National Conservation Area, authorized

by Congress in 2000, and additional areas established near Las Vegas in 2002 (fig. 5.1).

This portrayal of only modest pursuit of wilderness establishment on the public domain can be countered by a more positive interpretation. The bureau claims that it administers its wilderness study areas (17.2 million acres) as if they were statutory wilderness, a policy that preserves the final decision for Congress. Moreover, during the administration of Bill Clinton, additional acreage proposed for wilderness designation by citizen groups was similarly protected, but this policy seems to have been subsequently reversed (Jenkins 2004).

Wilderness enthusiasts nonetheless commonly express unhappiness with the bureau's policies. Reminiscent of the Forest Service and its invocation of the purity issue to reject large areas for wilderness evaluation, the Bureau of Land Management also uses the ambiguous definition of "wilderness" in the Wilderness Act to refuse further consideration of lands that may have had incompatible characteristics. Thus a dirt track violates the criterion for "roadless" conditions; evidence of early mining renders an area humanized and thus not "affected primarily by the forces of nature"; a small wilderness may place a visitor within sight or sound of human activities and therefore preclude the opportunity for "solitude." The decentralized nature of the bureau, with much discretion given to state and local offices, has facilitated the differential interpretation of the wording of the Wilderness Act, even though, by some analysis, that interpretation may be a violation of the spirit or the meaning of the congressional mandate (Greeno 1990). This characterization of the bureau as decentralized and thus susceptible to the pressures of its commodity resource users has long plagued the agency (Foss 1960, Vale 1979b).

The BLM's reluctance to add units to the wilderness system from the lands of the public domain is only one of the criticisms leveled against it. Like the wilderness areas on the national forests, those administered by the Bureau of Land Management continue the nonprotection (sometimes labeled "nonconforming") uses of hunting, trapping, livestock grazing, mining on existing hard-rock claims, and executive prerogatives to allow water development. Moreover, the characteristics of the bureau's protected landscapes (both potential and realized) lack broad variety, although the limitation differs from the constraint of forest types on the national forests: most of the bureau's lands lie in desert environments, and within these arid landscapes those most suitable for protection (and most sought by conservationists) are in mountainous terrain. Coastal landscapes and some forest environments may be included in some bureau wilderness, but the agency's major contributions to the National Wilderness Preservation System are typified by rugged red-rock canyons and dissected arid mountains. Like national forest wilderness, then, BLM wilderness testifies to the continued importance of monumental landscapes in nature protection.

THE NATIONAL PARK SYSTEM AND THE NATIONAL WILDLIFE REFUGE SYSTEM Wilderness designation on units of the National Park System and in the National Wildlife Refuge System precludes the construction of roads and other structures. Otherwise, as with the national forests and the public domain, the regulations of the administering agencies, in this case the National Park Service and the Fish and Wildlife Service, remain as dominant policy on the respective wildernesses. These agencies, too, reacted less than enthusiastically to the concept of congressionally mandated zoning for their lands. Nonetheless, reviews of potential wilderness and subsequent congressional actions have added major acreages to the wilderness system from the National Park System (forty-five areas in twenty states totaling about 44 million acres) and the national wildlife refuges (seventy-one areas in twenty-six states totaling about 21 million acres). Almost all of the major units administered by these agencies contain units of the wilderness system, with such conspicuous exceptions as Yellowstone and Grand Canyon. Particularly for the national parks, the designation of wilderness rarely generates controversy, testimony in support of the Park Service's contention during debates over the Wilderness Bill: the agency already was managing its existing wild lands as wilderness.

Reflections

Although the Wilderness Act was central to the political agendas of all the national nature protection conservation organizations, its passage dominated the work of one group in particular, the Wilderness Society. Howard Zahniser, the act's father, was also an active leader in the group from 1945 until his death in 1964. Dedicated to protecting individual wild areas and achieving a national wilderness policy, the society emerged from the minds of four prominent conservationists—including Robert Marshall—who, at a roadside rest area in Tennessee, discussed formation of a new conservation group to work toward preserving wild landscapes "free from mechanical sights and sounds and smells." Part of their immediate concern involved a proposal for roads in Great Smoky Mountains National Park and the failure of the Park Service to resist such recreational development (Fox 1984: 5, 1981/1985: 210) (see chapter 9). The specific focus of their anxiety was roads in national parks.

The Wilderness Society and thus the Wilderness Act, then, originated in a desire to protect landscapes neither from the traditional foes of commodity resource developments, such as grazing and mining, nor from such recreational activities as hunting and trapping. Nor did the beginnings reflect concerns other than those easily identified as contemporary, that is, worries over rare and endangered species, their habitats, and the functioning of natural ecosystems. The stress on freedom from perceptions of the "mechanical" world, moreover, suggests anthropocentricism, a focus on human experience. Thus when Watkins (1994a: 36) proclaims that the Wilderness Act represents the culmination of concern "with the needs of the land itself . . . [an expression of] respect [for] the land and those species with whom we are privileged to share the planet," he reads into the past the rhetorical motivations of the present. What seemed paramount in the minds of the conservationists who began the Wilderness Society, who led the effort to pass the Wilderness Act, was road building in the national parks.

In the eyes of wilderness enthusiasts, roads are still a critical threat to wild landscapes. Why else would we celebrate nature protection in wilderness areas that still permit livestock grazing, commercial trapping, and sport hunting, allow free-roaming pets and private recreational livestock, and remain vulnerable to mining and water development? A dense network of roads fragments a landscape, thereby threatening biodiversity values, but this fact fails to explain why conservationists hate all roads. The national parks offer clear and consistent policies against nonprotectionist uses, but the parks are criticized as failures; the Forest Service and the BLM restrict these activities in wilderness areas less stringently but do prohibit roads, and they are celebrated for their sensitivity to the natural world.

Why should roads be seen as such threats? From the modern perspective, which purportedly focuses more on natural process than on scenic spectacle, more on biological diversity than on scenery, more on functioning of ecosystem than on recreational opportunity, roads would seem to be hard to object to even as scars on the visual landscape. A single strip of pavement intrudes only trivially into a wild landscape otherwise protected, at least in these modern terms. That position may sound heretical, but it is easily defended (cf. Forman 2004). A road may allow access for commodity resource development—itself involving a supporting extensive road system—but if it does, it is alteration of the environment associated with that development, not the single narrow ribbon of asphalt, that threatens natural process, biological diversity, and ecosystem function. Grizzly bears survive in Yellowstone, for example, even with its road network (elaborate for a national park, modest for anywhere else) and the associated recreational development (again, the most extensive in any national park but as restrained as in any road-accessed major wild landscape in the country), because the species has been fully protected and because it is free to roam the expansive wild country, roadless and roaded, both within and surrounding the park. Moreover, the apparent increase in Yellowstone grizzlies over the late decades of the twentieth century reflects enhanced protection and nuanced management, certainly not road closures and limitations on visitors.

The perception of roads as key villains among conservationists suggests the continued importance of both the appearance of wild landscapes rather than their ecological functioning and of the humanistic meanings rather than the scientific purposes of those landscapes in nature protection. The framers of the Wilderness Society viewed roads rightly as mechanical intrusions into what they saw as *wild* places, not necessarily fully *natural* landscapes, and their perspective placed value on the ability of humans—anthropocentric, recreational humans—to be "free from [those] mechanical sights and sounds and smells." Today roads continue to be objectionable for their symbolism: the landscape with a road cannot so easily evoke sacred space, the nation's roots, a wild pleasuring ground, an ethical stage, or the other positive interpretations of wild nature. Roadless wilderness grazed by sheep or prowled by human hunters may not be as inviolate a sanctuary as a roaded national park, but to many observers it looks wilder and more natural. The contemporary criticism of national parks and the associated idealization of wilderness continue patterns of perception that extend back to the beginnings of national forest gestures toward protection of wild landscapes.

Wilderness represents not an ideal of nature protection but a compromise. The evidence, ironically, comes from the successes of recent wilderness establishment. Consider the major acreage of BLM wilderness authorized by Congress in 2000 and 2002 in Nevada. These reserves perpetuate the status quo: the prewilderness activities of livestock grazing, sport hunting, and other nonmotorized recreation continue; the Bureau of Land Management maintains administration of the lands; no recreational facilities need funding. Contrast the political difficulty, even the political impossibility, of transferring the same lands to the National Park Service, to be administered as more strictly protected national monuments with a few campgrounds, visitor centers, and nature programs. Jenkins (2003) interpreted the recent BLM wilderness creation as a compromise because the authorizing law also allowed the city of Las Vegas to expand onto public lands; but if the standard is the national parks, the nature protection offered by all wilderness on the national forests and the public domain is compromised.

Units of the National Wilderness Preservation System differ from those in the National Park System; their purposes and policies remain distinct. Neither system is necessarily better than the other; neither is a "higher refinement" of nature protection. To recognize the differences is not to say that both are unequivocal successes, without need for critical examination. The problems we see in either type of reserve will reflect what we consider most important in the protection of nature, and this variability in turn reflects the meanings that we choose in defining such concepts as "protection" and "nature."

Even the most enthusiastic defenders of the wilderness system, however, might learn the value of place identification from the national parks, particularly those grand old parks with their road systems and hordes of visitors. Americans carry in their heads images of these parks: Yellowstone, Yosemite, Grand Canyon, Mount Rainier, Crater Lake, Glacier. Each name resonates in the mind, even if the park cannot be described in accurate detail or located precisely on a map; each name stimulates an image of a particular locale, a type of landscape, a singular place. For all practical purposes, wilderness areas remain more generic wild spaces; the names fail to generate place-specific imagery, except for those persons who have personally experienced them. Watkins's attempt to illustrate the strength of the imagery evoked by the names of wilderness areas instead reveals the obscurity of the locales:

Consider the names. Let them roll off your tongue as part of the enduring poetry of the continent—Never Summer and Havasu, Black Fork Mountain and Golden Trout, Eagles Nest and Big Gum Swamp, Brigantine and Bisti, Middle Prong and Drift Creek, Linville Gorge and Turkey Hill, Table Top and Blood

Mountain, hundreds more, names that have been embraced by a system established with the passage of one of the most purely revolutionary acts in the history of American land legislation. (Watkins 1994a: 36)

The evocative force of the names Watkins celebrates exceeds Americans' sense of the places he names.

Wild nature enthusiasts would generate support within that part of the public indifferent or even hostile to their cause if the places they defend were indeed *places*. A handful of wilderness areas do enjoy singular identities—the Bob Marshall in Montana, the Frank Church–River of No Return in Idaho, the Boundary Waters in Minnesota come readily to mind—but most do not. Perhaps the fear lingers that the greater familiarity associated with place recognition will encourage tourism and use, thus threatening the solitude that obscurity protects. Such a vision is shortsighted; remember Glen Canyon, dammed because it was "the place no one knew" (Brower 1963: 8). Others might say that wilderness, precisely because it is not strongly humanized, cannot generate evocative place imagery; rich human history associated with a locale most easily generates place identities. For example, the Bob Marshall, the Frank Church, and the Boundary Waters all create a strong sense of place because of their long and extensive histories of recreational use (Proescholdt et al. 1995). But other national forest and BLM wilderness areas also have their human histories. The Gila Wilderness of New Mexico, with its sweeping slopes of ponderosa pine forest that so impressed Aldo Leopold, and the Flat Tops Wilderness in Colorado, where Trapper's Lake nestles beneath soaring mesa-like ridges, celebrate events as monumental in the history of nature protection as those associated with Yellowstone and Yosemite. The Ansel Adams Wilderness in California's Sierra Nevada not only commemorates a hero to nature protectionists but also embraces part of the most cherished landscape of John Muir. The Sylvania Wilderness of Michigan protects an area of mostly unlogged north woods landscape purchased in the late 1800s by wealthy businessmen as an extensive fishing and hunting preserve and bought by the Forest Service in 1967. The Kachina Peaks Wilderness sprawls on the San Francisco Peaks of northern Arizona where the biologist C. Hart Merriam developed his turn-of-the-century scheme of "life zones" to describe the altitudinal belts of vegetation and wild animals. The Dolly Sods Wilderness on a high ridge of the Allegheny Mountains of West Virginia protects an area of sphagnum bogs and dense mats of grass grazed by the livestock of the pioneering Dahle—or "Dolly"—family, as well as extensive areas of rounded, rugged rock bared by abusive logging and burning in the 1880s and now being recolonized by red spruce (Mohlenbrock 1987a: 77–79). The High Rock Canyon Wilderness not only protects part of the route of an emigrant trail through northwestern Nevada but also marks the landscape that George Stewart celebrates in his notable book of place-identifying interactions of people with nature, *Sheep Rock* (Stewart 1951/1971). Wilderness areas with human histories tie together the worlds of people and nature without demeaning or diminishing either.

A sense of place may also come from the characteristics of the nature that wilderness areas embrace. Even subtle appreciations of the natural world can enrich wilderness areas. The Otter Creek Wilderness of West Virginia safeguards an area of mixed forest where the West Virginia northern flying squirrel persists in stands of eastern hemlock and red spruce, all relics from the Pleistocene and isolated here when climates warmed 10,000 years ago (Mohlenbrock 1991: 74–76). The Hercules Glade Wilderness of Missouri secures grassland glades developed on shallow limestone soils, hot and droughty in summer, where grasses from western prairies extend their ranges eastward and where scissor-tailed flycatchers and roadrunners—both also from more open vegetation far to the west—make occasional appearances (Mohlenbrock 1985: 82–85). The Sycamore Canyon Wilderness of Arizona sits astride the edge of the Colorado Plateau, where Sycamore Creek has downcut into the suite of red and yellow sedimentary rocks that form the layers of the plateau and where mesquite and catclaw acacia from the lower deserts mingle with white fir and ponderosa pine from the higher forests (Mohlenbrock 1987b: 16–18). Maine's Great Gulf Wilderness protects the high ridges of the Presidential Range, home to record-setting winds, blanketed by alpine tundra, scoured by ice-age glaciers like no other landscape of the eastern states. Natural history learned enriches the wilderness experience and lends meaning to landscape.

Roadlessness—this characteristic more than any other binds together units of the National Wilderness Preservation System. But without intellectual elaboration, roadlessness seems a precarious basis for wild landscape protection. More positive, more constructive, more enduring, more likely to generate affection would be the articulation of positive, humanistic landscape meanings for these roadless landscapes. Stories of both human and natural history elevate the wild spaces to wild places. Every statutory wilderness needs its literary interpreter, its storyteller, its poet.

6 THE NATIONAL WILDLIFE REFUGE SYSTEM

Our views of national parks and national wilderness in previous chapters emerged from a kaleidoscope of shifting images—spoiled nature and place, false idol and sacred space, aristocratic castle and pleasuring ground. What of the third great group of federal lands dedicated to nature protection, the National Wildlife Refuge System? Certainly for Rachel Carson, the refuges no less than other federal reserves evoke powerful symbolism:

If you travel much in the wilder sections of our country, sooner or later you are likely to meet the sign of the flying goose—the emblem of the National Wildlife Refuges. . . . Wherever you meet this sign, respect it. It means that the land behind the sign has been dedicated by the American people to preserving, for themselves and their children, as much of our native wildlife as can be retained along with our modern civilization. (Carson 1947)

Carson expresses a sentiment a few others echo: the refuges represent "the most intensively managed system of reservations for the protection of wildlife in the world" (D. Butcher 1955: 12), "a major natural resource" (Watkins 1983: 3), a "testament to our national commitment to conservation" (Graham 2003: 40), and "a kind of monument to human repentance" (R. Mitchell 1983: 5). Yet such accolades remain rather scarce and somewhat hidden, testimony to the status of the refuges, less known, less appreciated, less engendering of sharply etched mental images than parks or wilderness. Nonetheless, the National Wildlife Refuge System stands as an equal to its more glamorous siblings (cf. Dolin 2003, R. Butcher 2003).

The Wildlife Refuges

Lands administered by the United States Fish and Wildlife Service sprawl in units large and small, from easternmost Maine to Guam, from Alaska's north slope into the Caribbean. Nonetheless, four regions account for the bulk of unit numbers (although not of acreage): the East Coast and the Florida peninsula, the Midwest and lower Mississippi River Valley, the state of North Dakota, and the lowlands in the Pacific Coast states (fig. 6.1). Formal refuges, waterfowl production areas, coordination areas—thousands of individual units totaling nearly 94 million acres defy simple classification or description. Consider specific areas notable for the times of their establishment or for their sizes. The first federal areas reserved for wildlife conservation purposes were in Alaska—the Pribilof Islands, protected by Congress in 1869 as a fur seal sanctuary, and Afognak Island, declared a "fish cultural and forest reserve" by presidential proclamation in 1892. (The Pribilofs today are part of the expansive Alaska Maritime National Wildlife Refuge; Afognak lies

Figure 6.1. The National Wildlife Refuge System, 2000 (most units are too small to map by area)

within the Chugach National Forest.) The area usually identified as the first national wildlife refuge is Pelican Island, proclaimed by President Theodore Roosevelt in 1903 as a "preserve and breeding ground" for brown pelicans; it initially protected but five and one-half acres of offshore mangrove on Florida's east coast. The largest refuge, the Arctic National Wildlife Refuge, covers 19.7 million acres of tundra on Alaska's north slope (it barely exceeds in size the 19.6 million acres of the Yukon Delta refuge, also in Alaska). The largest unit in the forty-eight states covers 1.6 million acres of desert terrain in southern Nevada, the Desert National Wildlife Refuge. The smallest unit, the half-acre Mille Lacs National Wildlife Refuge, embraces a north woods wetland in Minnesota. The state with the smallest Fish and Wildlife Service acreage, Connecticut, is also the only state with less than one thousand acres; it claims 733 acres, although being the second smallest state limits Connecticut's potential bragging rights. The state boasting the greatest extent of refuge land, Alaska, with 77 million acres, accounts for 82 percent of the system's total area, but those acres occur in only eighteen major units. The greatest acreage of waterfowl production areas is scattered over more than a quarter of a million acres in the prairie pothole country of North Dakota.

Growth of the system's area reveals both steadiness and episodic spurts (fig. 6.2). Between 1903 and 1910, acreage increased sharply with the Roosevelt administration proclamations, although the sizes of most of the "bird reserves" created in those years were reported by the secretary of the interior as "unknown." A major spurt in acreage in 1960–61 corresponds to several large refuges established in Alaska early in the Kennedy-Udall years; similar actions by Jimmy Carter, also in Alaska, explain the sharp rise in 1980.

The refuges initially were administered through the Department of Agriculture's Biological Survey, an agency with a strong focus on economic impacts of animals, as suggested by the survey's earlier name, Division of Economic Ornithology and Mammalogy. In 1939 the refuges were transferred to the Department of the Interior, where, in 1940, the new Fish and Wildlife Service became the administering agency; the word "refuge" was formally adopted for these lands at that time.

Criteria for Evaluation

Landscape quality, coherence as system, degree of elitism, strength of protection—these four standards suggest that the refuge landscape should enjoy an elevated status among people who value protected nature. Yet the national wildlife refuges seem immobilized on the fringes of the conservationists'

Figure 6.2. Millions of acres in the National Wildlife Refuge System, 1900–2000

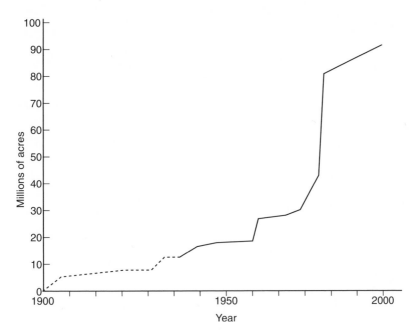

consciousness, only sometimes attracting the spotlight when commodity resource or recreational use threatens the imagery of wild landscapes.

LANDSCAPE QUALITY The landscapes within the national wildlife refuges are more difficult to characterize than those of either the National Park System or the wilderness on the national forests. The Bowdoin National Wildlife Refuge in eastern Montana, for example, noted for its expanses of freshwater wetlands and waterfowl, also embraces large areas of upland prairie and grassland birds. The Bosque del Apache refuge in New Mexico protects managed wetlands for wintering birds, including large numbers of sandhill cranes, although much of its nearly 60,000 acres is desert brushland. The Great Swamp National Wildlife Refuge, whose identity focuses on a notable New Jersey wetland, contains about 7,000 acres of "swamp woodland, hardwood ridges, . . . and grassland" (General Accounting Office 1989: 62). Categorizing any of these three units as "wetland"—although logical, given their primary purposes—would fail to capture their landscape character as Great Plains grassland, southwestern desert shrubland, or northeastern forest. Although similar issues might be articulated for national parks or national forest wilderness (e.g., grasslands occur in both Glacier National Park and the Flat Tops Wilderness), most units of the National Park System and the National Forest Wilderness System can be more easily characterized (e.g., the landscapes of Glacier and Flat Tops can be described only as western mountainous terrain). By contrast, the refuges often embrace areas with fine-grained diversity of landscape types.

Regardless of the complications, a classification of the landscapes within the National Wildlife Refuge System encourages comparisons with the other federal lands. About three hundred units—the best known, most often visited—form the core of the system, and their landscapes suggest the diversity of environment types administered by the Fish and Wildlife Service. About two-thirds of these refuges focus on wetlands, mostly freshwater marshes, whether in California's Central Valley, along the Mississippi River in the Midwest, or over the Yukon Flats of Alaska. This wetland focus suggests the primacy of waterfowl as the "wildlife" that forms the heart of the National Wildlife Refuge System. Another 10 percent embrace coastal habitats, some of which may include saltwater marshes and other wetlands but also rocky islands and barrier beaches. Somewhat less than 10 percent protect forested environments, largely in the eastern states, and a similar number preserve grasslands. Less than 2 percent protect arid mountain ranges and plains; although small in number, these units rival in size the huge refuges in Alaska. The remainder—about 7 percent—are located over a rich variety of landscapes—western mountains and mid-continent salt flats, rolling uplands and broken terrain, dunes and cliffs, tundra and meadow, tropical forest and boreal woodlands. The history of refuge establishment in these various landscape types, moreover, reveals unevenness: those in dry environments of the West—which are most of the refuges devoted to large mammals—date to the early decades of the twentieth century (fig. 6.3), whereas refuges in wetland and coastal landscapes have been established more evenly through time.

Compared to both the National Park System, often stigmatized as too focused on "mere" scenery, and the statutory wilderness on the national forests, particularly in the past defamed as protecting too much mountainous rock and ice, the national wildlife refuges cover a greater diversity of landscape types, a virtue in the minds of critics of parks and wilderness. Moreover, within that diversity, the emphasis of the refuge system on landscape types that occupy an elevated position in the hierarchy of contempo-

Figure 6.3. Establishment of national wildlife refuges created primarily for large mammals and in desert environments, 1900–2000

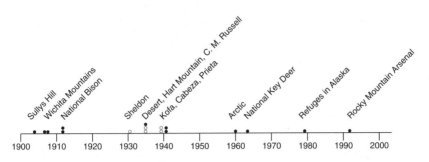

Closed circles indicate establishment dates for refuges primarily focused on large mammals; open circles indicate establishment dates for refuges primarily focused on desert environments.

rary environmentalist concern—wetlands, coasts, and grasslands—would seem to encourage special admiration for the refuge system. Given their stress on the biological in contrast to the scenic spectacle, the refuges might also be championed by modern lovers of protected nature. But in spite of these assets, the refuges do not enjoy a central position in the hearts and minds of environmentalists. Perhaps grand scenery and outdoor recreation continue to be important not only to "average" Americans but also to those who claim particular sensitivity to environmental qualities.

COHERENCE AS A SYSTEM The contingencies that play strongly throughout the history of the National Park System and early in the history of national forest wilderness—individual agendas of the politically powerful who acted without a systematic plan—are echoed in the actions that led to the first national wildlife refuges. A strong personality dominated early refuge establishment: President Theodore Roosevelt proclaimed not only the first unit (Pelican Island in 1903) but also fifty-two additional refuges before he left office in 1909 (Reed and Drabelle 1984: 8). The initial refuges were mostly carved from the federal domain, which constrained the nature of the landscapes protected. Exceptions included the purchase of lands for the National Bison Range in Montana with funds appropriated by Congress in 1909 and the donation of land by the Izaak Walton League for the nucleus of the National Elk Refuge in Wyoming in 1912. These exceptions are notable: the National Park System, recall, would not receive substantial federal funds for land purchases until the 1960s. Moreover, the early concern for bison and elk suggests that large mammals—monumental forms akin to the scenic spectacles in parks and wilderness—apparently stirred the imaginations of early-twentieth-century congressmen more than large landscapes or large wilderness. Presumably reflecting the peculiarities and limitations of such historical circumstance, additional refuges in the initial years "were made on an individual basis" (Clawson and Held 1957: 123), hardly testimony to the coherence of the refuge system.

A more systematically planned and diverse-landscaped array of refuges became possible in 1929 when Congress authorized the federal purchase of land for waterfowl refuges as part of the Migratory Bird Conservation Act. This authority became effective in 1934, when Congress approved the Bird Hunting and Conservation Act (the "Duck Stamp Act"), which imposed a federal fee on waterfowl hunters; the money generated by the sale of "duck stamps" was to be used to purchase land for waterfowl. Reed and Drabelle (1984: 9–10) suggest that initial funding for the Duck Stamp Act was facilitated by the failure of Senator Peter Norbeck of South Dakota to wear his false teeth when he delivered a supporting speech on the Senate floor: his words were unintelligible to his fellow senators, who then may have merely sympathized with their mumbling colleague. (Historical contingency structures human events!) Whatever the circumstances of its genesis, this program of wetland purchases, pursued by a staff of federal biologists and planners, diversified the collective refuge landscape, which increasingly reflected the perspectives of wildlife professionals. Initial refuges protecting wetlands included such varied environments as California's Central Valley (the Sacramento refuge), the mountains of Montana (Red Rock Lakes), the prairies of North Dakota (the Souris refuges), the north woods of Maine (Moosehorn), the coastal marshes of Delaware (Bombay Hook), and forested central Illinois (Chautauqua).

The influence of strong individuals did not end with the early years. Not only was Franklin Delano Roosevelt particularly active in invoking his proclamation powers to create new refuges, but potent leadership also emerged within the Biological Survey. Roosevelt's advisory committee on wildlife restoration in 1934 consisted of the publisher Thomas Beck, the biologist Aldo Leopold, and the Pulitzer Prize–winning political cartoonist Jay Norwood "Ding" Darling of the *Des Moines Register*. For eighteen months Darling also headed the Biological Survey during the beginnings of an expanded land purchase program for new wildlife refuges. He successfully amassed about $8.5 million for such purchases from various funds intended to retire farmland, to provide drought relief, and to invigorate the economy. But perhaps Darling's most important administrative action was his successful coaxing of John Clark Salyer II (whom he knew as a wildlife biologist in Iowa) to leave temporarily a Ph.D. program at the University of Michigan to head the invigorated refuge program (Poole 1971). Urged on by a deadline for expending some of the funds, Salyer "headed across the country to search out the best waterfowl areas he could find. . . . The days were for working, . . . the nights were for driving. . . . Within six weeks he had driven eighteen thousand miles and drawn up plans for 600,000 acres of new refuge lands" (Laycock 1965/1973: 6). Salyer would remain as head of the wildlife refuges until 1961, and during his tenure the protected acreage increased from less than 2 million to nearly 30 million (Poole 1971: 281). The label of "father of the national wildlife refuges" is appropriately applied to Salyer (Laycock 1965/1973: 11), who was as much a wildlife professional as a politically successful administrator.

The system also diversified with increased attention to the habitats of rare animal species. The early refuges for several large grazing mammals were followed by such units as, in 1935, Aransas, for whooping cranes wintering on the Texas coast, and, in 1954, National Key Deer, for a small subspecies of white-tailed deer in Florida. Still further diversification came with the Endangered Species Act of 1973 (and related legislation), which specifically authorized purchases of the habitats of rare and endangered species (Swanson et al. 1969). As a result, Fish and Wildlife Service specialists have added a rich array of refuges, many of them little known, varying from Moapa Valley in Nevada for the Moapa dace (a fish), to the Ellicott Slough in California for the Santa Cruz long-toed salamander, to the Oklahoma Bat Caves for several species of bats, to the Antioch Dunes near San Francisco for Lange's metalmark butterfly, Contra Costa wallflower, and Antioch Dune evening primrose. Taken together, congressional directives and strong wildlife professionals have elevated planning, rational decisions, and an image of cohesion in the National Wildlife Refuge System.

Such coherence—which critics have found lacking in the political happenstance that guides the growth of the National Park System and that seems an ingredient in at least the early history of national forest wilderness—should not be overstated. A second consideration, the pathways that lead to new refuge units, suggests divergent trails, sometimes following careful plans and sometimes not (Clawson and Held 1957, Drabelle 1983: 22–23, Reed and Drabelle 1984: 23–24). Two ways of establishing new national wildlife refuges reflect professional planning. First, the Fish and Wildlife Service may propose to establish refuges primarily for waterfowl on land purchased with funds from the sale of duck stamps to the Migratory Bird Conservation Commission, a body of eight individuals—the secretaries of the interior, agriculture, and transportation, two members from each house of Congress, and a representative from the natural resource agency of the state involved in the proposal. If the commission approves, the service proceeds with refuge development (Swanson et al. 1969). Although not entirely free from political considerations, this procedure emphasizes input from professional biologists and other specialists within the Fish and Wildlife Service. More than 4.5 million acres of refuge land have been purchased with duck stamp funds. Second, proposals for refuges focused on the habitats of rare and endangered species also emanate from the staff of the Fish and Wildlife Service, with funding coming from income from oil and gas leases in offshore areas that accumulates in the Land and Water Conservation Fund. More than twenty-five refuges have been established under this authority, although at least sixty refuges established by a variety of mechanisms specifically provide habitat for rare plants and animals. In both of these actions, then, professionals take the lead in planning and establishing new refuge units.

The three other means of creating national wildlife refuges reflect more strongly both the initiative of powerful individuals and the influence of political process, as opposed to perceptions of need derived from professional biologists. First, presidents have exercised their authority to withdraw federal lands, not only Theodore Roosevelt and Franklin Roosevelt but also Jimmy Carter in his 1978 proclamation of twelve refuges totaling 40 million acres in Alaska (Vale 1979a); these reserves formed the core of protected lands subsequently formalized by Congress under the Alaska National Interest Lands Act. Second, congressional action has created many national wildlife refuges, including the Upper Mississippi River National Wildlife and Fish Refuge in 1924, a project involving more substantial federal funds—$1.5 million—than those authorized for the National Bison Range. Congressional action is pursued for all refuge projects that involve the acquisition of private land and that have purposes other than protection of waterfowl or endangered species. Finally, refuges sometimes result from donations. These reservations range from the Trustom Pond refuge in Rhode Island, which began with a donation of 365 acres by a single individual (Anne Kenyon

Morse), to the Sevilleta refuge of New Mexico, derived from 220,000 acres donated by the Campbell Family Foundation.

Regardless of the specific mechanism employed to establish refuges, surprising sources have contributed richly to the system. Abandoned or purchased agricultural land, uneconomic or unproductive for commercial purposes, provided a foundation for the expansion pursued by John Salyer in the 1930s, whose legacy includes such units as the Necedah in Wisconsin, the Piedmont in Georgia, and the Turnbull in Washington (Holstine and Bruce 1991). Decommissioned military reservations provide an even more unlikely base for new refuges. Fort Niobrara in Nebraska closed as an Army post in 1912 and became a federal wildlife area, later named a refuge, home for donated bison, elk, and deer, with Texas longhorn cattle added in 1936. The Blackbeard Island National Wildlife Refuge in South Carolina developed from an 1800 Navy Department reservation established to protect timber for shipbuilding, and the Oxbow National Wildlife Refuge emerged from the phasing out of Fort Devens in Massachusetts. Perhaps even more striking are the refuges born from the Defense Department's particularly noxious involvement with atomic and chemical weapons—the Rocky Mountain Arsenal National Wildlife Area near Denver and the refuge lands on the Hanford Reservation of Washington.

The particular areas called national wildlife refuges, then, reflect systematic and professional planning as well as the quirks of individuals. But do they collectively form an integrated whole? Congressional action has repeatedly affirmed the purposes of the federal wildlife refuges. As early as 1906, the Game Bird Preserves Protection Act (also known as the Refuge Trespass Act) proclaimed it a federal crime to disturb birds or their eggs on federal wildlife reserves. In 1929 the Migratory Bird Act directed that refuge lands be managed as "inviolate sanctuaries" for migratory birds, a policy statement, according to Clawson and Held (1957: 123), by which "the refuges as a system became firmly established by law." Others demurred. Butcher (1955: 14) found the refuges to be inadequate both in number and in degree of protection, presumably consequences of too little centralized authority bestowed by Congress upon the Fish and Wildlife Service. Thirty years later, Drabelle (1983) found the 1966 National Wildlife Refuge System Administrative Act (a section of the Endangered Species Act) to provide a "clear direction for the system," a positive impression reinforced by congressional oversight (General Accounting Office 1989: 8–9). The Fish and Wildlife Service itself interprets this legislation as "formally establish[ing] the National Wildlife Refuge System . . . for the purpose of fish and wildlife conservation" (U.S. Fish and Wildlife Service n.d.). The Wilderness Society, however, continued to urge Congress to pass an "organic act" to "provide overall statutory guidance for the present and future management and use of refuge lands" (Wilderness Society 1983: 32). This action was also advocated by the 1979 Wildlife Refuge Study Task Force (U.S. Fish and Wildlife Service 1979). The same point continued to be argued more than a decade later. Williams (1996b: 38), for example, proclaimed that the refuges were "not really even a system" and the "agency [was] without an 'organic act.'" These actions, in their cumulative effect, might be viewed as recurring halfheartedness, a failure to forge unity and purpose for the refuge system. That view, however, contrasts with the imagery formed by the reading of history in which the laws over the twentieth century become "building blocks . . . filling gaps and adding strength" to an edifice of focused purpose. Bill Clinton's 1996 executive orders "to define the Refuge System's mission and guiding principles" and Congress's passage of the 1997 National Wildlife Refuge System Improvement Act, "organic legislation . . . [that] provides significant guidance for management and public use of the Refuge System" (U.S. Fish and Wildlife Service n.d.), might be seen as either continuing the hesitancy or finally creating a sense of coherence for the refuges (Gergely et al. 2000).

In spite of the ongoing dialogue over the need for statutory "guidance," the national wildlife refuges seem to enjoy strong input from their own professional staff on matters of new refuge projects, and this input may operate, overtly at least, in relative freedom from outside political forces. It is a freedom that is not enjoyed by new units in the National Park System, which may be proposed by the service but mostly flourish or die in Congress or on the president's desk, or by new units of national forest and public domain wilderness, which cannot transcend the boundaries of the lands administered by those agencies. The National Wildlife Refuge System, being more a product of professional design and open possibilities, may be the most coherent of the three major federal land systems.

DEGREE OF ELITISM The charge of elitism in national parks and national forest wilderness arose, in part, in the context of recreational use of those lands. As we have seen, the people who visit national parks and national forest wilderness are disproportionately educated, white, and affluent (Outdoor Recreation Resources Review Commission 1962a: 131–33, Hendee et al. 1968: 12–13, Heritage Recreation and Conservation Service 1979: 4, Wellner 1997: 38). By the criterion of visitor social class, the national wildlife refuges offer recreational assets to a wider segment of American society.

The national wildlife refuges host diverse outdoor recreation activities. Both the nature of the landscapes in the system and the general purpose of the refuges, however, mean that activities revolving around wildlife have long dominated recreation. Accentuating this dominance, the policy guidelines of the *Service Manual* (the policy guide for refuge managers, the first edition of which appeared in 1942) and the 1997 National Wildlife Refuge System Improvement Act state that wildlife uses shall receive emphasis in public use. The most widespread wildlife-oriented recreation on the refuges include wildlife observation (in 83 percent of the refuges), walking or hiking (77 percent), and environmental education (73 percent) (General Accounting Office 1989: 17), activities likely to be pursued by highly educated sectors of the population (Hendee 1969). But wildlife-oriented activity also includes fishing and hunting—more than half of the refuges provide fishing and more than a third offer hunting (General Accounting Office 1989: 17)—and both hunters and fishers "tend to have less education, lower incomes and occupational classifications than other outdoor recreationists" (Hendee 1969: 255). This demographic pattern has long been identified in recreation surveys (Heritage Recreation and Conservation Service 1979: 36, Wellner 1997: 38). This wide range of recreational activities, appealing to a broad spectrum of Americans, suggests stronger egalitarianism—at least potentially—in the refuges than in parks and wilderness.

The socioeconomic characteristics of recreationists on various federal lands support this speculation. Those who visit the national wildlife refuges disproportionately represent lower-income groups in comparison with those who use either the National Park System or the national forest wilderness. Moreover, among all the federal lands, the refuges attract the highest percentage of recreationists who identify themselves as African American (Heritage Recreation and Conservation Service 1979: 45, Dwyer 1994).

The spatial pattern of the units of the refuge system also might be seen as providing opportunities to a wide range of socioeconomic groups. Units of the National Park System and national forest wilderness are concentrated in remote parts of the western states, so that the expenditure of time and money required to get to them restricts users to the more affluent. To be honest, the National Park System expanded its mission during the latter part of the twentieth century to include "urban parks" (Foresta 1984, Conservation Foundation 1985), although the regional imagery of the Park System remains western. By contrast, national wildlife refuges are scattered throughout the country, often close to urban centers, and so may serve to satisfy the recreation needs of both rich and poor. Even the 1968 Leopold Committee Report on the system seems to recognize this egalitarian character: the refuges "offer the maximum number of Americans the chance to enjoy such spectacles as massed waterfowl against a sunset sky, a wisp of snipe power-diving down to a marsh, or a coyote mousing in a meadow" (Leopold et al. 1968). A "maximum number" may be a long way from universal, but it encompasses a good part of the American public.

The social justice issue arises only occasionally in evaluations of the national wildlife refuges (although such incidents may be increasing), perhaps because of their more egalitarian policies. Objections to refuge proposals voiced by local people, for example, can impress the political members of the Migratory Bird Conservation Commission and effectively end project development; witness the failure of the proposed Aldo Leopold National Wildlife Refuge in southern Wisconsin, opposed by local farmers in the 1990s. Moreover, commodity resources generally remain more accessible on refuge lands than in parks and wilderness, perhaps placating local interests; the standard histories of the Fish and Wildlife Service even celebrate such resource use (Reed and Drabelle 1984). On the other hand, the Flathead Indians covet control of the National Bison Range, which they feel was unjustly carved from their lands (Matthews 2003a); wildlife protection efforts generate stories that tell of reinventing local peoples as criminals (Jacoby 2001); and state wildlife landscapes have been interpreted as places of contestation between powerful government agencies and less powerful local and ethnic groups (Griffin 1992). Still, on balance, few observers see the refuge system as socially unjust, though that view may be attributable more to the obscurity of the refuges than to their egalitarian character.

DEGREE OF PROTECTION The refuges enjoy less strict protection from commodity resource development than units of the National Park System or national forest wilderness. Reed and Drabelle (1984: 55) suggest that the refuges are "dominant use" areas, in which the primary or dominant purpose focuses on protection of wildlife habitat, but that "secondary uses" are permitted if they do not conflict with the dominant use. Reed and Drabelle, seemingly pleased with such flexibility, also indicate that national parks are "single use" areas, although that phrase belies the long and persistent controversy over protection versus recreation in the parks. This concept of identifying a dominant use echoes a key element of a 1970 plan to consolidate and restructure the management of all federal lands (Public Land Law Review Commission 1970: 48). Traditional environmental groups opposed that proposal, seeing it as a means of strengthening the power of commodity resource users. Perhaps similar dissatisfaction with the de facto dominant-use vision of the refuges underlies the persistent call for stronger congressional guidance, in the form of an "organic act" for the refuge system—a call for a single-use policy.

The use of refuge lands for purposes other than providing wildlife habitat has a lengthy history. Commodity resource developments are common. During World War II the secretary of the interior opened certain refuge lands for fossil fuel production and bombing and gunnery practice (Reed and Drabelle 1984: 27–28). Ninety-five percent of the 860,000-acre Cabeza Prieta refuge in Arizona is overlain by the Barry M. Goldwater Air Force Range, one of the nation's largest training areas for military pilots. Apart from serious questions about the possible negative impacts on bighorn sheep and Sonoran pronghorn on the Cabeza Prieta, the use of the refuge for military purposes may have the positive effect—in some people's minds—of restricting more intensive recreational use. Mining occurs on more than two dozen refuges, including a contested production of natural gas on the D'Arbonne in Louisiana, where the creation of the refuge did not include the purchase of subsurface mineral rights. Executive order also permits livestock grazing on about 150 refuges. Most controversial is the grazing on large western refuges, such as Brown's Park in Colorado, Charles M. Russell in Montana (H. Fischer 1985), Malheur and Hart Mountain in Oregon, and Sheldon in Nevada; the latter two refuges have excluded livestock—at least temporarily—as part of their management plans (Durbin 1997, 2003a). Timber is cut on about eighty refuges; the logging on the St. Marks in Florida and the Seney in Michigan, for example, serves both to produce wood and to enhance wildlife habitat, at least according to the Fish and Wildlife Service (n.d.; see also General Accounting Office 1989: 75). Similarly, the selling of the right to harvest hay or grow crops on a "sharecropping basis . . . [with] the government's share of the crop . . . made available for wildlife" (Clawson and Held 1957: 125) sometimes promises a means to enhance wildlife habitat (Leopold et al. 1968). On some refuges the lack of unambiguous rights to water—necessary for wildlife purposes—

renders habitat quality vulnerable; the Bosque del Apache refuge in Arizona and the Stillwater refuge in Nevada are but two refuges in which adequate water supplies are tenuous.

The appropriateness of recreation on refuge lands and waters stirs no less controversy than that of commodity resource development. Hunting, particularly for waterfowl, has long been an accepted recreational use of national wildlife refuges. The model of the strict sanctuary, without hunting, originally dominated the vision for the refuges, but as early as 1924, when Congress established the Upper Mississippi River Wild Life and Fish Refuge, the law made allowance for hunting and fishing. Revisions to the Duck Stamp Act, beginning in 1949, allowed the secretary of the interior to authorize public waterfowl hunting on portions of refuges purchased with duck stamp funds, at first on 25 percent of the area of such a refuge, then on 40 percent. Today waterfowl hunting is a major activity on national wildlife refuges, occurring on nearly half of all units. Refuge managers hold much discretionary power in deciding whether and under what conditions hunting should be permitted, although they are guided by the principle that hunting should be prohibited unless "it contributes to or is not incompatible with the management objectives of the refuge" (U.S. Fish and Wildlife Service, Service Manual, link at http://refuges.fws.gov/manual.html, series 600, citation 631). Some critics have questioned the logical inconsistency of hunting on landscape reserves identified as wildlife *refuges* (D. Butcher 1955); others defend it both as a type of reward to hunters whose purchases of duck stamps have made possible the expansion of the refuge system (Reiger 1986/2001) and as an entirely "appropriate . . . [activity] to be encouraged" as long as refuge areas continue to protect "a bit of natural landscape where . . . native wildlife may find . . . a home" (Leopold et al. 1968). Under this precept, hunting of both large and small mammals and of upland birds is also permitted on at least half of the refuges.

Other types of recreation also have complicated the administration of the national wildlife refuges. Boating—which includes power boating on more than a hundred refuges—may sometimes conflict with the survival of wildlife, particularly nesting waterfowl. But once established as a recreational activity on a refuge, boating may be politically difficult to restrict or prohibit. Such use has been controversial in recent decades at the Des Lacs refuge in North Dakota, the Ruby Lakes refuge in Nevada, and the De Soto refuge in Iowa; on all three, however, boating has been successfully curtailed. More general recreation, including auto touring, picnicking, and water-based activities, may also sometimes counter wildlife goals on refuges. The heavy use of beaches by visitors and their off-road vehicles at Chincoteague National Wildlife Refuge in coastal Virginia has posed an ongoing threat to wildlife. Even though a 1962 law required that recreational use be compatible with the wildlife purposes of the refuges, the congressional directive apparently was too vague to constrain recreation that even the Fish and Wildlife Service considered harmful.

Designation of wilderness areas on the refuges, under the authority of the 1964 Wilderness Act, restricts many but not all nonwildlife uses and questionable recreational activities; timber cutting may be prohibited on refuge wilderness, for example, but livestock grazing continues, as does hunting. Moreover, the distribution of the more strongly protected refuge wilderness echoes the spatial patterns of the system landscape generally. About 21 million acres of the national wildlife refuges are within statutory wilderness, more than 90 percent of that total in Alaska. Refuge wilderness occurs in twenty-six states, including nineteen east of the eleven western states. The largest wilderness areas on refuge lands in the lower forty-eight states occur on the large units in the West—on the Kofa and Cabeza Prieta national wildlife refuges of Arizona—but also include the Okefenokee refuge of Georgia. Overall, wilderness designation does not substantially change the patterns of protection within the National Wildlife Refuge System.

In many people's minds the protection offered by the national wildlife refuges against both commodity resource development and inappropriate recreational uses, hardly stringent at any time in their history, reflects lack of strong guidance by Congress on the purpose of the refuge landscapes (Fink 1994); this issue thus merges with the argument over the coherence of the national wildlife refuges as a *system*. One consequence of the lack of strict congressional guidance is the elevation of presidential (or other executive branch) authority. During the administration of Ronald Reagan, for example, Interior Secretary James Watt proposed to expand commodity resource production on refuge lands:

We [i.e., the executive leadership] asked each region [of the refuge system] to identify expansion potential. The response we received was not satisfactory. . . . We believe that there is potential to expand economic uses in such areas as grazing, haying, farming, timber harvesting, trapping, oil and gas extraction, small hydroelectric generation, concessions, commercial hunting and fishing guides, guided interpretive tours and commercial fishing. (Quoted in Ryden 1983: 26)

An altogether different spirit is seen in Theodore Roosevelt's 1904 order to send a detachment of twenty marines to Midway atoll to protect nesting birds and their eggs from food-gathering humans, although Midway was not yet a formal refuge.

Congress and not the executive, though, formally institutionalized commodity resource uses on the refuges in 1966 with its passage of the National Wildlife Refuge Administration Act, which authorized the secretary of the interior to "permit any use of an area within the System for any purpose . . . whenever he determines that such use is compatible with the major purposes for which an area was established." The managers of individual refuges exercised primary responsibility for determining "compatibility" (General Accounting Office 1989, Curtin 1993), creating a decentralized and flexible decision-making structure, an arrangement much criticized by environmentalists (Williams 1996b) and underlying the "dilemma" of the refuge system (Reffalt and Barry, eds., 1992). The subsequent passage of the National Wildlife Refuge System Improvement Act received praise as the long-needed "organic act" by which Congress provides guidance and strength of purpose for the refuges (Gergely et al. 2000), although allowances for non-wildlife uses remain, with a continuation of the "compatibility" determination by refuge managers. Recreational uses also continue, with emphasis on wildlife-related activities, but this provision is hardly novel: formal policy of the Fish and Wildlife Service had already decided "to de-emphasize non-wildlife oriented recreation" (General Accounting Office 1989: 11). Regardless of statements in legislation, the stated purposes of national wildlife refuges seem inherently ambiguous. The dual purposes of protection and recreation in the refuges may equal the situation in the national parks, and thus the recurrent criticism, whether or not justified, may well continue.

COMPARISONS WITH NATIONAL PARKS AND WILDERNESS
When the criticisms of the national parks and national wilderness are applied to the National Wildlife Refuge System, the results are mixed. The refuges seem less vulnerable to the critique of either landscape quality or degree of elitism than parks and wilderness. The degree of nature protection, by contrast, is clearly less strong in the refuges. As for coherence as a system, although the refuges have leaned heavily on patron saints (Darling, Salyer), promoters (sporting goods manufacturers), and recreation interests (hunting and fishing), professional and centralized planning is not lacking in the refuge system. Overall, the critics of parks and wilderness may find in the national wildlife refuges at least some reason for celebration.

Reflections

The portrait of the national wildlife refuges offers much to the modern and sophisticated American who expresses concern for protected nature. The types of landscapes (the disproportionate importance of wetlands, coasts, and grasslands), the measure of landscape worth (the emphasis on biological values), the high degree of professional planning that goes into the creation of new units (the factor that imparts a sense of rational coherence to the system), and the greater appeal of many refuge lands to Americans in modest socioeconomic circumstances—all of these traits suggest that the refuges escape many of the characteristics that prompt criticism of national parks and national forest wilderness. Yet, in spite of these virtues, the national wildlife refuges hardly command center stage in the theater of environmental concern.

Several factors may discourage the placement of the refuges in such a preferential position, and these factors say more about the minds of Americans, particularly environmentally sensitive Americans, than about the refuges themselves. Both the typical refuge landscape that fails to offer scenic spectacle and the lack of diversified recreational opportunities that are available in national parks and national forest wilderness—backpacking, horseback riding, rock climbing, white-water rafting, bicycling, camping, lodging—must contribute to the secondary status of the refuge system. A detached observer might anticipate that both scenery and recreation would be important to a large segment of the general public but not to those who pride themselves on their environmental sensitivity. And yet admiration of both the sublime—fundamental to the imagery of wilderness as sacred space—and the pleasuring ground loom large in the motivations of even those who most value the protection of wild landscapes.

Still another factor that dilutes the imagery of the refuges comes as no surprise: the absence of more strict nature protection. Yet even here some sophisticated environmentalists use rhetoric that would seem to position the refuges above parks and wilderness as the ideal for protected landscapes. In an age when restoration ecology and ecosystem management have become preferred to hands-off preservation (wilderness as garden), when the notion of wilderness itself has emerged as the "wrong nature" (the false idol), what better model could we find than the active manipulation of refuge landscapes for enhanced nature values, an enhancement pursued in conjunction with compatible commodity resource uses? No one, however, points to the refuges, whether in fact or in promise, as expressions of just such a harmonized blending; rather, the resource development is deplored as a threat to nature protection (T. Williams 1996b; cf. Langston 2003). In sum, these interactions construct a tangled web. Those who criticize the imagery of sacred space as a false idol focus their attention on national parks and wilderness, where their critique is most effective, and ignore the national wildlife refuges, where the alternative to the false idol—the garden—captures the spirit of existing land use policy. By contrast, those who defend the sacred space image display the virtue of consistency: any commodity resource development or recreational use that threatens Edenic nature is anathema, whether in a national park, wilderness, or a national wildlife refuge.

In 1987 the Sierra Club offered a solution to the problem of too little protection for nature on the refuge landscape: designation of more formal wilderness (L. Rice 1987). It is a response not surprising, not unanticipated, but also not thoughtful. Statutory wilderness appropriately protects refuge lands that lack human artifacts or that require little active habitat management; much of the refuge landscape, however, contains the former and needs the latter. Rather than wilderness, the principle articulated in the 1968 Leopold Report on the National Wildlife Refuge System might serve as a superior guide. In promotion of the purpose of "the refuge as an oasis for wildlife," active manipulation of environmental conditions clearly plays a role: waterfowl refuges require "water control structures . . . roads. . . and agricultural crops"; refuges for large mammals or rare species benefit from "plant manipulation . . . water development . . . [and] development of food resources." But the Leopold committee recognized the potential for excesses, and called for "naturalism in refuge management . . . avoid[ance of] excessive artificiality," so that each refuge remains "a bit of natural landscape." It is a balancing act, an exercise in sensitivity, a plea for moderation. It is an answer that finds virtue—even protected nature virtue—in landscape conditions other than human-artifact-lacking wilderness.

Across the breadth of preservation sentiment, views linking nature and landscape range widely, but essentially everyone concerned with nature protection converges on a major point: the national wildlife refuges seem less worthy of attention than parks and wilderness. The names of even the heroes of the refuge system (Ding Darling and John Salyer) evoke no recognition comparable to those of the high priests of the national parks (Muir and Mather) or of wilderness (Marshall and Leopold). What is lost by this failure to recognize the virtues of the refuges, losses both to the collective sense of what has been and what might be accomplished in the name of nature protection and to the personal sense of appreciating wild landscapes, suggests sadness, even tragedy. No other protected landscapes—with the possible exception of the grand old national parks—have histories as varied and rich as the national wildlife refuges: stories of preprotection commodity resource use, of wildlife decline, of establishment as nature reserves, of habitat restoration, of wildlife resurrection, of recreational use, of conflicts between commodity uses and wildlife uses, and of successful efforts or continued struggles to resolve those conflicts. Blackwater and Moosehorn, Piedmont and Crab Orchard, Horicon and Seney, Wichita Mountains and Sullys Hill, Arrowwood and Fort Niobrara, Rocky Mountain Arsenal and Bitter Lake, Bear River and Kofa Mountains, Umatilla and Upper Klamath, Sacramento and Salton Sea—these refuges offer more than acres to some aggregated total of protected landscape, more than simply "wildlife habitat." They are places with stories, places to be celebrated.

ISSUES American
Wilderness

7   OUTDOOR RECREATION

"Climb the mountains and get their good tidings," John Muir exhorted us (Muir 1901: 56). And we Americans listened. In recent years, annual recreational visits to the National Park System totaled more than 270 million, to the national forests more than 280 million, and to state parks more than 730 million. We Americans have 16 million recreational boats and almost 2 million all-terrain vehicles. Hunting licenses exceed 30 million, and more than 40 million of us participate in freshwater fishing. As we watch for a new bird on a life list, peer for moose in a willow thicket, or walk a trail in hopes of finding a desert tortoise, we spend $18 billion each year for food and lodging alone. We have listened to Muir, and we have heeded his call.

Why, in a book about nature protection, does the matter of outdoor recreation arise? The answer is twofold. First, in issues involving the national parks particularly and protected landscapes generally, recreational activities are commonly seen as threats to the natural conditions being preserved. Yet the same accusation does not prompt me to discuss individual commodity resources, which clearly pose more threats to protected nature than recreation can. A second and more telling reason for the centrality of outdoor recreation in matters of nature reserves is more important: activities that we label as outdoor recreation are the means by which people involve themselves with—connect with—the natural scene in parks, wilderness, wildlife refuges, and other types of nature reserves.

Those involvements take a variety of forms. Some recreational activities clearly belong in nature reserves; some do not; many are ambiguous. In other words, what recreation appears appropriate for protected landscapes, or for a given type of protected landscape, remains a critical question because the way one answers it reveals how one perceives the purpose of such landscapes. In the absence of an extreme biocentrist perspective—a prohibition against any human contact with the nonhuman world in nature reserves—it will always be difficult to decide the appropriateness of outdoor recreation activities in nature reserves.

Outdoor Recreation Activities

The yearly *Statistical Abstract of the United States* provides data on participation by Americans in "selected sports activities," which include camping, fishing, and hiking, all of which are germane to nature reserves, but omits such equally appropriate activities as picnicking, bird-watching, and walking for pleasure. The occasional "national recreational surveys" or "outdoor recreation surveys" present more complete enumerations of activities usually considered suitable for parks and wilderness, and they also report on the unambiguously irrelevant, such as attending outdoor concerts and team sports events. To what degree do a large number of other activities—golfing, bicycling, water skiing, snowmobiling, jogging, motorboating, swimming in a constructed outdoor pool—pertain to a discussion of recreation in protected landscapes? Many activities may be legitimate in certain areas at certain times (e.g., waterfowl hunting on state wildlife land in the fall), ambiguous in others (e.g., deer hunting in a state park), and clearly inappropriate in still other circumstances (e.g., sport hunting of any sort in a national park). Some activities, such as running, may be a matter of indifference in regard to land use decisions, while others, such as downhill skiing, require a yes or no answer. Even the categories themselves influence the picture of the recreation being described; when, for example, does casual observation of nature, perhaps labeled "auto touring," differ from "sightseeing," and under what conditions does "sightseeing" become "bird-watching" or "nature study"? In sum, judgment and opinion influence what activities should be considered in an evaluation of recreation in protected landscapes, and, in a sense, that assessment is the core of the problem facing the makers of policies for land reserves.

Even though the reported numbers of adults who participate in various activities seem to reflect differences in the way data are collected and categorized, certain patterns emerge. First, sightseeing, particularly from the automobile, dominates as a recreational activity, an assertion hardly surprising to anyone who has visited a protected landscape, such as Yosemite or Yellowstone, that is accessible by road. Second, larger numbers of persons engage in simpler activities, such as picnicking and walking for pleasure, than in more skilled or specialized pursuits, such as hunting and skiing. Third, water-focused recreation, whether swimming, fishing, or boating, generates particularly large numbers of participants. Fourth, nature study such as bird-watching, as an explicit recreational activity, engages a growing but relatively small portion of the total recreationist population.

Hidden within these aggregated data lie differences among people of particular ages and ethnic groups (Dwyer 1994). Participation in most activities declines with age, particularly after the age cohort of 25–34; only bird-watching increases among older Americans, peaking with the age cohort of 55–64. Among racial or ethnic groups, whites are more likely than African Americans, Hispanics, and Asians to participate in most activities, even when such factors as income and age are held constant. In the context of recreation associated with wild landscapes, one group stands out as distinctive: African Americans are "significantly less likely than whites to participate . . . [in] rural and wildland activities (i.e., hiking, observe and photo nature, tent camping, driving for pleasure) . . . activities involving water, ice, or snow . . . and activities that are relatively expensive" (Dwyer 1994: 23). It is not clear whether these differences would be retained as expressions of group identity or lessened through acculturation if economic and social statuses were more uniform in society.

Regardless of the specific recreational activities that Americans seek in wildland environments, that use of wild landscapes has increased in recent decades far more rapidly than the population generally. Between 1950 and 1990, while the total population of the United States increased 66 percent, visits to the National Park System rose by 677 percent, recreational visits to the national forests swelled 690 percent, and visitation to state parks grew by 545 percent. Projections to the year 2025 suggest that still larger numbers of people, disproportionately nonwhites, will be participants in most wildland activities, but that there will be a decline in the percentage of the total population participating, perhaps reflecting changes in both the age and racial or ethnic structures of the American population.

"Appropriateness" of Outdoor Recreation in Nature Reserves

Commentators on nature protection commonly talk of human activities as either "appropriate" or "inappropriate" for protected landscapes. Such distinctions imply that not all recreational activities are equally desirable, even if we concede that a consensus on desirability eludes us. Such a value-laden assertion, seemingly elitist and exceptionalist, is broadly accepted, in principle, in American society. Everyone would recognize the appropriateness of walking and picnicking in national parks; some would question automobile sightseeing (which is allowed), while others would wonder about mountain biking or BASE jumping (which are not permitted); few would advocate hunting or golfing; fewer still would describe as appropriate the use of national parks for under-the-stars rock concerts or spectator team sports. (Imagine a proposal for a triple-A team for the San Francisco Giants—maybe the Sierran Grizzlies—playing in a stadium on the floor of Yosemite Valley.) The problem is not one of principle; that is, we expect neither categorical denial of human entry into nature reserves nor extreme egalitarianism in recreation activities on those landscapes—universal and unrestricted access to whatever anyone wishes to do in the name of recreation. Rather, we debate what is appropriate recreation and what is not.

The lack of perfect overlap between recreational activities and meanings of protected landscapes encapsulates the problem of identifying appropriateness for recreation in nature reserves; the lack of overlap suggests, moreover, two further points. First, recreation includes more than what is usually associated with the playground. To experience nature as sacred space or the nation's roots, to learn about nature as an evolutionary stage, to sense nature as ethical arena or place—all should be recognized as recreation, broadly conceived. Second, and more obvious, some recreation is not consistent with landscapes dedicated to nature protection. Although the two points interact on the stage where the dialogue for determining appropriateness is played out, the second usually occupies the spotlight. Discussions of the virtues and liabilities of encouraging nonplayground activities less commonly play a central role.

Several techniques help policy makers and citizens alike determine what recreation activities seem acceptable in protected landscapes. First, the assessment of ecological or environmental impact typically dominates the debate over whether a given activity should be allowed. Off-road vehicles damage vegetation, accelerate erosion, and pollute the air; roads alter drainage patterns of surface water and encourage the vehicles that increase air polution; unrestricted camping creates trampled ground and reduces accumulated organic material in soils. This approach underlies the identification of ecological carrying capacity and the "limits of accepted change" employed by the Forest Service to analyze the impacts of wilderness users (e.g., Hammitt and Cole 1987, Wuerthner 1990a, Cole et al. 1995, McCool and Cole 1997). Without denying the importance of these types of assessments, we must recognize that the common environmental impact study evaluates only the most fundamental types of impact and thus supplies only the most limited measure of appropriateness. This approach would not necessarily preclude helicopters for supplying recreationists, low-standard roads for mountain bicycles, or asphalt-surfaced camping pads for backpackers. Moreover, perceptions of environmental alterations caused by human activities vary from person to person. Whose perceptions should guide policy?

Second, user surveys to assess the goals and satisfaction of visitors to nature reserves, however informative in some limited sense, cannot determine the appropriateness of recreational activities (e.g., Hendee et al. 1968, Stankey 1973, Lucas 1985, Chavez 1993, Watson et al. 1993, Kane 2000). If this statement sounds contrary to democratic ideals, remember that everyone save the anarchist or extreme libertarian agrees on the need to balance individual and collective rights, and some sense of appropriateness is central to deciding where to strike that balance. In outdoor recreation, user surveys reduce policy questions to contests of popularity, inviting argument and counterargument over what is the proper public to be surveyed. For example, visitors to refuges, parks, and wilderness constitute populations already biased by established traditions of appropriateness. Waterfowl hunters account for a major part of visitors to many national wildlife refuges in the fall, so polling refuge users could only solidify the decision to continue such hunting on these lands; but would such a poll say more about inertia and political influence than about appropriateness? Snowmobilers constitute a major population of users in wintertime Yellowstone, but would polling January visitors to the park determine the appropriateness of snowmobiles or would it merely indicate who was in the park at that time? If bicycles were permitted in wilderness, how would they affect the surveys of wilderness users, and would the results speak to the appropriateness of bicycling in wilderness or to the interests of those users selected by prior policy decisions? Questions of appropriateness must consider more abstract or philosophical notions of landscape purpose, hopefully exploring some collective senses but extending beyond the popularity polls of user surveys.

A third approach to determining qualitative characteristics of phenomena addresses issues less directly, appears less precise, and encourages a dialogue rather than provides clear answers: appeal to expert opinion. We depend upon experts to enlighten us about a myriad of matters, and we do so when we question the wisdom that derives from either objective scalars or popularity polls. This dependence arises in situations that range from the trivial to the crucial. Hollywood critics give us rankings of movies, food experts of restaurants, sportswriters or coaches of sports teams; teachers identify the qualities of students, judges of courtroom discourse, social scholars of societal injustice; politicians assure us of their expertise in taking us to war. Any individual can reject the opinions of particular experts or seek out different spokespersons for wisdom, but we depend on the articulation of ideas by informed and knowledgeable people as at least an initial foray into complex issues that defy simple resolution.

This principle applies no less to the appropriateness of outdoor activities than to other issues. Exploring what thoughtful people believe about recreation in nature helps us to identify not only those activities that seem inappropriate in nature reserves but also those that might be encouraged. Now we are not only evaluating data from natural science or social science (without denying the importance of either) but considering the humanism of values. We are encouraged to assess the ways in which the galaxies of outdoor recreation and landscape meanings overlap.

Lest this discussion be misread as simply a class-based and moralistic vision of nature, let me again point out why it is appropriate to grapple with the issue of the appropriateness of recreation in nature reserves. The recreational uses of parks, wilderness, and refuges cannot encompass all activities desired by all people. We have to identify what should be allowed and what should not; and neither impact studies nor popularity polls confront this problem. Expert opinion helps clarify what outdoor recreation is appropriate for nature reserves.

Expert Opinion on Outdoor Recreation

Reasonable people may disagree about who should be included in the cast of experts, whatever the issue, from foreign policy to rankings of basketball teams for the NCAA tournament. Still, when the subject is outdoor recreation, some names seem uncontroversial.

ALDO LEOPOLD In "Conservation Esthetic," an essay in *A Sand County Almanac*, Aldo Leopold (1949/1970) presents his analysis of the purpose of outdoor recreation. Suggesting the motivation (the "motive force") for such activity to be "contacts with nature," he identifies five "components of the recreational process." First, "the simplest and most obvious," is a trophy or certificate: "a bird's egg, a mess of trout, a basket of mushrooms, the photograph of a bear, the pressed specimen of a wild flower, or a note tucked into the cairn on a mountain peak"—any object "that attests that its owner has been somewhere and done something." Second, "more subtle and complex," is a "feeling of isolation in nature," a component that Leopold suggests is diluted with "development of recreational resources." Third, "we may label 'fresh-air and change of scene.'" Fourth, "the perception of the natural processes, . . . evolution . . . and . . . ecology. . . . That thing called 'nature study' [is] . . . the development of the perceptive faculty in Americans." Leopold explicitly states that this component needs no Ph.D., no advanced education, no dollars. "He who has a little may use it to as good advantage as he who has much." Fifth and finally, Leopold identifies "the sense of husbandry . . . some art of management . . . applied to land by some person of perception."

Leopold presents his five components in an order that reveals his sense of their relative virtue, an order that emerges from his analysis of three threats to the components of the recreation process. First, "mass recreation"—large numbers of recreationists in an area of wild landscape—compromises the qualities of trophy and isolation in nature but threatens less, if at all, the other three components. Second, physical trophies consume the natural world, but other components do not; husbandry, in fact, distinctly engages nature in a creative way, the antithesis of consumption. Third, trophy hunting ("nothing to apologize for") "is the prerogative of youth," but it yields to the other components as an individual grows up. If a person continues to seek trophies and little more, "the capacity for isolation, perception, and husbandry is undeveloped, or perhaps lost." Ultimately for Leopold, the key to "qualitative" outdoor recreation depends on "building receptivity into the still unlovely human mind."

By describing the five aspects of recreation as "components," Leopold implies that they all belong to the unified experience of outdoor recreation. Even his lengthy defense of trophy hunting suggests that he wished not to dismiss the activity with a blanket condemnation but rather to link it with the other four components to complete an analytical understanding of what motivates people to have "contacts with nature." For example, sport bird hunting—an activity that Leopold pursued throughout his life—might involve all five of the components, and thereby elevate the qualities of the recreational experience above that sensed by the hunter for whom shooting pheasants merely results in dead animals. Similarly, walking becomes a richer outdoor activity with more components contributing to the experience, in contrast to a simple pursuit of speed and test of endurance, a sort of mettle trophy seeking.

Leopold's analysis—relatively ignored by Leopold admirers who favor his "land ethic"—provides a base for exploring other expert opinions. In a sense, certain of his components become central to these experts' ideas about outdoor recreation.

FREDERICK LAW OLMSTED Arguably the founder of American landscape architecture and without question the most notable landscape architect in the nineteenth-century United States, Frederick Law Olmsted also served briefly as the first commissioner for the Yosemite Grant, during which time he recommended to the state of California a rationale, and supporting policies, for the new reservation's recreational use (Olmsted 1865/1990). Joseph Sax (1980, especially pp. 17–26), interpreting the 1865 report, invokes Olmsted's thoughts as the basis for an analysis of recreation in the national parks, which might be conceptually expanded to include wild landscape reserves more generally.

For Sax, the essence of Olmsted's vision of recreational purpose was the opportunity for any visitor to enhance the "contemplative faculty," a phrase that combines two words employed frequently by Olmsted. Its characteristics defy simple articulation:

An opportunity for the mind to disengage from getting tasks done, and to engage instead on thoughts removed from the confinement of duty and achievement. . . . (Sax 1980: 20)

The attention is aroused and the mind occupied without purpose, without a continuation of the common process of relating the present action, thought or perception to some future end. (Olmsted 1865/1990: 504, quoted in Sax 1980: 20)

To clarify this elusive concept, Sax dissects some essential points in Olmsted's text. Recreation of this sort offers opportunities for working people, in particular, to free themselves from their labors in order to pursue "cultivation of certain faculties . . . [including] the power of enjoying beauty" (Olmsted quoted in Sax 1980: 21). It was this egalitarian notion of enhancing the options for the less privileged and less powerful that, in Olmsted's view, justified government action to protect wild landscapes. But it is more than just opportunity: the contemplative faculty marks "civilization . . . and taste that has been cultivated," in contrast to the world of the "savage . . . with a limited range of interests," for whom "the power of scenery . . . need[s] to be drawn out" (Olmsted 1865/1990: 503)—that is, the development of the faculty should be an explicit goal, *the* explicit goal, of recreation in protected landscapes. Perhaps anticipating the charge of elitism, Sax suggests that the effort to make the parks "democratic" threatens "their distinctive rhythms" (Sax 1976: 83–84). The contemplative faculty connects more to "aesthetic appreciation" (Sax 1980: 25) than to intellectual understanding. (Note that Leopold describes his fourth component, "nature study," with a similar-sounding phrase, "the perceptive faculty.") It elevates individual response, people reacting as individuals and at their personal paces, "outside the usual influences where [the] agenda [is] preset" (Sax 1980: 24). It seeks "not to serve popular taste but to elevate it" (Sax 1980: 25). It focuses not on biodiversity, not on charismatic megafauna, not on birds and butterflies, but on scenery: "The enjoyment of scenery employs the mind without fatigue and yet exercises it, tranquilizes it and yet enlivens it; and thus, through the influence of the mind over the body, gives the effect of refreshing rest and reinvigoration to the whole system" (Olmsted 1865/1990: 504). True to his profession, Olmsted offers the most overtly humanistic interpretation of the purpose of recreation in wild landscapes, one in which nature becomes a relaxing stimulus.

Compare the development of the contemplative faculty with Leopold's five components of the recreational process. Trophy, natural process, husbandry—none relates closely to Olmsted's idea; all perhaps even represent antithetical positions. Isolation in nature looms large for both experts, but Leopold's change of scene might capture one of the essences of Olmsted's contemplative faculty. It is the natural landscape, "the power of scenery," that elevates the human mind from those common tasks required to make a living, "small and petty details which are uninteresting in themselves" (Olmsted 1865/1990: 503–4). A change of scene (even that word suggests a strong linkage) from the workaday world to the natural landscape pivotally orients the development of the contemplative faculty. An observer might say that Olmsted's concept stresses one of Leopold's five components, perhaps enhances it (fig. 7.1).

ROBERT MARSHALL One of the twentieth century's most prominent enthusiasts for big and bold wilderness, Robert Marshall played critical roles in the development of protected wilderness on the national forests, in the formation of the conservation group known as the Wilderness Society, and in the articulation of still another purpose for recreation on wild landscapes. His rationale comes from neither a dissection of recreational activity nor a reflection on the virtues of natural scenery, but from a description of his own wilderness recreation. The autobiographical *Alaska Wilderness*

(Marshall 1956/1970) serves as the evidentiary portrait. That book's opening paragraph reveals Marshall's attitude toward wildland recreation:

The story of this book logically begins in New York when I was eleven years old [the year would have been about 1912] and in bed with pneumonia. . . . Someone read me a story by one Captain Ralph Bonehill entitled *Pioneer Boys of the Great Northwest*. . . . It was a splendid narrative of two lads and their fathers who accidentally joined the Lewis and Clark Expedition and went through the glorious adventures of the most thrilling of all American explorations. My ideology was definitely formed on a Lewis and Clark pattern . . . the great adventure. (Marshall 1956/1970: 1)

The sentiment continues over the following paragraphs, in which Marshall reflects on his life as a career forester (he earned his Ph.D. in plant physiology at Johns Hopkins in 1930), a career that allowed him to be in the natural world but that still lacked the critical element of thrill: "nowhere was there the adventure of Lewis and Clark." That adventure connected the mental and physical worlds: "Mental adventure and physical adventure were in reality the same thing" (Marshall 1956/1970: 2). His quest led Marshall to the wilds of Alaska, where he found a vast landscape suitable to his desires. On

Figure 7.1. Emphasis on any of three of Leopold's five "components of the recreational process" leads to a recreation "expert."

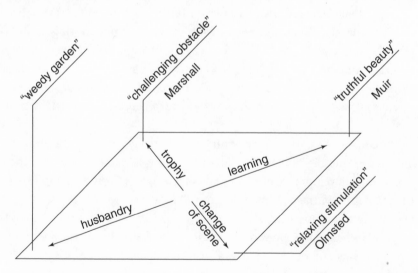

a seven-day backpack journey there, he and his companions covered ninety miles:

With brute strength we simply tore our way through the brush. . . . It was snowing steadily . . . [so that] our rests [were] chilly and uncomfortable and our footing [was] very slippery. . . . The sedge tussocks . . . would roll over, plunging us into the muck. . . . We would grit our teeth, gather energy, and pull ourselves up . . . only to do it all over again within the next twenty paces. Nevertheless, there was genuine exhilaration in triumphing over the toughest conceivable travel. (Marshall 1956/1970: 51–52)

Marshall makes clear his enthusiasm for the rugged and demanding in his outdoor recreation. In describing Marshall's teenage explorations of New York's Adirondack Mountains, Mitchell stresses the importance of speed and endurance in the experiences:

Bob and [his brother] George circled Lower, Middle, and Upper Saranac lakes afoot—a one-day stroll of a mere 41 miles. "It took us 698 minutes," Bob wrote with characteristic precision in one of his record books. "Taking out the [time] spent in stops . . . we covered the 41 miles in 613 minutes at the rate of a mile in 14 minutes and 57 seconds." Thus began Bob Marshall's extraordinary odometric account over the years of all his one-day hikes of 30 miles or more. There would be several hundred, more than sixty in the Adirondacks alone, a few running on incredibly to 60 miles or more. The man liked to walk. (J. Mitchell 1985: 14)

The longer the walk, the faster the walk, the more vertical the walk, the more unsettled the weather during the walk, the more difficult the conditions generally encountered along the walk, the better for Robert Marshall.

Comparisons with Leopold's five components suggest Marshall's strong linkage to the spirit of trophy. It was the achievement of success under difficulty, whether or not symbolized tangibly with an object, that marked his sense of wildland recreation (fig. 7.1). To be honest, he engaged the understanding of nature; on that first grueling Alaska trip he admits to sampling forest stands, testing tree seedling establishment, collecting rock samples, and evaluating animal feeding habits. He enjoyed the change of scene and relished isolation in nature, but the challenging aspects of travel and survival in a difficult natural world capture the essence of his outdoor recreation. For Marshall, nature was the challenging obstacle.

JOHN MUIR   As with Robert Marshall, the recreational goals of John Muir—prominently associated with the creation of Yosemite and other early national parks and with formation of the Sierra Club—are revealed by a consideration of the activities Muir pursued as his outdoor recreation. Although often considered either a wild adventurer engaging in spectacular stunts of mountaineering or a cloudy-eyed mystic pursuing obscure religious experiences, John Muir spent most of his time in a much more commonplace and accessible activity: nature study. Muir's first summer in the Sierra unrolls as a season of learning, what Muir describes as a time of "inexhaustible study and pleasure" (Muir 1911/1987: 50–51). Dissection of Muir's activities identifies seven characteristics, three of which seem particularly critical (the four not treated here are solitude, wildness, brotherhood, and breadth of the natural world). First, the characteristic of observation is the foundation underlying all the others. Early in his first summer, Muir eagerly anticipated the opportunity for "good centers of observation" from which he would be able "to learn something of the plants, animals, and rocks." Most of his subsequent days involved looking intensely at flowers and trees, domes and skies. He drew what he saw; he described in long passages what he saw: environmental situations, changing conditions, differences between superficially similar features. Second, the sense of discovery permeates Muir's continuing observation. Whether new tree species, new flowers, new birds, new cliff faces, new weather, or novel expressions of phenomena he had already encountered in his travels, Muir proclaimed a constant discovery of an infinitely rich natural world: "every tree calls for special admiration." Third, in spite of his penchant for invoking the divine, his feet remained solidly on the ground, his eyes on the flowers, his mind on science. I have characterized him as a "rational romantic," citing his embrace of conventional explanations for "mysterious odd things . . . the natural and common is more truly marvelous and mysterious than the so-called supernatural." In sum, Muir's outdoor recreation focused on study and learning: "I tremble with excitement in the dawn of these glorious mountain sublimities, but I can only gaze and wonder, and, like a child, gather here and there a lily, half hoping I may be able to study and learn in years to come" (quoted in Vale and Vale 1998: 22, 25, 94, 138). Think how different is Muir's attitude toward nature from that of Robert Marshall.

Among Leopold's five recreational components, the perception of natural process is most closely linked to the core of Muir's outdoor recreation (fig. 7.1). Change of scene, isolation in nature, even trophy—all were elements in Muir's activities, but the pursuit of understanding, beginning with scientific understanding, is its essence. Nature, for Muir, appeared less a relaxing stimulus or a challenging obstacle than a truthful beauty.

THE EXPERTS COMPARED Comparisons of the four experts encourage insights into American recreation in wild landscapes. Olmsted, Marshall, and Muir lay stress on different components of Leopold's vision. Olmsted stresses change of scene, Marshall focuses on trophy, and for Muir the prime consideration is perception of natural process. Each has his distinctive vision of the natural world—Olmsted sees a relaxing stimulus, Marshall a challenging obstacle, Muir a truthful beauty—and thus of recreational traditions. In teasing apart various motivations and elaborating on different themes, our experts suggest the richness of recreational behavior.

The remaining two components in Leopold's scheme raise confounding considerations. All four of the experts, and arguably everyone else who engages in outdoor recreation, elevate isolation in nature as a virtue, although the degree of removal from the human world they consider necessary to achieve ideal isolation varies enormously. It is a far cry from Robert Marshall's Brooks Range of Alaska to Frederick Law Olmsted's Yosemite Valley, genteel by comparison even in the 1860s. Even for Muir, solitude appeared as close as a saunter from camp. For Leopold himself "isolation in nature" happened in a tamarack swamp "just above the highway" in central Wisconsin or beside a frozen pond in the winter Iowa farm country (Leopold 1949/1970: 56, 120), although he also prized the bigness of such places as the Gila wilderness along the Arizona–New Mexico border.

The fifth component, husbandry, appears in a variety of contemporary recreational activities—Sierra Club work trips, Nature Conservancy restoration projects, the National Parks Conservation Association student conservation program, federal land agency volunteers, support groups for particular parks and other reserves, prairie planting festivals, savanna restoration parties, protective watches for rare spawning fish or threatened breeding birds. Nature, needing a nurturing human hand, becomes in this recreation tradition a weedy garden. Leopold recognized this component among wildland professionals: "We foresters and game managers might logically pay for, instead of being paid for, our job as husbandmen of wild crops" (Leopold 1949/1970: 175); he urged a "sense of husbandry" among farmers and conservationists alike. If his array of the five components in an ascending hierarchy of maturity, with the higher levels replacing the lower as sensitivity to nature develops, accurately anticipates outdoor recreation in the future, may

we all someday be planting willow sprigs on eroded stream banks or trapping cowbirds in Kirtland warbler habitat rather than hiking or white-water
rafting in wild landscape reserves?

Reflections

In spite of assertions that leisure activities represent only trivial and superficial behaviors (Lowenthal 1962, R. White 1995), outdoor recreation connects people to nature. The connections vary enormously, as we have seen.
Any individual observer may lament some activities or even disavow them
as heretical while celebrating others, but the richness of recreational encounters tells of more than something to be casually dismissed. Even Aldo
Leopold, recall, described the most general motivation for outdoor recreation as *contact* with nature.

Contact or connection, however, may assume vastly different forms. If
we assume that more gentle and constructive connections to the natural
world are to be desired—a virtue advocated by essentially everyone who expresses concern for the environment—how can we embrace equally all
of Leopold's components or all of the recreational traditions? Particularly
problematic are those activities that stress trophy seeking, human achievement pitted against the obstacle of nature (e.g., Coello 1989, Daniel 1990,
Davis 1993, Briggs 1996, Chavez 1996, Morrison 2003a). Is it possible that
recreations so commonly accepted, typically advocated, often celebrated by
those who consider themselves environmentally sensitive—rock climbing,
white-water rafting, endurance hiking, BASE jumping, bicycling—spring
from the same motivation as dirt biking, snowmobiling, ORV riding, jet skiing, and other amusements that appeal to the carnival-ride mentality? The
first group may lack the mechanical devices of the second, but both offer
opportunities to feel a sense of achievement gained through mettle testing
and thrill seeking *against* the natural world. How different are those activities that emphasize contemplation or scientific learning, pursuits that more
gently bond people to nature! (See Sax 1980 for a contrary perspective.)
John Muir may tremble with excitement to know and learn, but how many
of us respond?

Perhaps the same point underlies what several others suggest about
recreational development in the national parks. The geographer Stanford
Demars, in his thoughtful history of tourists and tourism in Yosemite,
defends the "average" visitor rather than idealizing the "wilderness" user
and observes that the "museum value [of the national parks] is likely to be

the most durable in the long run" (Demars 1991: 153). John White, the superintendent at Sequoia for periods spanning three decades, suggests that the "distinct" national park atmosphere should be considered paramount when we think about recreation in the parks. His invocation of atmosphere elevates the importance of motivation and experience, what Dilsaver and Tweed (1990: 157–58) equate with "education and enrichment." The same word highlights a cautionary comment by Carl P. Russell, longtime superintendent at Yosemite, whose sense prompts Vale and Vale (1994: 161) to suggest that "the tossing of Frisbees . . . threatens the atmosphere of [the parks] more than the presence of tent cabins . . . or strings of mules." The popular writer Ben Long (2001), in deploring snowmobiles in Yellowstone, may unknowingly be questioning a host of other recreations as well: "It's the carnival atmosphere that comes along with hundreds of zippy little machines [that] overshadow [and] out-muscle nature." Even the formal policy statement from the National Park Service rejects those recreation activities that "unreasonably interfere with the atmosphere of peace and tranquility of the natural soundscape" (National Park Service 2001). The character of the national park experience, then, rather than the impact on the natural world, dominates these interpretations.

When we analyze the appropriateness of recreational activities in nature reserves, then, it is not sufficient to array a list of recreational pursuits, evaluate the environmental impact of each, conduct user surveys to test preferences and acceptances, and set policy accordingly. Such considerations must be tackled by a mind sympathetic to the democratic tradition of nature reserves (Foresta 1984, Demars 1991, Rosenzweig and Blackmar 1992). Moreover, a single and universal identification of appropriateness, applicable across the array of protected landscape types, itself seems inappropriate. Nonetheless, thought should be given to the motivations that prompt various forms of recreation in any nature reserve and the desirability of encouraging one over another. Whether visitors ride in a car or walk, spend a night in a hotel or camp, wander a hundred yards from a road at Wisconsin's Horicon National Wildlife Refuge or trek a hundred miles over Alaska tundra in Gates of the Arctic National Park, a critical component of behavior and activity appropriate for wild landscape preserves is its contribution to growth and enhancement of the human heart.

8 CONSERVATION ORGANIZATIONS

In its annual assessment of conservation groups, *Outside* magazine typically lauds the small-scale, local, grass-roots organizations and jabs critically at the large, national, mainline associations. Crediting the Montana school-teacher Gene Sentz as the "driving force" behind the Forest Service's decision to ban oil and gas exploration in the Rocky Mountain Front, *Outside* identified a "change in the way environmental battles are waged": "In an era when some accuse the national conservation shops of corporate elitism and Beltway blindness, the Gene Sentzes of the world are gradually becoming biodiversity's new best friends. We've arrived at the age of the little guy" (*Outside*, April 1999: 65–66). Steven Fox similarly celebrates the "amateur tradition" of "the little guy," although he recognizes that amateurs need the work of professionals: "The radical amateur was the driving force in conservation history. The movement depended on professional conservationists and government agencies for expertise, staying power, organization, and money. The amateurs by contrast provided high standards, independence, integrity" (Fox 1981/1985: 333). Both *Outside* and Fox strike a contemporary cord: praise for local perspectives, cynicism about long-established institutions, faith that wisdom will emerge from amateurs. It is a view that cuts across twenty-first-century American society, almost without regard for an individual's political stance or the particulars of an issue.

Where nature protection is concerned, this view raises questions that reverberate within the worlds of both intellectual understanding and practical decision making: What is the collective structure of the nongovernment conservation movement? Do conservation organizations simply repeat each other in voice and policy? Does virtue in nature protection lie in individuals and groups detached from the centers of power and influence? Should admiration for organizations reflect the degree to which they are radical and aggressive? Underlying these questions is a more general and fundamental query: Who *should* speak for nature protection?

A Myriad of Groups

Hundreds, perhaps thousands of organizations populate the platforms on which nature-protection issues are debated (Wirth 1980, Ferguson 1985, Stegner 1985, *Conservation Directory* 2001). These groups range in size from a few individuals to the four million members of the National Wildlife Federation, in purpose from maintaining open green space to protecting biodiversity, in tactics from lobbying Congress to staging public spectacles. Some groups emerge to confront an enemy only to fade as controversy wanes. Others grow and strengthen, perhaps reinventing themselves to continue the battle on new fronts. Mainline groups offer organizational histories that tell much about American nature-protection sentiment and motivation.

THE NATURE CONSERVANCY In 1915 scholars who identified with the then-emerging science of ecology organized themselves as the Ecological Society of America (ESA); Victor Shelford, animal ecologist at the University of Chicago, and Robert Wolcott, at the University of Nebraska, joined to make the initial proposal. The group's first members—totaling 158—came largely from universities and the U.S. Forest Service. It had two purposes: to promote the scientific study of plants and animals in environmental contexts and to deal with the problem of disappearing natural areas—losses associated with the ongoing development of the American landscape— where such scientific study might be pursued. The tensions created by the contrasting purposes—should the society focus on scientific research or political activism?—led to a split in 1946. The parent group continued on as a professional scholarly association; the offspring, the Ecologists Union, dedicated itself to issues of nature protection. In 1950 the secondary group, renaming itself after a quasi-public association in Britain dedicated to land protection, became the Nature Conservancy (Behlen 1981, Blair 1991, Grove 1992).

Within a few years the conservancy initiated the activity that would become its distinguishing mission, the purchasing of land, and it did so by acting as a facilitator for another grass-roots organization. A five-person group spearheaded by Gloria and Tony Anable, the Mianus River Gorge Conservation Committee, had organized in 1953 to work against the development of a deep valley in New York. Lacking the funds it needed to complete the land purchase, the committee accepted a loan of $7,500 from the Old Dominion Foundation through the Nature Conservancy, with the stipulation that the money would be repaid to the conservancy for other conservation projects. In 1955 the Mianus River Gorge Preserve thus became the first sanctuary of the Nature Conservancy, which subsequently embarked on a program of lending money to local groups for land purchases; the local groups would then raise the funds necessary to repay the borrowed money to the conservancy's revolving fund. Wealthy sympathizers—early notables include Lila Acheson Wallace of the *Reader's Digest* and Katharine Ordway, a Minnesota mining heiress—donated funds to the conservancy, which engaged in a number of notable projects over the following years, including Dome Island on New York's Lake George and Sunken Forest on Fire Island, Corkscrew Swamp in Florida, Volo and Wauconda bogs in Illinois, and an area of mountainous forest along the Pacific coast, the Northern California Coast Range Preserve (Blair 1986, Grove 1992, Byers 2001).

The procedures established in the Mianus River Gorge project would be repeated thousands of times in the decades to follow. By the turn of the century, the national office had enabled local chapters to protect 12 million acres in the United States and more than 80 million acres elsewhere in the world. Individual projects have varied from less than an acre to more than 300,000 acres (the Gray Ranch of New Mexico). Biological science remains central to the Nature Conservancy's protectionist activities. State natural heritage programs—detailed databases on species and communities—allow activists to identify rare and threatened species and areas in need of attention. The conservancy's projects vary widely: they encompass land easements as well as outright purchases; agreements with landowners to donate biologically unimportant land that the organization may then sell to replenish its funds; and transfers of purchased land to other groups or government agencies. The 1,400 preserves administered directly by the Nature Conservancy make up the largest private system of nature reserves in the world. As might be expected of an organization whose activities require substantial sums of money, the Nature Conservancy depends as much on individual philanthropists and major corporations as on its dedicated volunteers and its million of dues-paying members (Gilbert 1986).

In sum, the Nature Conservancy remains wedded to the patterns it established in 1950. It prizes species and habitats (nothing excites the conservancy as much as a rare species), sees the virtues of scientific rationales (as befits its roots), focuses entirely on its program of land purchases, and maintains its organizational strategy of working through local chapters coordinated by a national office. No other major conservation group combines these characteristics.

THE NATIONAL AUDUBON SOCIETY Similar to the Nature Conservancy in both its focus on biological nature and its birth from a scientific association, the National Audubon Society arose from strikingly different motivation and activist strategy. Protection of wild birds, especially plume birds, from indiscriminate hunting emerged as one of the goals of the American Ornithologists' Union (AOU), a professional organization formed in 1883 to promote the newly crystallizing science of bird study. A leader of the AOU, George Bird Grinnell, formed in 1886 an "Audubon Society" to serve as a "popular arm" for the protection effort (Barrow 1998: 118) and a year later published the first issue of *Audubon Magazine*. Although at one time it had nearly 18,000 members, the society subsequently disbanded and the magazine died, in part because of the desire of professional ornithologists to continue collecting bird and egg specimens (Kastner 1986, Graham 1990, Fischer 2002). The bird-protection effort, revitalized within the AOU a decade later under the leadership of Harriet Hemenway, promoted the organization of the Massachusetts Audubon Society in 1896. Over the next few years at least nine more state Audubon societies were established. In 1905 the various state groups, now numbering three dozen, affiliated as the National Association of Audubon Societies for the Protection of Wild Birds and Animals (in 1901 they had agreed to a collective federation, then called the National Committee of the Audubon Societies). Under the strong leadership of William Dutcher, a successful businessman in insurance, the bird-protection effort this time persisted, a reflection of the strength of amateur bird-watchers, "a politically powerful interest group that was generally more aware of the threats facing native birds and often unsympathetic to the collecting demands of scientists" (Barrow 1998: 153).

Although linked through the national association, the state Audubon societies retained their autonomy. Each lobbied its state's legislature to adopt the "Model Law," an AOU document that articulated specific bird-protection goals: classification of birds as either game (ducks and geese, rails, coots, shorebirds, grouses, quails, turkeys, and pheasants) or nongame species, prohibition of the hunting of all nongame birds, and protection of eggs except for scientific collections. By 1901, eleven states had adopted such legislation. The Audubon societies also assumed responsibility for patrolling the federal wildlife refuges that Theodore Roosevelt had initiated, using funds raised by the artist and author Abbott Thayer. The 1905 murder of an Audubon warden, Guy Bradley, by plume hunters in the Florida Everglades became a cause célèbre of bird protectionists. *Bird-Lore,* an independent magazine begun in 1899 by Frank Chapman (avian artist, Audubon activist, and curator of birds at the American Museum of Natural History), eventually became the publication of the national association, transformed in 1941 to *Audubon Magazine,* and later more simply *Audubon* (Graham 1990, Orr 1992). But national issues—beginning with efforts to prod Congress to prohibit the commercial trade in wild birds, which culminated in the federal legislation of 1918—demanded a stronger centralized organization, which was realized formally in 1940 when the national association was replaced by the National Audubon Society. Still, it was not until after the Second World War that "a conscious effort by John Baker . . . reach[ed] out beyond the Northeast [to] finally establish . . . a truly national organization" (Graham 1990: 176). It was the 1960s before the organization initiated its first vigorous campaign for new members. Broadening of environmental concerns followed in the 1970s, although biological nature would remain its primary focus. Its main office remains in New York City, unusual for a national conservation group, perhaps reflecting the group's origins and its ties to funding sources and the publishing industry (Graham 1990: 239). Even with a strong central office, the group retains more than five hundred local chapters, some of them operating somewhat independently. Although never as active in buying land as the Nature Conservancy, the Audubon Society, including some active chapters, has expanded its sanctuaries from two small holdings in 1915 to more than 250,000 acres in 200 units. Its membership totaled 550,000 in 2000.

The National Audubon Society today preserves much of its original character, although it exhibits as well a more contemporary personality. It maintains a focus on wildlife, but so do most other groups, so National Audubon's emphasis seems less distinctive than it once did. Connections between living nature and other matters draw the organization into a wide range of environmental affairs. Its original humanistic motivation remains, now expanded by scientific rationales. The two perspectives of humanism and science may conflict: controversy arises within the membership over such matters as sport hunting and oil drilling on the society's land (J. Mitchell 1979–80). Its strategy of influencing legislation and promoting sensitivity through publications continues. The magazine *Audubon,* in the 1970s called "the most beautiful magazine in the world" and winner of National Magazine Awards, may not be quite as beautiful today, but it comes close. Its organization of active chapters united under a strong central office resembles its structure in the past.

THE NATIONAL WILDLIFE FEDERATION A third conservation organization also began with a focus on biological concerns but its origin differed dramatically from both the science roots of the Nature Conservancy and the antikilling base of the Audubon societies: it emerged from a Depression-era desire to maintain game populations for recreational hunting. In 1936 Jay Norwood (Ding) Darling, as head of Franklin Roosevelt's Biological Survey, arranged a national meeting to bring together groups interested in wildlife in order to encourage the development of a single, and presumably more effective, conservation voice. This first North American Wildlife Conference involved two thousand people, including "farmers, sportsmen, and representatives of Boy Scouts and Girl Scouts, 4-H clubs, garden clubs, and women's clubs" (Allen 1987: 27). Although Darling wanted the leadership of the subsequently formed coordinating committee to include such groups as the National Council for State Garden Clubs—whose members were more likely to criticize than to celebrate sport hunting—decision-making powers remained concentrated among "organizations of sportsmen active in conservation" (Allen 1987: 31). This hunting-and-fishing perspective dominated the new organization, which in 1938 called itself the National Wildlife Federation.

The initial organizational vision, as expressed in the first North American Wildlife Conference, formed the structure of the subsequent National Wildlife Federation. The private and public wildlife groups in each state organized coordinating state bodies, following Darling's positive impressions of an umbrella organization of 508 conservation groups in Indiana. The twenty-five or so state wildlife federations in 1936 expanded until virtually all states had developed such coordinating groups. Each of these umbrella organizations, called affiliates, held an annual meeting to set policy, pass resolutions, and elect a delegate to attend the national conference. At the annual national meeting those delegates would adopt positions and urge actions deemed important at the regional or federal scale.

For more than twenty years, then, the National Wildlife Federation acted as a body both populist (delegates were elected) but executive (no general membership existed). In 1960 the new leader, Thomas Kimball, argued successfully for the creation of a new sort of member, the associate, who could join the National Wildlife Federation by simply paying an annual membership fee; Kimball saw this as a way of increasing the federation's political effectiveness. Some members of the group resisted this move, fearing "hordes of unaffiliated garden club members and birders . . . seiz[ing] control of an organization dominated by . . . hunters and fishermen" (Allen 1987: 69). But, bolstered by the launching of a glossy magazine, *National Wildlife*, the membership drive succeeded. By 1968 "the print order for *National Wildlife* was 340,000" (Allen 1987: 74), and by the 1990s the dues-paying members numbered more than a million; the *Conservation Directory* for 2001 identifies more than four million members.

From its beginning, the National Wildlife Federation emphasized providing the public with information on wildlife issues and influencing Congress both by fighting proposals considered destructive of wildlife or wildlife habitat and by seeking funding for wildlife improvement projects. Publications, sometimes scientific but more commonly popular (e.g., materials for elementary school children, wildlife stamps, *Ranger Rick* magazine) have long been a cornerstone of its activities. The federation, moreover, has seen wildlife as a broad category, and in 1937 it favored continuation of the Civilian Conservation Corps, protection of the wild character of the Quetico-Superior country (the Boundary Waters) of northern Minnesota, and curbing of pollution. In the same year a proposed resolution calling for constraint on the trapping of fur-bearing animals generated much opposition, but eventually it was adopted.

Like most major conservation organizations, the National Wildlife Federation through the years has become a more catholic environmental group. Nonetheless, it retains its focus on wild animal species and their habitats, although the resolutions adopted at recent annual meetings cover such issues as concern for the inner city and political campaign finance reform. The group appeals to a broad range of environmental enthusiasts, continues to claim that its primary strategy is educational—it publishes as much material for all age groups as any conservation organization—and maintains its sense of a federation with a national meeting of delegates, although it supports a strong office near Washington, D.C., to interact with government officials.

THE SIERRA CLUB Unlike the Nature Conservancy, the Audubon societies, and the National Wildlife Federation—all of which focused on biological nature—the Sierra Club sought protection for "scenic lands" generally (H. Jones 1965: 5) and the Yosemite landscape specifically. In 1892, in San Francisco, twenty-seven individuals—all male, unlike the creators of the Nature Conservancy and the Audubon societies—composed articles of incorporation for their new Sierra Club. Their identities suggest professional backgrounds that link the Sierra Club more closely to the early Nature Conservancy than to the National Wildlife Federation, and those backgrounds are linked not to biology but to the earth sciences, which perhaps contribute to the focus on scenery. These initial leaders included Warren Olney (San Francisco attorney) and John Branner (geologist at Stanford), William Armes and J. Senger (both on the faculty at the University of California, Berkeley), Mark Kerr (U.S. Geological Survey), David Starr Jordan (president of Stanford), William Johnson (U.S. Geological Survey), and Robert Martin Price (in graduate school at Berkeley) (H. Jones 1965: 10). Only President John Muir, amateur naturalist, successful author, and professional orchardist, might be called nonprofessional. The group's initial interest was protection of the Yosemite "forest reservation," as it was called in the authorizing congressional act of 1890, which created a reserve around the already existent state park but provided little on-ground protection (Ise 1961: 58–65). But it also pursued the strengthening of forest reserve policies generally and realizing park status for Mount Rainier (H. Jones 1965: 15–18). The club would succeed in ceding the Yosemite Grant (the state park around Yosemite Valley) to the national park in 1906, but it would fail to stop Congress from authorizing the damming of Hetch Hetchy Valley by the city of San Francisco in 1913 (Cohen 1988, H. Jones 1965).

Together with its protection efforts on behalf of federal land issues in Yosemite and the Sierra, the early Sierra Club functioned as an outing group, resembling a chummy New England hiking club more than a strident environmental organization (Sierra Club 1989). The first "high trip," a multiweek camping trip for members, explored the Yosemite Sierra in 1901, and this outing "was for generations a fixture in Club life" (Sierra Club 1992: 56). In addition, the Sierra Club pursued a wide range of recreational activities. It constructed buildings for recreational use in the California mountains, including LeConte Memorial Lodge on the floor of Yosemite Valley in 1902, Muir Lodge in Big Santa Anita Canyon, Parsons Memorial Lodge in the Yosemite high country in 1915, an alpine lodge on Mount Shasta in 1922, Clair Tappaan Lodge on Donner Summit in 1934, and a ski hut on Mount San Antonio in 1935. It sponsored or cosponsored other recreational facilities, including the cable that enables hikers to ascend Yosemite's Half Dome in 1919 and a trail connecting Yosemite Valley with the northern part of the park in 1921. It organized mountaineering trips and local walks. Its members, including David Brower, became innovators in the technological hardware that today is so much a part of modern rock climbing (Sierra Club 1992: 56–65). These recreational activities were not simply a means of generating public support for the club's landscape-protection aims, although club leaders recognized that they served such a purpose; they were an integral part of the reason for the club's existence. The original expressed purposes of the club identify recreation as a central reason for the group's existence: "to explore, enjoy, and render accessible" the wild lands of the Sierra. It seems reasonable to view the early Sierra Club as a group dedicated as much to recreation as to nature protection.

But this characterization fails to capture the personality of the Sierra Club after mid-century. The transition from a club narrowly concerned with California mountains, with camping trips, with protecting certain landscapes but embracing development generally (Schrepfer 1976, 1980) to the most sweeping, most strident, most skeptical, and most influential of major conservation groups developed after 1952, when the governing board created a new position of executive director and hired David Brower to fill it. Brower, involved with the club since the early 1930s, led the Sierra Club into national conservation battles and new arenas of debate: wild landscapes remained dominant—in the 1950s, Echo Park and the Wilderness Bill; in the 1960s, Glen Canyon and Grand Canyon, Redwoods and the North Cascades. But, in addition, the Brower-led organization pursued an aggressive publishing program of exhibit-format books, beginning with *This Is the American Earth* in 1960. It approved a resolution against pesticides in 1965, its first major policy position on an issue other than wild places. It initiated litigation on behalf of the wildness of Mineral King in the southern Sierra in 1969. It opposed nuclear power and economic growth in general in the late 1960s. The friction generated by these policies flared into a civil war over the Diablo Canyon nuclear power plant on the Southern California coast. This debate centered on whether the Sierra Club should seek accommodation with development interests (in this case a public utility)—honoring previous commitments to embrace construction, accepting the inevitability or even the desirability of growth—or should resist economic development in principle and pursue "a more militant, evangelical form of environmentalism" (Schrepfer 1992: 214). Although Brower was forced out as executive director in 1969, the Sierra Club remained on a course charted more by his vision than by his opponents': it opposed supersonic transport planes in 1971; held an urban environment conference in 1979; gave priority to city transportation in 1982; opposed the nuclear arms race in 1986; and expressed concern about genetic engineering, world trade, and human rights in the 1990s. At the close of the century the club became less alarmist in regard to human population growth, a reflection of its increasing commitment to traditionally liberal or left-wing politics. The organization retains its image as a "radical" mainline conservation group (T. Turner 1990). In 1996, club members elected a twenty-three-year-old as president, a sign of continued concern for change (Keegan 1996). Membership in 2002 reached more than 700,000, distributed among 65 chapters and 396 working groups.

Perhaps no conservation group has changed more than the Sierra Club. Over its lifetime, its focus has broadened, its motivations have diversified, its strategies have intensified. Only its organization has retained the spirit of its founders; it has always been strongly centralized, with headquarters in San Francisco, but since 1905 it has encouraged the creation of local chapters.

THE NATIONAL PARKS CONSERVATION ASSOCIATION Similar to the early Sierra Club in its focus on national parks and scenery, the National Parks Association emerged from a vision of one of the first leaders of the National Park Service. From 1917 Robert Sterling Yard—publisher, editor, and friend of Steven Mather—sat as informal chief of the new park service's informal education division. Mather, forever the benefactor of the national parks, paid his friend's salary. The position title was coined by Yard, who promoted the concept of the units of the National Park System as museums of natural history, museums that would popularize the study of natural science in the public schools and universities. Stymied by what he saw as indifference within the Park Service, however, Yard gathered nine other men, among them Charles Walcott, president of the Smithsonian Institution; the geologist Wallace Atwood of Harvard University; and the zoologist George Bird Grinnell, to form a separate nongovernmental body, the National Parks Education Committee. The new group's statement of its purposes, which included expansion of the park system, articulated its educational image for the parks: "to educate the public [about] . . . national parks . . . [and] to further . . . the national parks as classrooms and museums of Nature." Its first meeting, with seventy-two members, "all . . . leaders in science and education," was held in 1918. The following year the committee renamed itself the National Parks Association, but its primary purpose remained the same: "to interpret and popularize natural science by using the conspicuous scenery and the plant and animal exhibits of the national parks, now prominent in the public eye, for examples" (Miles 1995: 18, 25). Even the 1925 revision of its goals retained the "original emphasis on education," although the National Parks Association would become concerned with supporting the National Park System more generally.

An issue that dominated the work of the organization through most of its history was that of park standards. The National Parks Association, while defending the grand parks against commodity resource development, also actively opposed new parks in landscapes that it considered too common or that had inappropriate boundaries or authorized uses. The list of parks that the group opposed reads like a list devised by the National Cattlemen's Association or the American Mining Congress: Shenandoah, Mammoth Cave, Great Smoky Mountains (if its boundaries were to expand too far from the heart of the rugged mountain core), Grand Teton (its expansion onto the floor of Jackson Hole), Kings Canyon (without the canyon valleys desired by dam builders), and Olympic (an expansive park that would include commercially valuable forests). It also opposed many proposed parks that did not receive authorization, including those in a part of the Ouachita Mountains of Arkansas, the area around Mount Katahdin in Maine, and the Green Mountains of Vermont. In the 1930s, in fact, the association felt that the "National Park System was essentially complete" and that continued growth represented merely "bureaucratic expansionism of the Park Service." The reasons for such adherence to high standards reflect both a conviction that only the most extraordinary scenery should be protected within a national park and a fear that too aggressive a policy would generate a backlash against all parks (Miles 1995: 87, 92).

In the 1960s, under the leadership of Anthony Wayne Smith, the National Parks Association embarked upon a broadened mission with concerns outside the park system—watershed management, ecological forestry, pollution control, environmental protection, urban growth, suburban development, industrial expansion, and population growth. Appropriately, it changed its name to the National Parks and Conservation Association in 1970. Miles (1995: 214) suggests that this transformation was facilitated by the structure of the group as a "centralized, Washington, D.C.–based organization," presumably lacking a spatially dispersed and thus goal-fractured leadership. Fiscal crisis later in the 1970s prompted changes, a retrenchment in goals, and a refocusing on the National Park System. Its membership in 2000 totaled about 500,000.

In summary, then, through most of its history the National Parks Conservation Association (it has dropped the "and") has focused on the National Park System, defending both its landscapes against commodity resource and often recreational development and its integrity, as perceived by the association, against units it considers inferior. The group's initial motivation, revolving strongly around a vision of parks as natural history museums, has muted with time, although the association has remained committed to a sense that park landscapes serve human purposes (Miles 1994). Through much of its history, in fact, this group, like others, saw nature protection as part of the general development of American society, development that required a transformation of nature beyond the boundaries of landscape reserves. To realize its strategy of strengthening the National Park Service, the association has maintained its centralized organization in Washington, D.C., where it has access to both the legislative and executive branches of the federal government. It has no chapters or affiliates but it does have regional offices. The conclusion to the association's published history captures its vision:

The founders were of a privileged class of Americans. They were an elite—men who had achieved success in their professions, who were civic minded, and who sought to improve their society and the world. . . . They believed that people needed places where they could encounter and study nature, where they could be inspired and educated. They saw the national parks as an institution dedicated to this high purpose. (Miles 1995: 332)

THE WILDERNESS SOCIETY The Wilderness Society grew from a concern over, ironically, the popular success of the national parks. The story is told that in 1934, on a field trip in Tennessee during the annual meeting of the American Forestry Association (a group that promotes forest management), four men began to argue about the possibility of a new conservation group. The four men—Benton MacKaye and Bernard Frank, TVA foresters; Robert Marshall of the Office of Indian Affairs; and Harvey Broome, an attorney and leader in the Smoky Mountains Hiking Club—agreed that somehow, among all of the existing conservation organizations, none was really focused on wild landscapes protected against both commodity resource uses and recreational development. They contacted four others they thought to be like-minded: Harold Anderson, active in the Potomac Appalachian Trail Club; Ernest Oberholtzer, defender of the Quetico-Superior landscape of northern Minnesota; Aldo Leopold, wildlife ecologist at the University of Wisconsin; and Robert Sterling Yard, leader in the National

Parks Association. The following year they had a new conservation group, the Wilderness Society.

The organizers agreed that members should be few and "carefully selected" (Fox 1984: 9); no large membership was sought (Cohen 1988: 111). Leadership initially rested largely with Marshall, who ran the group as "a virtual oligarchy" (Fox 1981/1985: 211). But other leaders also acted from firm convictions and strong wills: a robust suspicion of capitalism permeated the thinking of at least two of the most prominent and energetic of the organizers, Marshall and MacKaye (Sutter 1999), and the obstreperous Yard had antagonized his fellows at the National Parks Association, whom he found too conservative and accommodating. Both symbolically and literally, the leadership of the new Wilderness Society marked a change in American conservation: what had been a concern nearly exclusive to moderate Republicans became a political activity attractive to the Roosevelt administration and Democrats both mainline and radical.

The vision that united the original eight, however, was neither political nor prompted by disdain for landscapes with dammed rivers and logged forests (although they did disdain them); it emanated from their outrage at recreational development in national parks. Their anger especially zeroed in on roads, the most vile of evils that had compromised even the parks: "The craze is to build all the highways possible everywhere . . . to barber and manicure wild America. . . . Our duty is clear" (*Living Wilderness*, first issue). The society's distrust of the National Park Service ran deep, and it looked to another agency, the Forest Service, as the best means to keep wild landscapes free of roads. The linkage between the Wilderness Society and the Forest Service involved personnel as well as the common enemy of the National Park Service: five of the thirteen councilors that governed the society in 1937 either worked for or had been employed by the Forest Service. Perhaps the society's allegiance to the Forest Service is responsible for its opposition to the creation of Kings Canyon National Park in 1939: the Forest Service opposed the park because with the park's creation it would lose control of a large piece of southern Sierra Nevada landscape (Dilsaver 1990: 117–19; Dilsaver and Tweed 1990: 210). Park advocates suggested the Wilderness Society should be renamed the Bewildered Society. Even as recently as the 1960s, the society, focused on the Wilderness Bill and fearful of alienating the Forest Service, only reluctantly worked for the creation of the North Cascades National Park, a project that would transfer lands out of the national forest system (Cohen 1988: 313).

Through the 1940s and into the 1950s, however, the Wilderness Society grew to become, in one historian's words, one of the two (along with the Sierra Club) "most innovative, militant forces in conservation" (Fox 1984: 14). It would grow to have goals and strategies similar to those of the Sierra Club (Cohen 1988: 111–12). The society fought the National Park Service over units unworthy and excessively developed (Ise 1961: 437); it championed the Quetico-Superior wilderness; it fought salvage timber sales at Olympic National Park; it helped lead the successful fight against Echo Park Dam in Dinosaur National Monument. Its celebrated cause during this time, and perhaps its crowning achievement, was the passage of the Wilderness Act in 1964. The Wilderness Society's strong advocacy of this legislation drove a wedge between the group and the Forest Service, perhaps also evidence of "innovative militancy" (Fox 1984: 13).

Suggesting much less innovation, much more the values of the conservative mainstream, the early Wilderness Society leaders wanted roadless landscapes in part for leisure time, for recreation. Consider six of the founding eight: Robert Marshall, the very model of the wilderness trekker; Benton MacKaye, conceiver of the Appalachian Trail; two leaders of eastern hiking clubs; Robert Sterling Yard, promoter of wild landscapes as outdoor museums; and Aldo Leopold, promoter of wilderness for the maintenance of "primitive arts" (Leopold 1949/1970: 193). The society never developed into an outing club, a promoter of the elaborate outdoor recreation activities so much a part of the Sierra Club, although for a while it did sponsor trips in a program called "A Way to the Wilderness." The suggestion that recreation was important to the society does not mean that other purposes served to mask a focus on elitist leisure-time activities. Compare these men's interest in recreation with the typical environmentalist's disdain for any suggestion that recreation is a legitimate purpose of national parks and other wild landscapes.

Into the 1960s and 1970s, the Wilderness Society, like so many other conservation groups, experienced fiscal problems and endured quarrels between leaders and governing boards. Recovery in the 1980s and 1990s led the group into a somewhat broadened set of concerns, although not nearly so extensive as those that engaged either the Sierra Club or the National Audubon Society. Wild landscapes remained its primary focus. In recent years it has promoted a "network of wildlands" to facilitate protection of wild landscape as "a part of everyday life," notably in the Chesapeake watershed (Beach 2001; see also Watkins 1994b). Unlike any other major conservation group, it ceased publication of its major magazine in 1995—initially *Living Wilderness,* after 1982 more simply *Wilderness*—citing the general awareness of wild landscape issues in American society as sufficiently strong to no longer require still another fund-demanding magazine. The society's membership in 2000 totaled about 300,000.

In sum, the Wilderness Society has been a group dedicated to protecting roadless areas on the federal lands. It initially stressed roadless recreation, although ethical rationales increased. True to its goal of influencing the federal lands, the society has maintained a strong central office in Washington, D.C. Perhaps not so much as the National Parks Conservation Association but more than the Sierra Club, the Wilderness Society remains largely true to its name.

SOME OTHER MAINLINE GROUPS The history of the *Defenders of Wildlife* tells much about its initial focus and its subsequent motivation (Herscovici 1985, Jasper and Nelkin 1992, Cecil 1997). It began in 1925 as the Anti–Steel Trap League, an organization dedicated specifically to eliminating the trapping of wild animals and more generally to treating all animals humanely. The group's creation story attributes its founding to the outrage of the adventurer Edward Breck when he came upon a trapped bear in Nova Scotia, but other people concerned about inhumane treatment of animals were also instrumental in its founding. Lucy Furman, for example, who campaigned against the selling of chicks and ducklings at Easter, served as an officer in the league's early years. Too, part of the reason for the group's formation may have been a desire to draw attention to animals in wild and rural landscapes, in contrast to the humane societies' preoccupation with pets and urban draft animals. In 1947 the group reorganized and became the Defenders of Furbearers, but the campaign against trapping continued; in the 1950s, the defenders criticized First Lady Mamie Eisenhower for wearing fur, recalling the turn-of-the-century protests against bird feathers in women's hats. The humanistic leanings of the organization also remained. The group's newsletter offered a revealing mix of exposés of the cruelty of leg traps and of sport hunting with stories of wild animals befriended as household pets. Renamed the Defenders of Wildlife in 1959, the organization gradually moved away from an emotional appreciation of animals to a more detached and scientific perspective.

In highlighting the group's major concerns today, a spokesperson identifies support for biodiversity and international wildlife generally and protection of bears, wolves, dolphins, and porpoises specifically; defense of endangered species legislation; support for the public lands; and support for constraints on predator control programs (Cecil 1997). The group cooperates with other conservation organizations in national efforts and its name appears among the plaintiffs in wildlife lawsuits. It publishes a periodical, *Defenders,* claims 250,000 members, and operates from headquarters in Washington, D.C.

Like the Defenders of Wildlife, the *Izaak Walton League* began with a focus on wild animals, although its motivation was nothing like the Anti–Steel Trap League's: it championed a constant supply of fish for the creel (Fox 1981/1985; see also Robinson 1975, Searle 1978, Graham 1990). Spawned in 1922 by a Chicago advertising man, Will H. Dilg, the Izaak Walton League appealed especially to midwestern men who liked to fish and hunt, activities that seemed threatened by modernity. They were given to "a fretful looking back to the old fishing hole" and were moved to act by "a dawning sense that modern progress was polluting it, filling it in, paving it over." Although the league's organizational framework included a nine-person executive committee ("mostly business and professional people of middle income from the Midwest"), Dilg remained its policy maker, its energizer, its visionary (Fox 1981/1985: 161, 162). From Chicago, Dilg—far ahead of his time—worked with campaigning rhetoric and a provocative magazine, after 1923 called *Outdoor America,* to generate a national membership. By 1925, when other conservation groups counted members in the hundreds or a few thousand, the league claimed more than 100,000, organized into regional chapters and state divisions. No other group came close to the league in size. Nor did other conservation groups share the league's breadth of issues: bag limits on waterfowl, cleanup of polluted waters, wetland protection, forest fire control, reforestation. Fox (1981: 168–69) suggests that its first major achievement, reflecting Dilg's energy and political connections, was securing congressional authorization for the Upper Mississippi River National Fish and Wildlife Refuge in 1924. Arguably at least as important was the league's work to keep roadless the national forest land in northern Minnesota, land that would become the Boundary Waters Canoe Area Wilderness, thereby inspiring the national forest primitive area policy of 1929; Aldo Leopold and Seth Gordon, both league members, arranged a compromise agreeable to opposing factions in the Boundary Waters dispute (Searle 1978).

The league declined in influence thereafter. In 1926 Dilg was removed from leadership by an executive committee unhappy with his fiscal policies—

a common tale in the histories of conservation groups. The committee opposed the creation of Kings Canyon National Park unless the boundaries
omitted two potential dam and reservoir sites, a position perhaps resulting
from its alliance with the antipark Forest Service and American Forestry
Association (Fox 1981/1985: 214). In adopting this position, the league
became an adversary of the Sierra Club and the National Parks Association,
both of which for a time opposed the Kings Canyon National Park proposals but for the opposite reason—the *omission* of those same dam sites. During the 1940s, led by Kenneth Reid, the league returned to national prominence as the leading opponent to the proposed transfer of federal lands
in the West to state administrations, a cause championed in the popular
press by Bernard DeVoto, who effectively borrowed Reid's term "land grab";
DeVoto would describe the league as his "favorite conservation group" (Fox
1981/1985: 226). As Reid's health declined, so did the league (Fox 1981/1985:
252–53), although it joined with other conservation groups in the classic
battles over Echo Park and the Wilderness Bill. A mark of modernity, even,
may be seen in the appearance of the league's name in lawsuits filed in
opposition to clear-cutting on the national forests and mining in Forest Service wilderness (Robinson 1975: 79; 191).

What began as a group of midwesterners organized to perpetuate the
manly recreational activities of their boyhood, then, evolved to embrace such
concerns as wilderness, public lands, and water pollution. Today the league
operates from a central office in suburban Washington, D.C., has nearly two
dozen state divisions, and lists a modest membership of 50,000.

Another conservation group rallied around goals located at the opposite end of the political spectrum. The roots of *Greenpeace* are wrapped
around protests against underground nuclear testing by the United States in
1971 (Brown and May 1991). Jim Bohlen, a peace advocate and former U.S.
military careerist, joined the Quakers Irving and Dorothy Stowe and Paul
Cote, a law student, on a trip by small boat from Vancouver, British Columbia, to the bomb test site on Amchitka Island, in the Aleutians of Alaska.
Their action, prompted partly by the Sierra Club's failure to stand against
the violation of Amchitka's wild landscape, was inspired by both the general
Quaker tradition of "bearing witness" to objectionable human activity and
the specific Quaker action of sailing a boat into the hydrogen bomb testing
grounds on the South Pacific's Bikini atoll in 1958. They christened their
boat *Greenpeace,* a word that linked concern for the environment with sentiment against war. Although the bomb test was carried out, the American

military canceled subsequently tests on Amchitka, perhaps in response to press coverage of the protest. A couple of years later, the Vancouver group received a call for aid from activists in the South Pacific, headed by David McTaggart, a former California ski resort administrator who planned a boat venture to the atoll of Moruroa, where the French planned to conduct above-ground tests of hydrogen bombs. The ensuing protest, involving a ramming of the protest boat and beatings of its crew, led to a promise by the French that they would engage only in below-ground blasts. The link to more conventional environmental concerns followed in 1975 when protestors against whaling, initially organized as Project Ahab, adopted the strategy of using small boats to harass Soviet whalers in the Pacific. Disagreements developed between Greenpeace members who wanted to broaden their efforts to include the whaling issue and those who preferred a narrower focus on antinuclear efforts.

The outcome of the dispute gave us the modern organization. In essence, environmental matters became not just an additional concern but the primary focus. In 1976, in addition to organizing boats to harass whalers, Greenpeace began protesting the harvesting of harp seals on the ice of the Canadian Arctic, continuing the style that had proved effective in the whaling protests: confrontation, harassment, public display, and strong news coverage. The publicity apparently generated a positive response among people concerned with the environment, and "within the next couple of years groups calling themselves Greenpeace independently sprang up from Tennessee to Saskatchewan" (Brown and May 1991: 39). But the ad hoc nature of this blossoming led to rivalries between groups, disputes over issues and strategies, and growing debts. These controversies reached their peak when the Vancouver group, money-poor but claiming chronological primacy, sued the San Francisco group for violation of trademark, and the San Francisco group countersued for slander. By the late 1970s, the still centrally positioned McTaggart arranged a truce and compromise: a new umbrella office in the Netherlands, called Greenpeace International, would coordinate the autonomous local groups, which would continue their particular campaigns, send representatives to an international council, and contribute a portion of their income to the central office.

With that reorganization, the history of Greenpeace shifts to its most alarming incident: in 1985 French commandos sank its boat *Rainbow Warrior,* killing a man on board. The number of issues Greenpeace tackled expanded to include dumping of nuclear wastes and burning of toxic materials at sea; river and air pollution; and protection of tropical forests, Antarctica, endangered species, and fur-bearing animals. Whatever the issue, the Greenpeace strategy remains consistent, with a focus on the news-catching public display—balloons overhead, banners draped from smokestacks, signs on buildings, people costumed as animals or dressed in the protective suits worn by people who must handle toxic materials, as well as nonviolent harassment by people on foot or in boats. Its decentralized structure persists. The Greenpeace membership in the United States totals 420,000.

Sharing skepticism about modernity with both conservative Waltonians and the more radical Greenpeacers, the founders of *Friends of the Earth* embraced the conventional strategies of the former with an ideology closer to the latter (Brower 1990, Cohen 1988). When David Brower was removed as executive director of the Sierra Club in 1969, he organized three new groups to pursue his activist environmental policies—a think tank, a group to disseminate voter information, and a more classic pressure group— and he took much of the Sierra Club's senior staff with him (Cohen 1988). Whether inspired by a line of John Muir's or a suggestion of Brower's wife, Anne, Friends of the Earth became the name of Brower's new conservation organization; the acronym, FOE, was seen as suggesting the group's opposition to all who would despoil the planet. Friends of the Earth was known for greater stridency and fewer compromises than Brower had been able to manage as leader of the Sierra Club, which he described as "so eager to appear reasonable that it goes soft, undercuts the strong grassroots efforts . . . as if the new professionalization and prioritization requires rampant tenderization" (Brower 1990: 439; cf. Gifford 1995, Olin 1995). FOE issued a magazine/journal, paperback books, and ten exhibit-format books. It generated three dozen affiliated groups in other countries and an umbrella organization, FOE International, to coordinate what Brower described as a "beautifully decentralized activist environmental organization" (Brower 1990: 246).

After a decade of growth, during which debt disappeared and membership approached 200,000, financial problems escalated, bills went unpaid, and programs were cut. In 1989 FOE merged administratively with two other environmental groups. By the end of the century, Friends remained viable, even strong, with an office in Washington, D.C., organizations in sixty-three countries (the "largest international environmental network in the world," according to its own promotion), and a list of issues that clearly distinguishes FOE from other conservation organizations: community support, corporate accountability, tax reform, international debt relief, International Monetary Fund revision, trade investment changes, and World Bank reform, as well as the more familiar pollution and biodiversity. Perhaps no group discussed here so clearly aligns itself with progressive political ideals, with the possible exception of the Sierra Club (an ironic comparison, given Brower's 1969 ouster).

Pursuing a slate of issues as broad as that of Friends of the Earth, the *Natural Resources Defense Council* attempts to affect policy with a specific and contemporary strategy: litigation. Fox captures the spirit of this strategy when he suggests that their motto is "Sue the bastards!" (Fox 1981/1985: 304). The group coalesced from the Scenic Hudson Preservation Conference, formed by a dozen activists in the 1960s to fight the construction of a hydropower plant on Storm King Mountain, along New York's Hudson River. Led by the attorney Stephen Duggan, his wife, Beatrice Abbott Duggan, and the environmental lawyer David Sive (one of the first to pursue what subsequently would be called environmental law), the conference sued the electric utility involved, Consolidated Edison (Con Ed). Con Ed argued that environmental citizen groups had no legal standing, but the court upheld the conference's right to bring the suit, based on its "aesthetic, conservational, and recreational" interest in the area (Natural Resources Defense Council 1995: 1). After a decade of fighting, Con Ed eventually abandoned the proposal. In 1970 the Duggans, Sive, and several others formally organized the Natural Resources Defense Council to pursue lawsuits in defense of environmental causes; the council thereby paralleled another new group, the Environmental Defense Fund, which had formed in 1967 from a class-action suit over the aerial spraying of DDT, also in New York. Joining the Duggan-Sive group, several young law students from Yale became the council's core staff. They focused on selected cases not only to establish legal precedents but also to improve the public visibility of particular issues and to demonstrate the inadequacy of existing laws; for these purposes, the group employed public advertisements and formal reports, as well as legal actions in the courts. Over the ensuing decades, the council's actions spanned the breadth of environmental concerns: suits against Bethlehem Steel and Texaco for water pollution, defense of the Clean Water Act, protests against carcinogens in foods, controls on emissions from coal plants of the Tennessee Valley Authority, arguments linking reductions in waste to increasing energy supplies in the Bonneville Power Administration, and participation in the international controls on nuclear weapons. In 1973 the council challenged clear-cutting on the national forests, which the courts declared illegal. That decision led to the 1976 National Forest Management Act. Other achievements followed. It authored a 1980 report identifying below-cost timber sales on the national forests; it pursued the 1982 effort that led to environmental impact statements and management plans for potential wilderness within the national forest system; and it spearheaded the 1991 action that led Congress to prohibit petroleum drilling in the Arctic National Wildlife Refuge. The council publishes a periodical, *Amicus Journal,* as well as some books and reports. Although it is not perceived as dependent on a large membership, it does claim 400,000 members, and operates from headquarters in New York City.

Characterization of Groups

The ten groups reviewed here have differed from one another, sometimes strongly during their formative years, in focus, motivation, and strategy/organization (fig. 8.1), although many have become more similar over time. Still, with the proliferation of groups, the diversity within the conservation movement expands; the 2000 *Conservation Directory* lists more than 1,300 mostly national groups active in some part of the environmental arena. Still other groups, often local and obscure, may remain little known. The Center for Biological Diversity, a Tucson-based, lawsuit-happy group, eagerly sues anyone anywhere who engages in actions that threaten rare plants and animals (Skow 1999). The Greater Yellowstone Coalition, a Bozeman-headquartered group with 7,500 members, works to preserve the wild characteristics of the region centered on the Yellowstone Plateau. Wild Alabama, operating out of Moulton with a thousand members, adopts a strident tone: "Those woo-woo vegetarian urban eco-weenies are afraid to take a stand against industry!" (*Outside* 1999). The Quincy Library Group, a locally based and informal gathering—even the word "group" suggests too much organization—brokered an agreement among users, including nature protectionists, of land in a large area of national forest in northern California, and in 1998 persuaded Congress to approve its plan (Little 1998). The National Resource Information Center, in Eagle, Idaho, with a tiny staff pursues lawsuits and forges volunteer efforts to improve watershed conditions and fish populations (*Outside* 1994). Range Watch, a one-person "group" (Jane Baxter), videotapes environmental abuses in California's Sierra Nevada from "a Rube Goldbergesque four-wheel-drive truck mounted with a tiny pop-up conference area and editing studio" (*Outside* 1994). Nature-

Figure 8.1. Location in the space that defines environmental concern occupied by mainline conservation/environmental groups in their formative years

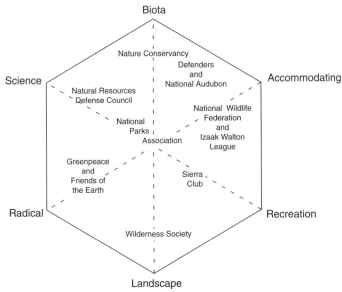

protection sentiment, like mushrooms after a fall rain, pushes out from its Earthly base in endless diversity.

Generalizations about Groups

The particularities of environmental organizations are not the whole story. Five patterns emerge from their operations over the years.

CONVERGENCE Clearly conservation groups have not remained static in their concerns and activities. The Sierra Club's concerns today extend far beyond the parks of the Sierra Nevada; the contemporary Wilderness Society champions causes other than vast, roadless landscapes; the modern National Audubon Society promotes issues other than bird protection. In fact, from disparate beginnings the mainline environmental groups have converged to champion similar values, promote similar agendas, and adopt similar strategies.

PERSISTENCE OF HISTORICAL IDENTITIES Persistence is as characteristic of conservation groups as change. The Nature Conservancy, Greenpeace, and the Natural Resources Defense Council remain faithful to the strategies they initiated decades ago: land purchases, public spectacles, and legal proceedings, respectively. Even among groups that have converged from disparate beginnings, past patterns may persist or reappear. Natural history topics are much more likely to appear in the publications of the long-established biologically focused organizations, notably the National Audubon Society and National Wildlife Federation, than in those issued by groups that traditionally have focused on scenery. Similarly, recreation topics grace more pages of the Sierra Club's *Sierra* than the magazine of the Nature Conservancy, with its roots in science.

SIMILAR INTERESTS, DIFFERENT CAUSES Critical of the Sierra Club's studied avoidance of confrontation, Greenpeace was determined to "bear witness." The Izaak Walton League defended the Boundary Waters area and later the public lands of the West, both at times when other groups seemed uninterested. The Wilderness Society battled roads in the national parks when the National Parks Association and the Sierra Club seemed ready to accept recreational development (in 1936 even David Brower favored a ski lift on Mount Hoffmann, in the center of Yosemite National Park). Conservation groups adopted different stances in debates over the creation of many national parks, particularly Kings Canyon, Olympic, and Grand Teton. The strong progressive stance of many groups contrasts with the Nature Conservancy's appeal to corporate America.

The distinctiveness of conservation organizations continues to appear in a variety of issues. The role of animal rights groups in debates on nature protection confounds the simple dichotomy of protection versus development: Earth First! and the Fund for Animals cooperate to protect Yellowstone's bison, but the bond quickly dissolves in the details of that debate: are the bison wild creatures inhabiting wild landscapes or domesticated animals living in soulful coexistence with humans? A strategist for conservation, moreover, urges caution in making common cause with animal rights groups, "lest the ever-elusive big picture doesn't get miniaturized into portraits of battered puppy dogs" (M. Knox 1991: 37). Similarly, although most mainline groups refuse to oppose sport hunting, their enthusiasm for it varies enormously (Amory 1974, Mitchell 1979–80, Brower 1990).

MUTUAL INTERESTS, MUTUAL ANTAGONISM The singularity of conservation groups may cause them not only to embrace different causes but also to confront one another in outright hostility over issues that one would expect to unite them. Schrepfer (1980) explains in admirable detail the antagonism between the Sierra Club and the Save-the-Redwoods League over the preservation of coast redwoods, a story told more briefly by Vale (1974a). The Friends of the Earth and some Audubon chapters opposed captive breeding programs for California condors (Brower 1990, Cohen 1990), a strategy accepted by other conservation groups, including National Audubon. Audubon's San Francisco Bay chapter, opposed to the captive breeding effort, considered "joining Friends of the Earth in a court case against National Audubon and the Fish and Wildlife Service" (Cohen 1990: 273). The bitter divisiveness between personalities and organizational levels within the Sierra Club unfolds in a story of the New Melones Dam in the northern Sierra Nevada (J. Mitchell 1980), an echo of earlier disputes that led Rosalie Edge and her Emergency Conservation Committee to spearhead opposition to mainline conservation groups over animal trapping. Cohen (1990: 201) quotes a leader in National Audubon as saying that "Rosalie Edge hates us and we hate her."

INTERNAL FRICTION   Strong personalities and fiscal crises contribute repeatedly to heated disputes within conservation groups. David Brower's ouster from the Sierra Club and later from Friends of the Earth are the classic examples, but comparable situations appear in the histories of the Izaak Walton League and the National Parks Conservation Association. The rivalries within Greenpeace and between central offices and local affiliates recur in the history of the conservation movement. Nor is such friction entirely a result of increasing complexity in the contemporary world: even the early twentieth-century Sierra Club held a referendum among its thousand members because of substantial support for the flooding of Hetch Hetchy Valley in Yosemite National Park.

Reflections

Nature-protection groups represent a diverse array of motivations and strategies, reflecting different perspectives on the connections between people and nature. The conservation movement, then, can hardly be characterized as simple and monolithic, as a bunch of tree-huggers, a gaggle of highway-hating backpackers, or a hotbed of socialists. From the perspective of nature protection, this diversity is an asset; much is lost if purges in pursuit of purity reduce the groups' ranks.

In his book *At Odds with Progress*, Bret Wallach (1991) identifies disguises behind which nature-conscious Americans hide their apprehensions about dominating nature. Behind all the disguises is general anxiety about economic growth and the resulting development of the wild landscape. By implication, recognition of the basic unease should make it possible to work toward what really matters to those Americans who hide behind the disguises, thereby unifying efforts of conservationists around the common goal of stopping growth. However appealing this no-growth future may appear—and I have issued my own antigrowth message (Luten 1986)—any attempt to reduce the diversity of motivations not only simplifies the intellectual understanding but also reduces the potential for maximizing support for nature protection. Easing the complexity paints nature protection as nothing more than sentimentality or self-indulgent recreation or progressive politics, whereas in fact the concern emerges from far more complex motivations. Mainline and oddball, amateur and professional, humanistically leaning and scientifically inclined, conservative and radical, conservation groups of all stripes strive to protect nature not only in our own country but throughout the world.

9 BIOLOGICAL NATURE, BIODIVERSITY

Consider the PBS television series *Nature*. A typical program headlines mammals, with supporting roles for birds or invertebrates (particularly insects) and certain plants, especially as they relate to the featured animals. Weather may have a bit part as its seasonal characteristics influence the biota. A rock formation or a stream-flow event may appear in a cameo role, notably as a factor that contributes to the animal narrative. Tectonic or volcanic processes (more likely) and soil formation (less likely) may make walk-on appearances. But throughout the hour, the story line rarely strays from its spotlighted stars. In this emphasis, the program reflects a common American sense of the natural world: the focus is on biological species, and the broad and varied nonliving creation serves as the setting for the living things. The stage is the ecosystem.

American Attitudes toward Animals

The work of Steven Kellert (1976, 1980, 1982a, 1982b, 1985), whose questionnaire surveys began in the 1970s, is the most sweeping exploration of the structure and diversity of attitudes toward animals within American society. Kellert first developed a typology of these attitudes and identified ten categories. He then studied a national sample to determine the presence or absence of these attitudes in societal groups and the strength of their association with those groups. He plotted his findings on linear scales that reveal the links between attitudes and demographic characteristics. Kellert discovered the tendency of certain attitudes to appear in certain parts of the population. Individuals hold multiple attitudes; the mix of attitudes varies with the group; and the groups to which individuals belong vary. Therefore, any given individual in any particular group may or may not conform to that group's characteristics.

In the American population as a whole, certain patterns emerge for eight of the ten types. Two proved not useful: the neutralistic attitude (indifference to or avoidance of animals) and the aesthetic attitude (artistic symbolism of animals). The four most frequent attitudes, reflecting the most fundamental bases of Americans' connection to animals, suggest to Kellert two attitudinal poles. First, utilitarian and moralistic attitudes represent opposite feelings about the degree to which animals deserve to be respected. Do human needs justify the exploitation of animals regardless of our impacts on them? Or should human activities not cause animals to suffer or die? Hunting, trapping, and laboratory experimentation generate approval or scorn in this pairing. Second, humanistic and negativistic attitudes reveal degrees of affection for animals: "intense emotional attachment to individual animals [versus] indifference or incredulity toward the idea of 'loving' animals" (Kellert 1980: 116). The naturalistic attitude, associated with fondness for the outdoors, and the ecologistic attitude, linked with the idea of nature as a interconnected system, appeared strongly in parts of the population but weakly in the total. Two additional attitudes appeared less frequently than the other six: dominionistic, a desire to control animals, and scientistic, an interest in the physical functions of animals.

The attitudes expressed by various segments of American society reveal some surprising patterns and many expected ones. Young people express strong humanistic and moralistic impulses; elderly people are more likely to reveal utilitarian and negativistic attitudes. Women tend to be humanistic and moralistic, men dominionistic and utilitarian but also naturalistic. A rural childhood is associated with dominionistic and utilitarian attitudes (but not negativistic ones), whereas an urban upbringing seems to favor naturalistic tendencies. But this urban-naturalistic relationship is not linked to the inner cities of our largest metropolitan areas: the naturalistic attitude is tied to persons raised in towns with populations of 10,000 to 50,000. College education tends to favor naturalistic and ecologistic attitudes, but not necessarily moralistic ones. Unskilled workers and farmers are likely to reveal utilitarian tendencies. Unmarried and childless individuals favor humanistic and moralistic attitudes. Bird-watchers score high on the naturalistic, ecologistic, and scientistic scales. Hunters are likely to reveal ecologistic and dominionistic attitudes. Professional trappers score high on naturalistic values.

Most generally, education and gender provide the strongest explanatory power of American attitudes toward animals. Educational achievement appears as "the most sensitive indicator of appreciation, concern, affection, knowledge and respect for animals. . . . Respondents with less than a sixth grade education were very nearly the opposite of those with a graduate education in basic perceptions and understanding of animals" (Kellert 1980: 71). Moralistic and humanistic tendencies are much stronger in women; men are stronger in naturalistic attitudes and knowledge about animals (fig. 9.1). In all these patterns, moreover, Kellert consistently extends the attitude variables from simply "animals" to "the natural world."

The data on knowledge about animals suggest that Americans' factual understanding of living things is "extremely limited" (Kellert 1980: 115). Knowledge scores are high among bird-watchers, members of conservation organizations, and hunters, who value close contacts with nature; college education is closely associated with enhanced knowledge. Low knowledge scores are linked with both advanced age (over 75 years) and youth (under 25), residence in a large city, and less than a high school education.

The surveys reveal that Americans, whether "well-informed" or not, express willingness to sacrifice certain material gains in order to protect the natural world. A majority of Americans, sometimes a strong majority, are willing to pay more for energy in order to preserve populations of bald eagles, eastern mountain lions, and silverspot butterflies; wish to limit logging to protect grizzly bear habitat; would impose constraints on housing developments on wetlands needed by waterfowl; would reduce livestock grazing on public lands to enhance wildlife; and favor restricting the use of off-road vehicles for wildlife protection (Kellert 1980: 112–13).

Kellert also documents the unevenness of concern for wild animals across taxonomic groups and the relatively weaker regard for plants than for animals. For example, in his surveys of public interest in specific species that represent more general groups of organisms, protection of the bald eagle enjoys strong support—9 of 10 Americans not only favor preserving it but also express willingness to accept increased economic costs to do so—and 64 percent indicate similar backing for a butterfly species, the silverspot. Much lower levels of sympathy are expressed for snakes (eastern indigo snake), invertebrates (Kauai wolf spider), and plants (Furbish lousewort). Kellert suggests that many factors contribute to this differential support, including the aesthetic appeal of species, their phylogenetic closeness to humans, the reasons for low population levels of species (direct killing by humans is linked to increased sympathy), cultural meanings, and knowledge about species.

Figure 9.1. Attitudes of Americans toward animals and knowledge about them, by education, gender, and ethnicity, as found by Kellert. (Adapted from Kellert and Berry 1980, pp. 60, 64, 74)

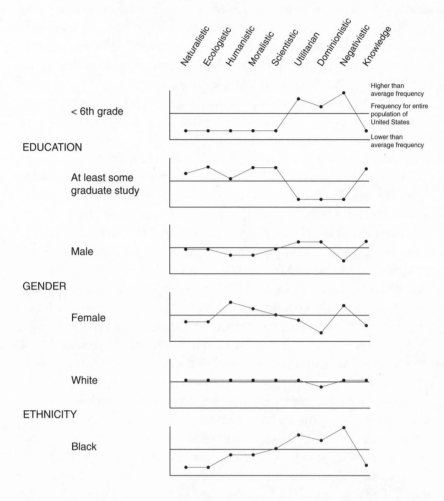

The most sweeping conclusion to be drawn from the Kellert surveys is that Americans generally, if not universally, are committed to wildlife conservation: "Wildlife [is] not just the concern of an esoteric and elitist minority, but, instead, [has] broad appeal to many, if not most, Americans.... An abundant, diverse and healthy wildlife population contributes ... to a high standard and quality of life" (Kellert 1980: 123). Arguments for both the diversity of motivation for nature protection and the strength of Americans' support for it are supported by Kellert's findings.

The Institutionalization of Concern for Wildlife

The political mechanisms that regulate and conserve wildlife in the United States include both landscape reserves, which protect and control habitat, and government regulations, which apply to landscape independent of land-ownership. Although our primary focus has been on the reserves, as areas set aside for nature protection, the regulatory laws may be more sweeping in their effect on wildlife.

THE LEGAL STATUS OF WILD ANIMALS   Many wild animals (fewer wild plants) occupy a unique position in the United States: they are a public sector resource with a legal status independent of the human owners of the land on which the animals live. You may own a particular piece of the landscape (say a quarter section of forest in Georgia or a suburban lot in Wisconsin), with the right to use the land, subject to the regulatory powers of the state, in ways that you consider desirable. But your ownership does not include rights to many of the wild animals that may live on your land: songbirds and white-tailed deer, for example, remain public resources, *ferae naturae,* the property of no one. This legal status, extending back in Western thought to the Roman Empire, was adopted by the earliest American colonists, who consciously resisted the feudal European idea that wildlife belonged to the landowning nobility. Egalitarianism, rather than elitism, has long ruled access to wildlife in American society. Private ownership is gained only when a wild animal has been captured or killed. Governments obviously regulate access to this means of possession, but such regulation is superimposed on the fundamental commons character of wildlife. Access to wild animals was even specified as a guaranteed liberty in William Penn's 1683 charter for Pennsylvania.

This status of wild animals is unique among natural resources in the United States (cf. Luten 1986). Food, energy, and nonenergy minerals are all private sector resources, with production rights associated with the owners of the land on which the resources are located. Exceptions come to mind: fish in the sea, unlike dairy cows, remain resources of the public commons; nonmetallic mineral resources on federal lands are leased for development, rather than transferred in fee title to private companies; subsurface mineral rights can be independent of surface land use rights. Yet the fundamental rights of private landowners to use these resources on their land remain dominant. Timber products derive from both public and private lands, although production is entirely by private companies, with decisions about forest uses linked to the agency or company that legally administers the land. Water may be a resource of the commons, but riparian rights link landowners with access to the resource; appropriative rights alter this tight linkage, but the public trust doctrine more clearly maintains the commons character of the water resource. Recreational land resources exist in both the private and public sectors, whereas park and wilderness uses of land are almost entirely activities of the public sector. In all these amenity land uses, the resource is intimately linked with landownership. Perhaps only the functioning of the atmosphere as an assimilative resource resembles the commons character of wild animals: no one owns the air, which remains, even when used to assimilate wastes, a resource of the commons.

Wild plants enjoy little of the special legal status of wild animals. Landownership generally carries unequivocal rights to the plants rooted in the owned land, except for those species protected under laws covering rare and endangered species; but even those laws differentially protect animals and plants (Bartel 2001, Roberson 2001). Lack of mobility, more limited functioning as human food, less association with amenity sport, greater taxonomic distance from the human species (Luten 1986)—these characteristics apparently make wild plants less deserving of protection than wild animals.

STATE AUTHORITY From the property of no one to the property of the public—a public for whom governments should protect and otherwise regulate wild animals for the common good—seems a logical progression in legal authority that might explain how government agencies became responsible for wild animals. Yet the emergence of that authority reflects a pathway more aristocratic than egalitarian: authority over wildlife passed from the exclusive hunting rights of European feudal lords to, in England, the similarly restrictive rights of the king, to the regulatory powers of Parliament, to the authorities of individual colonial governments in America, to, finally, the state governments in the United States. State authority would be challenged by both advocates of private rights and federal agencies, but it remains today preeminent in power over wildlife.

The colonies exercised their authority over wild animals modestly, in laws both to constrain the taking of species considered desirable and to encourage the destruction of species thought to be undesirable. The Rhode Island town of Portsmouth declared deer to be off limits in the summer of

1646, and most colonies had established similar laws by 1720. Constraints were placed on spearing or snagging of spawning fish in parts of Virginia in the 1680s; New Jersey offered bounties on wolves in 1697; Massachusetts and New York established protection for the heath hen in 1837. Feeble and erratic, these wildlife regulations pale in comparison with modern laws, and the states' authority to legislate in wildlife matters long remained uncertain. That authority was challenged in the courts. The first case to reach the Supreme Court involved the right to take oysters in certain New Jersey mudflats; the Court upheld the regulatory power of the state, invoking the tradition of Britain's king, and thus the state, as holder of the public trust in navigable waters and the lands beneath them. Overall, however, in spite of incipient state regulation, wildlife remained essentially an unregulated free good until the last quarter of the nineteenth century.

The need for regulations is often interpreted as a consequence of the long decline in the abundance of American wildlife, which reached a sort of nadir in the 1880s. Sport hunters rose to become the most influential group advocating restrictive wildlife regulations, although the distinction between hunters and nonhunting wildlife enthusiasts was much weaker then than now. Many people identified as nature lovers—John James Audubon, John Burroughs, George Bird Grinnell, William T. Hornaday, Frederick Law Olmsted, Robert Ridgway, Henry David Thoreau—frequently hunted or fished, as did the founding members of groups such as the Nuttall Ornithological Club and the American Ornithologists' Union. As early as 1844, the New York Sportsmen's Club posited three goals: limiting or prohibiting market hunting, eliminating spring shooting, and otherwise strengthening wildlife laws. In 1865 Massachusetts established the first precursor to today's state fish and game agencies, a fish commission whose authority was later extended to game birds and mammals. Advocates of private rights challenged protective laws in the courts. The key case of *Geer v. Connecticut* (1896), involving the state's authority to regulate traffic in wildlife, established state ownership of wild animals "as a trust for the benefit of the people" (Bean and Rowland 1997: 14). The states' exercise of their authority continued to be uneven, however, and in the 1930s two statements were issued to encourage uniformity in state laws: the American Game Policy, authored by Aldo Leopold and presented at a 1930 game conference, and the Model Game Law, drafted by Seth Gordon, president of the American Game Association. The Model Game Law called for creation of state wildlife agencies as "nonpolitical, nonpartisan" commissions with the responsibility to set policy, within guidelines from the legislatures, and to appoint directors. These structures are common in states today. As in early wildlife protection efforts, hunting enthusiasts led the way in the search for uniformity in state wildlife law.

THE EXTENSION OF FEDERAL AUTHORITY Around the turn of the twentieth century, a combination of factors prompted wildlife enthusiasts to consider the virtues of federal laws regarding wild animals: the mobility of wildlife, which might cross state lines; the movement of wild animal products from state to state, whether or not they were derived from legally killed animals; the perceived problems of introduced species, such as the starling and house sparrow, clearly beyond the power of individual states to influence; the success of the U.S. Fish Commission, established by Congress in 1871 to investigate causes of fish decline; and an absence of strict regulation and enforcement by at least some of the states. The legal basis for the federal usurpation of state responsibilities, however, remained uncertain, and the courts often found in favor of state authority. A Supreme Court case as late as 1912, for example, found that state rights prevailed over federal authority in matters of wildlife. Eventually three acts of Congress would permit federal action.

First, a federal property power was established with the Lacey Act of 1894, sometimes called the Yellowstone Park Protection Act. This law prohibited hunting in Yellowstone National Park; made illegal the possession of dead animals in the park or their transportation from it; created a commissioner of the U.S. circuit court to enforce the law; set a schedule of fines; and authorized the building of a jail to house violators. Most generally, it asserted that the wildlife of Yellowstone National Park was a responsibility of the federal government, not of Wyoming.

Second, the Lacey Act of 1900 made it a federal offense, under the power of the U.S. government to regulate interstate commerce, to transport animals killed illegally in one state into another state. Although this legislation overtly enhanced the authority of the states, it modestly established a federal presence in the general arena of wildlife regulation.

Third, federal treaty-making powers saved efforts to provide national protection for migratory birds. In 1913 Congress had passed the Weeks-McLean Migratory Bird Act, which invoked interstate commerce authority as the basis for federal power to protect birds. President William Howard Taft signed the act, but as he had feared, a district court ruled it an unconstitutional extension of federal authority. A 1916 law authorized the president to enter into international treaties for such purposes; the initial agreement, with Great Britain for Canada, became law when Congress passed enabling legislation in 1918. Subsequent treaties were signed with Mexico and the Soviet Union. The courts upheld this power.

What a reversal over a few years! In 1886 even wildlife enthusiasts observed that "Congress has no power" to enact legislation to protect wildlife (quoted in Tober 1981: 226). Yet twenty years later, federal authority had been extended to end "spring hunting . . . the sale of migratory game birds . . . the hunting of plovers, sandpipers, and most other shorebirds . . . [to protect] all migratory insectivorous birds and songbirds [and to regulate] the hunting of ducks, geese, woodcock, snipe, doves, and other game birds at the discretion of the Secretary of Agriculture" (Trefethen 1966: 28).

Thus established, federal powers in wildlife matters have increased, particularly in recent decades. The laws fall out as icons of wildlife protection: the Bald Eagle Protection Act of 1940, the Wild Free-Roaming Horses and Burros Act of 1971—which was declared unconstitutional by a lower court but upheld by the Supreme Court—the Marine Mammal Protection Act of 1972, the Fishery Conservation and Management Act of 1976 (regulating oceanic fish), and, particularly noteworthy for its breadth and impact, the Endangered Species Act of 1966 and its subsequent reauthorizations. Also influential as federal intrusions into state wildlife programs have been the incentives and coercions associated with the Cooperative Wildlife Research Unit Program, initiated by Ding Darling in 1935 to advance the science of wildlife management, and the Pittman-Robertson Federal Aid in Wildlife Act of 1937, which not only returned to the states for wildlife purposes revenues generated by a federal sales tax on sporting arms and ammunition but also required states to apply their hunting license fees to fish and wildlife agencies. Nonetheless, in spite of this history, typically narrated as a drama of success, the states retain the primary right and responsibility to regulate and manage wildlife, and they defend this primacy vigorously.

INTERNATIONAL ACTION Biological nature—not spectacular scenery, not representational landscapes, not recreational opportunities—drives protectionist concern on the international scene. The high regard for nature protection in the Western world makes it all but inevitable that the technology-rich countries of North America and Europe will turn their attention to the species-rich tropics. They have descended on the tropical world in force with scientific investigations, Nature Conservancy projects, government aid and development programs, United Nations initiatives, international conventions. All of this activity reflects what rarely is recognized: the relatively recent assumption that "nature" means "biodiversity."

TAXONOMIC ENTITIES AND WILDLIFE LAW Biological taxa form the basis for regulation of wild animals. Colonial laws focused on particular animals; groups of birds appear in the Migratory Bird Treaty Act; specific species or arrays of species are protected under several federal laws; endangered species legislation depends on a list of taxa organized by degree of rarity. This scheme seems obvious, logical, scientific, yet in no other arena in the natural world do we find a taxonomy of protected forms. Perhaps the current stress on whole ecosystems and habitats suggests a move away from a focus on taxa and a shift of attention to a land-based, territory-bounded, nature-reserve strategy.

Four Themes of Contemporary Concern

Shunning both mere scenery and mass recreation, environmentalists proclaim the primacy of biological concerns in nature protection. In those concerns we can identify four themes: the rights of animals and of nature, biophilia, conservation biology, and restoration ecology.

ANIMALS' AND NATURE'S RIGHTS Over the course of the twentieth century, concern for the humane treatment of animals came to be extended from household pets and farm animals to wild species, to spectacular birds and large mammals, to fur-bearers and predators, and eventually to such unglamorous creatures as frogs and beetles. The moralistic motivation (in Kellert's terminology) or the ethical stage (in mine) receives increasing intellectual attention and expands to include more of the natural world.

The most thorough historical analysis of this theme is found in Nash's *Rights of Nature* (1989). Nash sees the conviction that nature has moral rights as an extension of a long tradition of progressive thought, which in the United States has recognized inalienable rights to exist in an ever-broader community—first for white men other than an elite, then for laborers, slaves, women, Native Americans: "One can regard environmental ethics as marking out the farthest limits of American liberalism. . . . [It] can be understood not so much as a revolt against traditional American ideals as an extension and new application of them" (Nash 1989: 4, 12). In setting forth the thesis and tracing its history, Nash attempts to place the "most radical fringe" of American environmentalists, those who advocate legal rights for the nonhuman world, as central not only among those concerned with nature protection but also among Americans generally.

Itself a radical idea—that is, the positioning of nature's rights in the mainstream of both liberal politics and nature protection—Nash's thesis appeals to anyone who seeks to view nature protection as consistent with the loftiest progressive traditions of American society. Certainly, critics on the left remain unconvinced. Imperialistic nature-protection efforts, they say, commodify nature in an inherently destructive capitalistic system, foster the separation of people from the nonhuman world, deflect attention from the destruction of nature going on outside protected areas, and succeed only in creating picturesque playgrounds for an idle aristocracy. Apart from this critique, however, Nash's thesis seems somewhat overstated and, ironically, exclusionary. First, in an attempt to make icon personalities exemplify the idea, he interprets them selectively. John Muir, for example, is said to have "camouflaged his radical egalitarianism" because "he got into politics and became pragmatic" (Nash 1989: 41), whereas Muir may simply not have seen protection and recreation as incompatible (Vale and Vale 1998). Similarly, Aldo Leopold, characterized as "the intellectual touchstone" for the environmentalism that includes recognition of nature's rights, remained dedicated to sport hunting, hardly an activity embraced by animal rights advocates (cf. Reiger 1986/2001). Second, Nash wishes to dismiss all but those who participate in "ethically impelled environmentalism," stigmatizing everyone else as being "on the other side," advocates of "anthropocentric ethics and [thus] environmental exploitation" (Nash 1989: 213). Such a position hardly furthers the mainstreaming of modern environmentalism.

Questions remain about the positioning of persons who advocate the rights of nature within the political world of American nature protection. Do such environmentalists represent the vanguard of the future, as Nash suggests, and if so, what is the likelihood of finding common ground for them and the earliest spokespersons for wild animals, the sport hunters? On the other hand, should mainstream environmental groups ignore or even reject groups that press for the ethical treatment of animals and all nature, without regard to human concerns, and in so doing deny some of the richness of attitude that explains the strength of American nature-protection sentiment? The questions echo similar queries raised earlier about which conservation groups most effectively and honestly speak for nature protection.

BIOPHILIA A little book by the noted biologist Edward O. Wilson introduced a word and articulated a notion that have become keystones in nature protection: "biophilia." Biophilia, Wilson says, is an "innate [human] tendency to focus on life and lifelike processes" (Wilson 1984: 1). He simply suggests that humans, reflecting their genetic history, feel affinities to certain landscapes ("open tree-studded land on prominences overlooking water" [p. 110]), to the activity of observing nature ("the naturalist's trance was adaptive: the glimpse of one small animal hidden in the grass could make the difference between eating and going hungry" [p. 101]), to a mental fusion of the humanistic arts and the natural sciences ("Arcturian zoologists visiting this planet could make no sense of our morality and art until they reconstructed our genetic history—nor can we" [p. 114]). We need to understand this link between our evolutionary development and our tendency to "cherish and protect life": "Ranging from awe of the serpent to the idealization of the savanna and the hunter's mystique, and undoubtedly others yet to be explored . . . [biophilia] grows into a form true to its long, unique evolutionary history" (p. 139). The idea's own evolutionary history continued with subsequent explorations and elaborations (Kellert and Wilson, eds., 1993). Its general argument expresses wilderness as evolutionary arena; its numerous manifestations (Kellert 1997) resemble the many meanings of wilderness.

Biophilia appeals to many nature enthusiasts for its suggestion that aesthetic sensitivity has an innate genetic basis, so that both love for and protection of biological nature become necessary consequences of being human. Perhaps, though, the idea is too restrictive. If we do have such bonding to other organisms imprinted as a consequence of our evolutionary heritage, maybe we have similar linkages to parts of inanimate nature. We may have sealed in our genes appreciation for the sunny weather that stimulates our body's manufacture of vitamin D, for the low-light hours of dawn and dusk that may improve the chances for success in the hunt for food, for rivers that provide a variety of needed resources and a means for travel, for mountains that furnish refuge from lowland drought or disease or predators, for dark organic soils that support the growth of desirable food plants, for wetlands where animal foods abound. Instead of being driven by Wilson's biophilia, we humans may be genetically subject to Tuan's topophilia, an "affective bond between people and place" (Tuan 1974: 4). After all, the most common subject of human conversation—among friends or strangers, regardless of the season of the year, throughout the country (and the world?), independent of the conversants' social status, in all types of group situations—is not the plants nearby or the animals recently seen, but the weather.

CONSERVATION BIOLOGY If animal rights and biophilia represent humanistic themes of biological nature protection, conservation biology epitomizes natural science's expression of that concern. Since it appeared as the title of a 1980 book (Soule and Wilcox 1980), "conservation biology" has become increasingly common as a denominator of a scientific approach to understanding the characteristics of species with limited ranges and/or small populations, with the added goal of using that understanding to create policy that will increase the likelihood of such species' survival (Western and Pearl, eds., 1990; Fiedler and Jain 1992; DiSilvestro 1993; Soule and Orians 2001). Soule and Wilcox (1980: 1) articulate what was for them an incipient field of inquiry but what has since blossomed into a bumper crop of scientific research: "Conservation biology is a mission-oriented discipline comprising both pure and applied science. . . . It focuses the knowledge and tools of all biological disciplines, from molecular biology to population biology, on one issue—nature conservation." (Note that the "nature" in "nature conservation" means "biological species.") The application of science to the mission of protection, moreover, reflects not just some vague sense of responsibility but a zealous passion: conservation biology is "an emotional call to arms. The green mantle of Earth is now being ravaged and pillaged in a frenzy of exploitation by a mushrooming mass of humans and bulldozers" (Soule and Wilcox 1980: 7).

The topics of central concern to conservation biologists are familiar to anyone even remotely aware of the issues concerning rare species: the hazards that rare plants and animals face, the variability (genetic and otherwise) that structure animal populations, the spatial patterns of species' occurrence (often at regional and continental levels), the impacts of habitat fragmentation (particularly associated with human use of the landscape), the design of nature reserves that further survival of species, the various strategies employed to aid species' recovery. Usually grouped together within the category of biodiversity, these topics appear in the journal *Conservation Biology* (inaugurated in 1987), in new college courses, and in the constant flow of books and reports, more often than not with a case study of a species or other taxon or a treatment of a region (e.g., Ricketts et al. 1999). Although they sometimes reflect on the humanism of the "call to arms" or on the political/cultural worlds linked to rare species, these outlets far more typically deal with the natural science of rarity and the human response needed to aid species' survival. According to the discipline's practitioners, moreover, the science of conservation biology must be rigorous (see Lyman 1998, Fitz-simmons 1999).

One expression of this human response takes the form of "gap analy-sis," an effort to compare spatial patterns of protected areas against bio-logical data—species richness, major habitat types, ecoregions, biomes—in order to identify gaps in the distribution of landscape reserves, gaps that need filling with new protected areas. Among the first such efforts, Crum-packer et al. (1988) compared Kuchler's (1964) potential natural vegetation types in the United States against the federal lands; of the 135 types, 9 had no representation and 24 had what they judged to be inadequate representa-tion. Forest Service lands, whether or not protected from commodity re-source development, encompassed 98 of the types (perhaps partly reflecting the abundance of forest types in the classification), the National Park Ser-vice 90 types, the Bureau of Land Management 71 types, and the national wildlife refuges only 63 types (a modest representation probably reflecting the classification system and the coarse scale of the data). The U.S. Geolog-ical Survey Gap Analysis project (Scott et al. 1993) and the Managed Areas Database (McGhie et al. 1996) preceded the Protected Areas Database (Della-Sala et al. 2001), which forms the empirical base for an exhaustive biodiver-sity assessment for North America north of Mexico (Ricketts et al. 1999). This evaluation identifies "globally outstanding ecoregions requiring imme-diate protection of remaining habitat and extensive restoration" in four regions: southeastern forests extending through Florida, tall-grass prairie of the upper Midwest, southwestern lands along the Mexican border from cen-tral Arizona beyond the Big Bend country of Texas, and the mountains along the Pacific coast, including California's Sierra Nevada (Ricketts et al. 1999). On a finer scale of "globally outstanding" ecoregions, and assessing simply the percentage of each ecoregion that lies within strongly protected reserves, the Protected Areas Database ranks Central Tall Grasslands, Flint Hills Tall Grasslands, and Aleutian Islands Tundra as highest in need (none of their areas are protected), followed by Southeastern Mixed Forests (less than 0.1 percent) and Appalachian Mixed Mesophytic Forests (0.3 percent) (DelaSala et al. 2001). Although a humanistic critic might observe that not all species appeal equally to all people and that large mammalian predators justifiably deserve attention regardless of general spatial patterns of biodiversity (Kareiva and Marvier 2003), the hot spots of concentrated biological richness remain a focus for conservation biology.

Conservation biology is known for its distinctive concerns; for example, species that may not have much appeal for most people, collective measures of species richness, large spatial areas. But more general themes have long appeared within the discipline of wildlife management or wildlife ecology: concerns for rare animals, for the impacts of human use of landscapes on those animals, for management plans designed to increase the populations of desired animals, and, critically, for generating and applying scientific understanding to the cause of species survival. Wildlife management, effectively articulated by Aldo Leopold in his pioneering *Game Management* (1933), emerged during a period of alarm over rare animals, notably species important for sport hunting, in the first decades of the twentieth century. The threads that connect caring people with wild animals, of course, extend much further back in time.

RESTORATION ECOLOGY Closely paralleling the meteoric rise of conservation biology, restoration ecology has risen to a prominent place in contemporary concern for animate nature. The fundamental premise of restoration ecology is that active human management is needed to create, recreate, and maintain desired conditions of vegetation and ecosystems; it is not enough to protect landscapes against commodity resource use. The natural science foundation for the view rests with the ecological work of Frank Egler, who argued that vegetation characteristics of a locale reflect at least in part the conditions existent at the time of its establishment, that those characteristics have a certain inertia through time, and that change tends to be concentrated during periodic episodes of disturbance. In many ways, then, he challenged the dominant views of Frederick Clements and his model of succession (Egler 1954; Vale 1982, 2002). For example, an abandoned midwestern cornfield will not become a prairie if no one plants and otherwise cares for prairie species. An overgrazed western range will not revert to pregrazed conditions without human manipulation of the vegetation. A southeastern pine forest, even after the reintroduction of long-suppressed fire, will not necessarily resemble its pre-European form without active attention to the ways in which process (burning) and structure (form of the forest) interact. The extinction of wolves in a southwestern pine forest cannot be reversed without purposeful reintroduction of the species. The interactions between prey and predators in northeastern forests may not require the presence of all of the fifteenth-century predatory species; their effects on the prey populations could be simulated by other types of predation—that is, active management. If desired conditions of the natural world are to be protected, this view asserts, people and their management programs must be involved.

Born as a perspective with the now-familiar name in the 1980s, restoration ecology gained prominence particularly as a result of efforts by ecologists at the University of Wisconsin Arboretum to recreate and maintain midwestern prairie vegetation. Sharing with conservation biology the sense of developing natural science understanding and of using that science to further nature protection, restoration ecology has expanded with books (William Jordan and his colleagues' *Restoration Ecology* [1987] may have been the first to use the term), conferences, college courses, and journals (*Restoration Ecology, Ecological Restoration*). The University of Wisconsin Arboretum remains home to both Jordan and his journals (Jordan 2003).

Among Jordan's precursors was the forest ecologist Edward Stone, at the University of California at Berkeley, who argued for the development of "vegetation-preservation management" in the 1960s (Stone 1965). Stone's recommendations coincided with those of the Leopold Report (Leopold et al. 1963). Fire ecologists recognized the need for purposeful burning in southern pine forests as early as the 1930s; a 1970 eulogy honoring the pioneering fire ecologist Herbert Stoddard testifies to this history:

Forty years have passed since Stoddard stated in his book . . . his convictions on the use of fire . . . in southern pinelands. . . . Long ago he was aware of the complex nature of "fire ecology" though the term is of recent usage. . . . The Fire Ecology Conferences [of his Tall Timbers Research Station in Tallahassee, Florida] are an expression of [his] influence, an attempt to develop an ecological understanding of fire in nature. (Komarek 1971)

Even more distant in time, George Perkins Marsh argued for active human agency to reverse the destructive actions of people; David Lowenthal, in his eloquent biography of Marsh, suggests that this argument is one of the "great lessons" of Marsh's *Man and Nature*: "Once subdued and then abandoned, land did not revert to its previous plenitude but remained impoverished, unless taken into human care. . . . Neither disdaining nor despairing, Marsh cautioned that civilization required enhancing, not abdicating, dominion over nature. If men could ruin nature, they might also mend it" (Lowenthal 2000: 297–98). Marsh is one of the great heroes of strident environmentalists. His recognition as an early restoration ecologist should please them. The designation of restoration ecology as an expression of human "dominion over nature" may please them not at all, but the phrase does capture the core of the perspective.

Reflections

The narrative of wildlife conservation in the United States often tells of successes, of saving animals from perpetual rarity or extinction (Matthiessen 1959, Wilcove 1994): white-tailed deer in the nineteenth century, midwestern duck populations in the 1930s, a substantial number of species after mid-century—trumpeter swans and bald eagles, elephant seals and sea otters, California condors and peregrine falcons, maybe even grizzly bears and whooping cranes. Certainly problems of survival remain, challenging resource managers and the concerned public, and regardless of the successes, the focus remains on crises (Wilcove 1994, Chadwick and Sartore 1995, Ricketts et al. 1999). Even the histories that raise "many dark and troubling questions" (Warren 1997: 182) about the pursuit of "environmental justice at the expense of social justice" (Jacoby 2001: 198) do not negate the sense that protectionist sentiment has generated accomplishments.

Whether the history of wildlife conservation in the United States is read as an "elite discourse" (Jacoby 2001: 3) or a saga of crises followed by "remarkable comebacks" (Wilcove 1999: 230) and of "getting there" (Chadwick and Sartore 1995: 143), the meanings that people see in wild animals, the history of human efforts to protect wild animals, the contemporary concern for wild animals—all suggest that the human species is strongly linked to the rest of animate nature. The bonds are expressed in attitudes both humanistic and scientific, consumptive and contemplative, aristocratic and common, passive and active. Possibly we sense that wild animals are not so different from ourselves. Maybe we feel the kinship that Darwin told us is in fact real.

But as a focus and rationale for nature protection more broadly, biodiversity constrains as much as the concept of wilderness, and for much the same reasons. Persons who denigrate the idea that the ideal natural world is wilderness emphasize how the concept separates people from nature both mentally and physically: people must go far to find wilderness, meanwhile ignoring and neglecting nature close at hand, in the everyday landscape. This is the criticism of wilderness as false idol.

Biodiversity values may generate the same effect: we think of biodiversity as existing only in distant tropical forests or in the species-rich and threatened tall-grass prairies and forest reserves far beyond our urban and suburban homes. Does our strong valuation of biodiversity prod us to think of both common biological species and systems simplified and modified by human activities as lacking in "natural" values, thus unworthy of our attention and affection? One rejoinder serves for the critics of the pursuit of both wilderness and biodiversity: People should develop sensitivity to common nature, but this development need not be at the expense of affection for uncommon nature. Nothing logically precludes concern for both obscure endemic subspecies and pan-world plants or animals, for both tropical forests and weedy urban vacant lots. Such heightened sensitivity requires effort, but nothing inherent in the task renders the outcomes necessarily contradictory.

A heightened appreciation of living nature, moreover, increases the likelihood of a stronger regard for nonliving nature. Conscious and sustained effort enhances any kind of sensitivity. Imagine, for example, a new kind of unit for the National Park System. It might be given a new name, such as the national natural area, or it might retain the name of national monument, invoking the intent of the Antiquities Act to establish national monuments to protect "objects of scientific interest." The novelty would be in the conceptualization of nature, a broadening of the nonhuman world to include specifically objects or events of scientific interest beyond scenery or biology—weather and climate, soils, hydrology, landforms, Quaternary history, perhaps interactions of humans and nature. Already we have national monuments for paleontology and archaeology; why not for other types of natural phenomena and for people-environment linkages? The possibilities seem without limit. Let us create the Downpour National Monument to celebrate and interpret the world record for one-minute rainfall, achieved on July 4, 1956, in Unionville, Maryland, when 1.23 inches fell in 60 seconds (Riordan and Bourget 1985). Consider the recreational facilities at this monument: a visitor center, located ideally at the site of the rain gauge, where displays would explain the specific conditions that led to the event, as well as more general information about rainfall-causing factors; an interpretive trail that focused on water cycling in the earth-atmosphere system but might also present all manner of natural history information, as most such walks do; a picnic area; and perhaps a gift shop and lunch counter. How about a series of monuments that feature each of the major soil orders, such as the Vertisol National Monument, perhaps in east-central Texas, "the most notable area" of such soils in the United States (Buol, Hole, and McCracken

1997: 363), where the interpretation might emphasize the specific suite of environmental characteristics that contribute to the development of these clay soils that swell and heave upward when wet and shrink and crack when dry. Monuments could highlight both typical and notable stream-flow events or characteristics, maybe a Fall Flood National Monument on Fish-eating Creek in central Florida, as an interpretive unit for the unusual phenomena of peak stream flows in the autumn (*National Atlas of the United States* 1970). Units might protect and present landforms, whether common or unusual; perhaps a Carolina Bays National Monument centered on the shallow oval depressions on the Carolina coastal plain, or a Blackhawk Canyon Debris Slide National Monument on a spectacular five-mile mass of debris that slid away from the San Bernardino Mountains out onto the floor of the southern California Mojave Desert (J. Shelton 1966). Monuments could focus on Quaternary events, perhaps a Lake Bonneville National Monument in Utah or a Channeled Scablands National Monument in eastern Washington, a landscape scoured by a lake-draining flood when a wall of water 2,000 feet high, moving 8 to 10 cubic miles of water per hour, drained away in a matter of days (Alt and Hyndman 1984). We should have a unit to present the Holocene history of southwestern Wisconsin—a Driftless Area National Monument, to interpret the post–Ice Age climate variability and environmental response of streams and vegetation, perhaps involving the impacts of nineteenth-century mining and farming on both stream flow and vegetation cover (Knox 1995, 2001). The possibilities indeed seem endless.

This broadened sense of the natural world would be appreciated by the ever-traveling American public, who would revel in visiting and learning about the natural United States. One impact of this conscious effort to expand the concept of national monuments might well be an increased appreciation of nature, not only of spectacular scenery, not only of rare plants and animals, but also as it appears in various phenomena, in various landscapes and situations, the nature to be found almost everywhere.

10 THE "NEW" NATURE PROTECTION

In evaluating nature-protection efforts at the turn of the twenty-first century, the geographer Karl Zimmerer finds fault with the twentieth-century ideal, the inviolate landscape reserve. Calling the human actions to create such preserves "territory making," he looks upon this behavior with more than a little disdain: "A plethora of conservation abuses and injustices have resulted from territory making. . . . Territorial designations often precipitate the loss of access to social-environmental entitlement among residents and resource users alike" (Zimmerer 2000: 359). Rather than concentrating on strongly protected areas, Zimmerer advocates a focus on human needs: the boundaries of areas where human activities are permitted or prohibited should be determined by the specifics of human needs, and decisions about the placement of those variable boundaries should be made by reference to spatial and temporal scales appropriate to the activities. Only with such recasting of the nature-protection effort can societies move beyond "the proclivity towards parks and other protected areas, and toward the fuller understanding of utilized or 'second nature'" (Zimmerer 2000: 364). From this perspective, focusing on social justice, Zimmerer sees protected landscapes as aristocratic castles, and he advocates instead the garden. He seems to oppose outright the concept of protecting "first nature"—or, more constructively, he seems to advocate other forms of nature protection.

Zimmerer describes his ideal as "nature-society hybrids," which form "new conservation areas." His scholarly discourse accurately echoes events that have appeared throughout the nature-protection movement in recent years: a "new kind of national park," the "new forestry," the "new BLM," "new mining rules" in a "new West." Collectively, nature protection seems to have become a "new conservation."

Protected Nature as Unreal, Unjust, and Unwise

The intellectual foundation for the contemporary ideal of the garden image rests on three pillars of thought: wilderness as unreal (no landscape is natural; all landscapes are humanized), wilderness as unjust (nature-protection efforts lack a sense of social justice), and wilderness as unwise (by focusing on pure nature in wild places, society neglects modified nature in everyday places). All three often appear together in scholarly treatments of nature protection, at least those treatments in the social sciences, though any one may dominate a particular dialogue.

The three assertions reflect hyperbole more than nuanced truth. Consider each one separately. *Unreal:* The belief that native peoples modified the pre-Columbian landscape everywhere in North America is so common that its articulation often goes unqualified (Denevan 1992, McCann 1999, Kay and Simmons 2002); its exaggeration fails to recognize a *geography* of Indian impacts and a resulting mosaic in the landscape of 1492, which included natural as well as humanized areas (Vale, ed., 2002; cf. Grayson and Meltzer 2002, 2003). *Unjust:* The identification of an undesirable elitism and thus a fundamental injustice in nature protection (Duncan and Duncan 2001) similarly simplifies complex situations (the *dicto simpliciter* fallacy) by implying that injustice appears only when someone promotes a nature reserve, that the interest expressed by wealthy and powerful elites in nature protection proves the basic injustice of the interest (*argumentum ad hominem*), and that the magnitude of the injustice associated with parks—if it exists—explains why societies have poor and powerless groups (a fallacy of cause and effect, *post hoc, ergo propter hoc*) (but cf. Melosi 2000). *Unwise:* The assertion that an obsession with wilderness blinds us to nonwilderness nature (Lowenthal 1968b, Cronon 1995a) seems contrary to experience: in the American political arena, the folks concerned with wilderness are the same ones who worry about pesticides and water pollution and the legion of environmental issues in the everyday world. As with many hyperboles, some truth lies in the exaggerations—we need to keep in mind the impacts of native peoples on the North American landscapes of 1492, to consider social justice as an element in decisions about nature protection, to seek sensitivity toward nature in nonwilderness landscapes—but hyperbolic simplifications obfuscate rich and complex realities.

New Models for Reserves on the Federal Lands

When President Bill Clinton proclaimed new national monuments in several western states in the late 1990s, environmental activists cheered as loudly as local ranchers bellowed in outrage. Apparently neither group noticed that the executive actions changed the potential uses of the affected landscapes only modestly. The monuments represent the sort of flexibility that increasingly characterizes the new nature protection on the federal lands.

THE NATIONAL PARK SYSTEM Flexibility appears in units administered by the agency with the strongest protectionist tradition, the National Park Service. In 1974, when Congress created Big Thicket and Big Cypress national preserves, the National Park System initiated reserves with less than complete protection as a formal type of system unit; with the 1980 Alaska National Interest Lands Act, the national preserves became a major part of the total acreage of the entire park system. Hunting, trapping, mining, livestock grazing, off-road vehicle use—such activities are acceptable on at least some national preserve lands, with constraints permitted for protection of natural characteristics. Moreover, the loss to the National Park Service of the exclusive authority to administer reserves called national monuments began in recent years with the Forest Service's administration of two 1980 national monuments in Alaska and of the 1989 Mount St. Helens Volcanic National Monument in Washington; the Bureau of Land Management assumed responsibility for national monuments beginning in 1996. These actions suggest the appeal of making territorial designations without denying uses incompatible with Park Service traditions. Historic irony accompanies these new national monuments: in 1933 Franklin Delano Roosevelt simplified the administration of the federal lands by consolidating areas called national monuments—some had been administered by the Forest Service—under the National Park Service. An even more dramatic deviation from the traditions of the National Park System appear with the Tallgrass Prairie National Preserve, a 1996 unit whose landscape is owned by a nongovernment (albeit nonprofit) organization, the National Park Trust, with a number of additional "new conservation" arrangements: oversight provided by an advisory committee and a board of trustees, commitment to continue livestock grazing (as part of the prairie's history), and rhetorical proclamations of "partnerships" with "good neighbors" to create a "model for the nation." Similarly, the Blackstone River Valley National Heritage Corridor, in Massachusetts and Rhode Island, involves no land owned or managed by the Park Service, instead relying on public-private "partnerships" to protect the area's "special identity." Such cooperative administration between the Park Service and other bodies is hardly novel; the Canyon de Chelly National Monument, for example, established in 1931, is jointly overseen by the Park Service and the Navajo Nation, which continues to own the monument's land. Nonetheless, the number of recent units that proudly proclaim partnership administrations hint at the popularity of "new conservation": New Bedford Whaling National Historic Park (Park Service and city of New Bedford), Petroglyph National Monument (Park Service and city of Albuquerque), Cayahoga Valley National Recreation Area (now a national park; Park Service and local park agencies), Ice Age National Scenic Trail (Park Service imprimatur on lands administered by local governments or private owners), City of Rocks National Preserve (Park Service and State of Idaho), Nez Perce National Historic Park (Park Service and Nez Perce government), Boston Harbor Islands National Recreation Area (Park Service and a variety of other public and private groups), Channel Islands National Park (where the Nature Conservancy continues to own substantial acreage).

Perhaps the strongest expression of flexibility in Park Service policy emerges with provisions for access to system lands by Native Americans. A 1970 decision to exclude Chippewa lands from the proposed Apostle Islands National Lakeshore has been described as a "watershed" for its recognition of contemporary Indians as no longer "invisible" (Keller and Turek 1998: 16). This action was followed, in 1975, by boundary revisions to Grand Canyon National Park, which transferred 185,000 acres of park land to the Havasupai, and the creation of a "traditional use" zone for Havasupai commodity resource development within the park. These provisions, obviously intended more to give residents access than to protect nature, pale in comparison with what the Havasupai initially wanted: freedom to use the park lands in any way they wished and construction of Hualapai Dam in the Grand Canyon itself (Keller and Turek 1998: 181). Similarly, the creation of the Timbisha Shoshone Tribal Homeland within Death Valley National Park will permit tribal members to manicure mesquite stands, set up overnight camps, harvest piñon nuts, clear springs of shrubs and trees, and gather plant materials in a large area of the park, and to construct residences (dare anyone label them a subdivision?), an administrative center, a cultural center, and an inn/gift shop in the Furnace Creek area. Throughout the system, Indian groups covet access to park resources: the Miccosukee for housing in Everglades, the

Hoh for elk in Olympic, the Hopi for eagles in Wupatki; various Native Americans desire plant materials in Organ Pipe, Death Valley, and Yosemite. On a grand and more sweeping scale, the units of the National Park System created under the 1980 Alaska National Interest Lands Conservation Act permit subsistence activities (the key being hunting), hailed by one observer as a "different conceptualization of humankind in nature . . . an inhabited wilderness . . . strik[ing] the right balance between the inhabitants' desire for freedom and the wilderness users' desire for the primitive" (Catton 1997: xviii–xix, 220). "The right balance"—such compromises in nature protection in the National Park System mark the "new conservation."

BUREAU OF LAND MANAGEMENT LANDS The emergence of landscape reserves within the Bureau of Land Management testifies to the strength of the new model that extends protection to landscapes in use while maintaining those uses, though they are not ordinarily associated with reserved lands. Wilderness designation, for example, became the focus of protectionist efforts on the public domain in the 1980s, even though such areas permit livestock grazing and sport hunting. The congressionally established national conservation areas (the first being the King Range in northwestern California, established in 1970) generally allow commodity resource uses that are interpreted as benign to natural values, but that may include everything from hunting, mountain bicycling, and free-roaming recreational animals to livestock grazing and mining. The Clinton administration's declaration of national monuments on the public domain, beginning with the Grand Staircase–Escalante in southern Utah in 1996 and followed by many others by the end of the decade, similarly represents flexible nature-protection actions. The monuments are typically closed to new mineral entry and off-road vehicle use but open to livestock use, hunting, bicycling, and recreational animals (Durbin 2003b, Nijhuis 2003, Tobin 2003); these less than strict policies, in fact, are touted as a virtue of the BLM reserves (Larmer 1999, Stuebner 1999). Moreover, in an effort to enhance its role as a manager of areas identified as "protected," the BLM proclaimed the National Landscape Conservation System as an umbrella administrative structure for its various reserves, an action that calls to mind the virtue seen in "systems" elsewhere on the federal lands. Finally, in promoting this new role for the bureau, Interior Secretary Bruce Babbitt emphasized the importance of interactions between the federal agency and local human communities, "partnerships" in which visitors are encouraged "to see the [reserve] landscape in the context of the history and tradition of the entire region" (Babbitt 2000).

Although environmental groups may continue to press for a more protectionist BLM (Maffly 2003, Morrison 2003b), Babbitt's statement sounds similar to urgings for a "fuller understanding of utilized or 'second nature.'" The
notion of cooperation even outlived the Democratic administration to
become a boast of the subsequent Republican leadership (Scarlett and Watson 2004).

NATIONAL WILDLIFE REFUGE SYSTEM Some recent national wildlife refuge projects also reveal attempts to accommodate land uses other than
wildlife enhancement. The Rachel Carson National Wildlife Refuge consists
of ten separate units of wetlands within an area of development along
Maine's southern coast. What distinguishes this refuge is its scattered small-
holdings and its lack of a large, contiguous block of protected landscape.
Even more striking is the Silvio O. Conte National Wildlife Refuge, authorized by Congress in 1991 for the Connecticut River drainage, a project that
involves some land purchases but that focuses on involving "the people of
the watershed, especially landowners and land managers, in environmental
education programs and cooperative management projects" (U.S. Fish and
Wildlife Service, http://www.fws.gov/r5soc). In one sense, these types of
"new" refuges, characterized by dispersed landholdings and cooperative
agreements among various groups, simply use the long-established programs of the Fish and Wildlife Service to fit their protectionist efforts into
working landscapes, perhaps typified by the habitat purchases of waterfowl
production areas. In another sense, however, if the Conte refuge characterizes future refuge projects and if national wildlife refuges become less blocks
of landscape than arrangements for cooperative management, this development may herald a focus as much on social-environmental entitlements as
on wildlife.

In northern Florida, the Merritt Island National Wildlife Refuge serves
as but an anchor for a program to improve habitat for the Florida scrub jay,
and in the lower Mississippi River an ecosystem team works with various
partners on projects in matters of nutrient loadings and wetland enhancement. While applauding these goals and praising cooperative agreements
with local residents, a conservation skeptic might wonder if the justification
reflects political compromise rather than what is best for nature protection.

Less clearly compromising policies for nature reserves, in designating
areas as "critical habitat" for threatened and endangered animal species the
Fish and Wildlife Service embraces the broad spatial perspective associated
with the Conte refuge model or ecosystem conservation. Such designations

initiate constraints on the use of federal land and even of private land tied
to federal funding or permits. They also encourage the development of habitat conservation plans, which prompt creation of landscape reserves within
otherwise developed or modified environments.

BIOSPHERE RESERVES AND OTHER VISIONS Whether within the
National Park System, the public domain of the Bureau of Land Management, the National Wildlife Refuge System, or the national forests (Reese
2003), the emergence of new models for nature-protection areas, with pride-
ful embrace of lenient regulations and local human involvement, suggests
an application of the biosphere reserve model, typically touted for societies
in the developing world. With their core areas receiving the greatest degrees
of nature protection, biosphere reserves also include zoned regions with various degrees of commodity resource use and landscape modification, all
"intended to integrate the preservation of biological diversity along with
economic development" (Povilitis 1993: 18). It is a vision of a world where

Figure 10.1. *Wild Earth's* Sky Islands Wildlands Network Conservation Plan
(Adapted from Foreman et al. 2000)

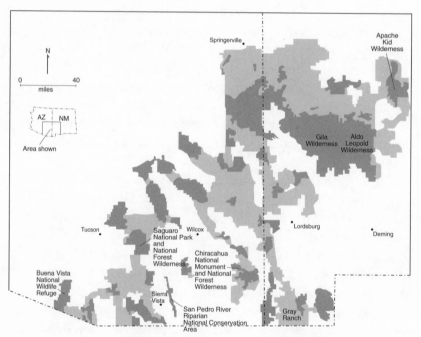

Dark shading indicates core areas of strong protection; many are already protected. Lighter
shading indicates lands needing some lesser degree of protection.

societies can have both nature protection and development, without conflict; everyone wins. No wonder the rhetoric has such wide appeal!

A surprisingly parallel perspective emerges as the Wildlands Project from Wild Earth, surprising because this environmental organization seeks a "wilderness recovery" (or, more provocatively, a "re-wilding") of North America by land zoning and land protection. Corridors of wild landscape would be linked together across large areas of the continent (but especially in the West), protecting landscapes "free of mechanized human use and the sounds and constructions of modern civilization," enabling the unfolding of natural processes such as fire, allowing the persistence of biological species small and large, allowing "grizzlies in Chihuahua [to] have an unbroken connection to grizzlies in Alaska" (Butler 2000: 4). What sounds like the most strident of protectionist proposals may appear less radical on a map. The Sky Islands Wildlands Network in the region astride the Arizona–New Mexico border, for example, reveals a system of protected areas with various types of permitted uses, virtually all on public lands, but with essentially no constraints on the landscape more generally (Foreman et al. 2000, Foreman 2004) (fig. 10.1). Liberal social reformers and conservative economic growth enthusiasts alike should be able to embrace this plan, designed as territory making but hardly representing injustice to residents and resource users.

Redirection of Policies of Federal Land Agencies

The blossoming of specific and named landscape reserves consistent with visions of "second nature" and "access entitlements" has paralleled contemporary trends more generally in the management of the federal lands. These trends can be seen in both the Forest Service and the Bureau of Land Management.

THE NATIONAL FOREST SYSTEM Across the federal lands, the once-dominant commodity resource users (the "lords of yesterday," in Charles Wilkinson's [1992] provocative phrase) increasingly yield to amenity resource users, including those who build remotely located ranchettes on private lands adjacent to the federal domains, thereby contributing to the crisis of land development (R. Knight 1997). With a focus on biodiversity values, the powerful gathered strength during the 1970s and 1980s, and by the early 1990s seemed to influence the U.S. Forest Service, which announced a policy shift toward a "new forestry," with "new perspectives" based on "ecosystem management." Sometimes attributed to the old-growth forest scientist Jerry Franklin and his colleagues in the Pacific Northwest (Lindenmayer and

Franklin, eds., 2003), the "new forestry" represents "a reasonable alternative to the harsh choice between tree farms and total preservation" (C. Fiedler 1992: 4), an alternative that "accommodates ecological values, while allowing for the extraction of commodities" (Franklin 1989: 37–44). Decried by some critics as antiscientific (Atkinson 1992) and by others as too weakly applied to change the traditional emphasis on timber extraction (Alverson et al. 1994), the proposals seem to others as simply "sustainable forestry" (Maser 1992). One commentator even interprets the ideas as a postmodern evolution from belief in the "one right forestry" to faith in a blending of "rationalism . . . [with] romanticism, as well as classicism and primitivism" (McQuillan 1992: 19, 20). However characterized, the movement has generated a new type of Forest Service administrator, typified by Jack Ward Thomas and Michael Dombeck, who during the 1990s spearheaded policies more attuned to the new visions (Drabelle 1994, T. Wilkinson 1998, Dombeck 2003). The effects cascaded throughout the forests: rates of timber removal plummeted; road building temporarily ceased; commodity resource interests criticized forest plans; wilderness and recreation increasingly dominated decisions on Idaho's Nez Perce (Doherty 1992); local Hispanic groups in New Mexico become "a powerful incentive for reforestation and responsible grazing stewardship" (Wright 1997: 14); and, on the Lewis and Clark National Forest, Supervisor Gloria Flora prohibited natural gas exploration on Montana's Rocky Mountain Front (Matthews 1997, Montaigne 1998). By the end of the decade, a Forest Service mission statement prepared by an advisory committee of scientists called for "preeminence to preservation of biodiversity . . . [and] more collaborative relationships with local communities and groups" (Quinn 1999: 12, 13). This stance achieved a sort of institutional legitimacy in 2001 when the Forest Service issued its "Sierra Nevada Framework" (Marston 2001b).

"New forestry," postmodernism, enlightened administrators—such policies clearly seem to conform to the "soft" and flexible notion of the new conservation. But even the wild-forest ideal proposed as a guide for preserving biodiversity on the national forests, in many ways a strident reaffirmation of traditional "hard" nature protection, reveals a silky side. On the one hand, the wild forest is seen as critical to maintaining biodiversity: "wild" and "unengineered" forests, rather than new technologies in forest management, are portrayed as necessary to stem the loss of biodiversity. Moreover, the fundamental basis for biodiversity protection is said to rest with "the idea of wilderness," recast with biodiversity values in mind and expressed as

"Diversity Maintenance Areas" dedicated to "wild forests where human influence is kept to a minimum." On the other hand, such protected areas would be open to human uses that do not threaten biodiversity values, including "snowmobiling or subsistence logging for firewood" and the harvesting of fir boughs and edible plants. Moreover, where sport hunting is necessary to reduce undesirable browsing and grazing by ungulates, it "should not only be permitted but actually be increased" (Alverson et al. 1994: xviii, 150, 173–74, 193, 243). National forests reinvented as biodiversity reserves might be interpreted, ironically, as testimony to the ideal of flexibility in the new conservation.

Although celebrations of environmental protection attitudes among old-timers in the Forest Service persist (Doig 1984, Wallach 1988), the proposals for diversity maintenance areas come from natural scientists critical of the traditional Forest Service policy. The 1990s "roadless initiative," however, emanated from concerned Washington bureaucrats also critical of that policy. T. Williams (2000) reports that Forest Service chief Dombeck was determined to reverse the federal subsidy to timber cutting on the national forests, which created both below-cost timber sales and road building, and from that concern emerged a program to constrain the road network on the national forests. In 1999 President Clinton ordered a study to evaluate "appropriate long-term protection for most or all of [the] currently inventoried 'roadless' areas," more than 40 million acres. By the end of 2000, the Forest Service issued its plan to prohibit most road construction and timber harvesting on 49.2 million acres; the total was to increase to 58.5 million acres in 2004, when Alaska's Tongass National Forest would be included in the program. Irony again looms in this story: For decades, nature-protection groups sought congressional oversight on wilderness protection on the national forests—meaning mostly protection from roads—because executive authority was seen as uncertain, and they succeeded in 1964 with passage of the Wilderness Act. But by the end of the century, those groups were praising the use of executive power to more than double the national forest acreage protected from road building. Irony follows upon irony: the Bush administration then reversed the roadless decision.

If the trends toward increased protection continue—and they show no signs of reversing, no matter who resides in the White House—the national forests will become increasingly like national parks while the areas of "total preservation" become increasingly like national forests. Ed Marston, editor of *High Country News* and Colorado resident, sees the Forest Service as

clearly committed to a stronger protectionist impulse, and he implores resisting westerners who long for the days of fewer constraints on resource
extraction to recognize that regional interests must conform to "the national will. Anything else consigns us [westerners] to the same backward
status as the South in the decades after the Civil War, before that region was
freed by the civil rights movement" (Marston 1999: 1).

BUREAU OF LAND MANAGEMENT LANDS   Less conspicuously but
no less importantly, the general policies of the Bureau of Land Management
over recent decades suggest increased protectionist trends consistent with
those of the Forest Service (Conniff 1990). Long before the emergence of the
new conservation it was evident that the BLM was moving away from its traditionally tight relationship with large ranchers (Foss 1960) toward a more
diverse mix of landscape users, including those who championed nature
protection (Vale 1979). That movement seems only to have continued over
the ensuing decades, although the magnitude of the agency's transformation hardly pleases environmental groups (Darlington 1989, Wuerthner
1990b). Nonetheless, authorized livestock grazing on the public domain's
grazing districts, consistently maintained at 15 million animal unit months
from the 1940s into the 1960s, gradually decreased thereafter to less than 9
million in the late 1990s, a drop of more than 30 percent (*Public Land Statistics*, 1965–99). The admittedly crude estimates of overall range conditions
indicate improvements: the percentage of the public domain landscape in
"good" or "excellent" condition rose from about 20 in the 1970s to nearly 40
in 1990 (Vale 1979; *Public Land Statistics* 1990). It is tempting to see a causal
link between the decrease in cattle and sheep on BLM lands and the rise in
the number of pronghorns from fewer than 200,000 in the mid-1960s to
nearly 400,000 in the late 1990s (*Public Land Statistics* 1965–99). The BLM's
Great Basin Restoration Initiative (Bureau of Land Management 1999) promises an effort to reestablish a more natural vegetation cover in the interior
West, where alien plant species have encouraged wildfires that degrade ecosystem productivity for livestock and native animals alike (Trimble 1989).
One commentator suggests that the initiative is "one of the most ambitious
ecosystem restoration projects in the West" (J. Christensen 2000: 8). Whether
one admires the initiative (L. Jones 2000) or dismisses it as simply appease-
ment of ranchers (Tweit 2000), one cannot miss the contrast of both the
rhetoric and vision with the explicit boosterism of the "rangeland improvements" of earlier decades (Vale 1974). Also telling is the continued talk of
banning all livestock from the bureau's domain: although politically prob-

lematic, not only because of the influence of ranchers but also because of the landscape identity linked to range livestock activities (Starrs 1994), such action seems only marginally more dramatic than ending logging on virtually all roadless areas in the national forests, a policy realized with Clinton's roadless initiative. Even the privileges most sacred to the "lords of yesterday," those bestowed by the 1872 Mining Law, may be constrained: BLM rules announced in 2000 so strengthen the agency's oversight and regulatory powers over mining that the National Mining Association has denounced them as "detrimental to hard-rock mining and mineral development" (quoted by T. Watson 2000). Perhaps the public domain and the Bureau of Land Management, like designated wilderness, simply lag behind the Forest Service and the national forests: both seem to be a part of the new conservation.

Marston's warning that people who resist constraints on the uses of the national forests are doomed to a "backward status" (Marston 1999) should be heard by people linked to the public domain. Local folks in rural parts of the interior West, in Nevada, Utah, Wyoming, and New Mexico, find themselves caught between a romanticized view of "local control" and the shifts in national demands on western lands. Throughout the 1990s, Secretary of the Interior Bruce Babbitt championed consensus creation, admiring successful BLM projects that generated conversations among people with different interests in the public domain. In northern California he spoke glowingly of the prospects for such a creative coming together: "I'd like to know what it is in the water that lets you people cooperate. If I could, I'd bottle it and take it around to the rest of the West" (Bureau of Land Management 1993: 4). Cooperation requires appreciation of change. The critical issue may be less the creation of decision-making structures open to "residents and resource users" than the willingness of local people to embrace the opportunities still available to them to participate in the decision-making process (Marston 2000b).

Privatization

The new conservation expands the role of the private sector and encourages cooperation between private and public sectors. Fitzsimmons (1999: 278) argues against a strong federal hand, urging "democratic institutions, individual liberty, decentralized market-based decision-making, and guaranteed rights for owners of private property." The promise of a "fuller understanding" of nature appears today in both traditional areas of protected nature and newer models involving less than strict protection.

CONSERVATION GROUPS Several older conservation groups have

histories of land purchases, but none better exemplifies the strategy of buying natural areas or otherwise controlling development on pieces of landscape than the Nature Conservancy. With leadership and funding from corporate America, the Nature Conservancy had resounding successes during the 1990s under John Sawhill, once dean of New York University School of Business and a member of several corporate boards of directors. Many of its land projects have rivaled or exceeded in scope those of even the federal land agencies: 70,000 acres in the Mount Hamilton area of central California, 18,000 acres in the Davis Mountains of Texas, 32,000 acres in the Pascagoula Swamp of Mississippi, 185,000 acres on the St. John's River of Maine, the 55,000-acre Niobrara Valley Preserve in Nebraska, the 45,000-acre Virginia Coast Reserve of Virginia, the 32,000-acre Tallgrass Prairie Reserve in Oklahoma, and the massive 320,000-acre Gray Ranch of New Mexico.

In addition, the Nature Conservancy has moved toward programs that situate its land purchases in the contexts of surrounding landscapes (Margolis 2000a), even seeing its projects as protecting nature "while allowing compatible uses, like farming" (Byers 2001: 20). The Conservancy's project in the Texas hill country, for example, attempts to "stitch together a quilt of healthy natural habitat and settled areas . . . [even] allowing development to proceed around [existing cities]" (W. Stevens 1992). Having bought the Gray Ranch, the Conservancy then sold it with restrictions and easements to a wealthy ranching family, organized as the Animas Foundation; the concept was "responsible ranching," a laboratory "to show how people could respect land and still make a living from it" (Weisman 1993, Page 1992). At the still larger scale of the borderlands along the Arizona–New Mexico state line, the Gray Ranch is involved in a partnership of thirty-five ranchers, who together with the Nature Conservancy and federal land agencies have formed the Malpai Group, "dedicated to protecting two things . . . a vital ecosystem and the cattle-ranching way of life" (Klinkenborg 1995: 36). Attacking the wilderness enthusiast as "hand-in-hand with the real estate developer" ("Now the enemy is . . . backpackers, anglers, hunters, new housing and resorts"), one environmental activist in Colorado praises the efforts "to add local people and economies" to conservation goals (Marston 2000b: 15). The examples reveal a perspective that is more than mere rhetoric: the new conservation flourishes with such accommodation to residents and resource users.

LAND TRUSTS The recent popularity and promotion of land trusts as a landscape-protection strategy similarly suggests expansion of private-sector conservation activity. Two virtues of land trusts, which involve the donation or purchase of development rights to land, are commonly identified: control of conservation policy by local people and maintenance of private property. More than 1,200 land trusts are scattered across the United States; more than 500 were organized in the 1990s alone. The strongest concentrations are in the urbanized regions of New England, southern Florida, Chicago–Milwaukee, Puget Sound, and the San Francisco Bay Area (Wright 1993: 16, Biondo 2000: 28, Merenlender et al. 2004). By the year 2000, nearly five million acres had been included in land trusts in the United States. The names of the trusts, revealing affection for places, deserve to be recognized as readily as major federally protected areas: Big Sur Land Trust, Aspen Valley Land Trust, Colorado Open Lands, French and Pickering Creeks Conservancy, Society for the Protection of New Hampshire's Forests.

An extension of the land trust idea appears in conservation easements on private commercial forest land (Matthews 2003b). Such easements, sometimes involving hundreds of thousands of acres, permit continued timber harvesting but with constraints designed to protect nature, especially biodiversity. Federal funds flow through the Forest Legacy Program to these projects in at least thirty-three states.

Enthusiasm for land trusts is found in widely separated sectors of the political spectrum. John Wright (1993: 257), for example, argues strongly in their favor and against government land purchases from what seems to be a conventionally conservative political stance: "Attempts to reach environmental goals through excessive civil control will spawn further injustice and social unrest . . . [because it] will be injurious to basic constitutional rights." Individual land trusts occasionally boast that their protection of environmental qualities supports economic vitality; for example, the McDowell-Sonoran Land Trust in Arizona observes that saving the mountains also preserves "the economic benefits that they bring." The Desert Foothills Land Trust, by contrast, is dedicated to opposing the uncontrolled exercise of private property rights in land development: the Arizona landscape needs protection because "bulldozers are moving onward." The Vermont Land Trust is certain that the New England landscape should be focused on "farming, forestry, and wilderness." The Central Maryland Heritage League Land Trust warns that the Maryland countryside is threatened by "the march of development." The Central Indiana Land Trust wants to "protect natural spaces in the face of urban sprawl" (http://www.lta.org/regionallta/index). The land trust may be seen as a realistic protectionist response to ongoing growth in a capitalist system or as evidence of naive faith that nature can be protected while economic development proceeds unabated. Whatever value is assigned to these efforts, it strongly conforms to the spirit of accommodation that is central to the new conservation.

HABITAT CONSERVATION PLANS   A procedure for protecting rare and endangered species while also allowing landscape development has become a cornerstone of American biodiversity policy (Noss et al. 1997, Rolfe 2001, T. Davis 2003). The 1982 revision of the federal Endangered Species Act authorized consultations between the U.S. Fish and Wildlife Service and nonfederal and nongovernment bodies to develop plans to mitigate the "incidental take" (i.e., habitat destruction) of protected animal species on private lands; these plans became known as habitat conservation plans (HCPs). The approach promises "to integrate conservation with planning for appropriate development, and relies on a partnership between local government and private interests" (DeSimone and Silver 1995: 33). Initially focused on individual species, HCPs increasingly turned toward multiple species and large geographic areas. The federal government's agreement to abide by the terms of the HCP even if unforeseen circumstances should suggest attempts to protect a species increased the appeal of the process. By August 2000, 313 plans involving 20 million acres had been approved, allowing various types of commodity resource use and landscape development to proceed, testimony to the appeal of flexibility in endangered species protection.

The critics of HCPs focus on that very flexibility. Some environmentalists worry that the compromises can only endanger rare species (Kling 1997, Mann and Plummer 1997). Accommodation is seen as weakness: "Adversarial wrangling . . . has fallen out of favor, replaced by . . . the negotiating table" (Luoma 1998: 39). Others see the planning process hampered by the conflicting goals of the political bodies involved, none of which is wholeheartedly dedicated to protecting species (DeSimone and Silver 1995) or inclined to question the limitations of capitalist politics (Feldman and Jonas 2000). Finally, the on-ground application of not only HCPs but also efforts to protect species more generally remains tied to what is described as the false people/nature dichotomy: too much attention is still paid to "inviolate reserves" and too little to "finding practices and metaphors that embrace biodiversity . . . while refusing to accept as inevitable . . . the ideological and spatial gap between humans and the natural world implicit in contemporary social constructions of nature" (Proctor and Pincetl 1996: 704). It seems that even the segmentation of nature into a mosaic of protected and developed landscapes, as envisioned by regional HCPs and as promoted by spokespersons for the new conservation, fail to free the dialogue from established visions of wilderness. Is it inevitable that any expression of concern for species survival derives from some emotion that might be called the sacred, and that any criticism of that emotion, whether outright dismissal or nuanced questioning, hides behind the intellectual mask of aristocratic castle or false idol? For those who care about species extinctions, the ethical stage is nothing for which to apologize.

Community

An intellectual foundation for the new conservation, for a focus on "second nature," for constructing links between local human populations and the natural world, builds on the everywhere-popular vision of community (e.g., Western and Wright, eds., 1994; Ghimire and Pimbert, eds., 1997; Kusel and Adler, eds., 2003). Do not establish strict nature reserves cut off from the needs and wishes of the people who live nearby, those who take this perspective assert, but pursue policy that connects nature and people in constructive ways, even in ways that involve resource extraction. The bonding so created, if honestly fashioned to fit "devolved" local desires, generates self-interest in restoration and sustainability, in healthy interactions between nature and people, in caring communities. Tourism and luxury living destroy such relationships, as "community identity and values [yield] to the demands of intro- and extra-regional capital, visitors, and incoming residents" (Rothman 1999: 198). No positive relationships, the argument concludes, develop from landscape reserves focused on an ideal of pristine nature as valued and imposed by powerful outside elites.

A rationale common in the developing world, particularly in situations involving people identified as "indigenous," the community perspective also underlies much recent thinking in the United States. It is the vision that prompts "consensus-building" as a means to resolve controversies over protection versus development on the federal lands (Babbitt 2000). It is the reason for celebrating the success of the Quincy Library Group (Marston 1997). It is a message articulated by contemporary writers as the core of future environmentalism across the United States and throughout the world (Schoonmaker et al., eds., 1997; Neumann 1998; Zerner, ed., 2000; Kemmis 2001; Shabecoff 2000).

A vision of community informs the persistent message of Ed Marston, editor of *High Country News*. Before sentiment for nature protection became central to so much of the rhetoric of environmentalism, Marston worried that the environmentalists would win the West, perhaps beating back the forces working to save the region from becoming an "Appalachian dark night" of poverty but ensuring that it would become merely "another suburb" of parkland. To protect western nature and western landscapes, he urged, continue "the way of life that makes it unique" (Marston 1988). By the end of the century, he was still arguing the importance of a functioning rural West: "the main force in the rural West today is restoration. But restoring a healthy landscape requires a healthy, creative and prosperous rural society. . . . We need urban help . . . [but more to the point] urban-rural cooperation . . . to restore what is now a plundered land" (Marston 2000b). Others argue the same point, even defending the landscape most symbolic of western plundering, the irrigated field:

. . . the loss of the agricultural landscape and culture will be tough to stomach. Like Dorothy returning to Kansas, we will watch the vivid green pastures fade out to dull tans and grays. Sagebrush and rabbitbrush will return with a vengeance around the sodded courtyards of new homes. The great cottonwoods will wither and die, their skeletons providing roosts for eagles and vultures. . . . Some forms of life have adapted just fine to this watered desert. (Larmer 2001)

The same enthusiasm for local community and the environmental wisdom linked to it prompts Daniel Kemmis (2001) to suggest that the federal government no longer needs a strong presence in the American West, that today the interior West should gain its sovereignty and govern itself.

The rhetoric is seductive, ready to draw in the uncritical reader. Whatever virtue lies in the perspective, history tells us that environmental sensitivity, environmental wisdom, environmental knowledge derive not from the parochial, inward-looking, locally bounded community but from the national perspective. Jon Margolis, also of *High Country News,* cautions against blind faith in the local view, which counters not only environmental progress but enlightenment thinking more generally:

American history has been a progression from parochialism to nationhood, and the path toward nationhood led toward equality; it has been the national community—meaning the federal government—that has taken the lead in enforcing racial equality and enhancing economic justice. . . . The latest version of Western devolution is inspired largely by money and bitterness. . . . The bitterness leads folks astray; they think their "way of life" is threatened by the federal government, when it is threatened by the consolidating trends of the private economy. (Margolis 2000b)

The history of conservation in America, including the nature-protection impulse, is a story of actions by governments, typically against local desires. The successes in the 1990s by Bruce Babbitt and the Clinton administration affirm that history (Turner and Gregory 1997a, Mockler 1999, Marston 2001a). Do not misread the point: Marston, Larmer, and Margolis all speak truth. A sense of local community enriches the world and its landscapes, but it is romantic blindness to assume that alone and by itself the local view is sufficient for progressive environmental policies. Urban attitudes and national forces, tied to so many problems of people–nature interactions, provide the only hope for environmental wisdom, for nature protection.

Reflections

The new conservation, which seeks models other than strict and territorially bounded nature preserves, broadens the playing field for the contestation over the preservation of the natural world. But however promising the new perspective, its constructive contribution should be seen as augmenting the possibilities, not simply replacing the old traditions with something necessarily better. Glitz appeals mostly to the myopic eye.

The new conservation teaches us the importance of place, place identity and place sensitivity, throughout the nature-protection landscape. Novel nature-society hybrids appeal not only because they promise salvation for both the natural world and human society but also because the worlds thus linked, in the modern view, are in need of coupling. But even strictly protected, rigidly bounded nature reserves speak of human intention, reflect human creation, and thus express a connection between people and nature. The wildness of Yellowstone and Okefenokee, no less than Canyon de Chelly and Silvio O. Conte, no less than Gates of the Arctic and the Central Indiana Land Trust, tell of human links to the natural world, even if the nature involved in the various areas differs in degree of remoteness from the influences of people. To recognize the bonding that all of the areas represent, moreover, is to appreciate the locales as places, and by understanding them as such, we enhance the potential for greater sensitivity toward nature everywhere—not by belittling the vast wilderness as somehow apart from us, but by embracing the natural world in both the immense and the minute, in both the pure and the modified.

"legitimacy . . . and

. . . connection"

FINAL REFLECTIONS   We who cherish wild landscapes may not share an identical list of personal or social concerns. Mexican food, Japanese cars, Robin Williams, Barry Bonds, Starbucks coffee, *Star Wars* (all episodes)—those of us who love Yellowstone or Linville Gorge may or may not find ourselves agreeing on the relative virtues of an endless array of such personal matters. So, too, with social issues: fondness for Yosemite or the Wichita Mountains does not necessarily correlate with commitment to National Public Radio, increased taxes for education, and affirmative action, nor need it connect with opposition to NAFTA, English as the national language, or the Star Wars missile defense system. People who love Wisconsin's Blue Mounds State Park and its nearby Nature Conservancy reserve on Thousand Rocks Prairies may not burn with similar passion for federal water-pollution controls or soil-erosion abatement. Some of these connections are more likely, *much* more likely, than others, but the point remains: as a human motivation, concern for protecting wild landscape is sui generis.

To assert this point is not to deny the importance—even for preservation enthusiasts—of personal and social issues other than nature protection. Each of us bundles together diverse purposes—hopefully complementary, sometimes conflicting, occasionally contradictory—but the aggregation of the bundle remains just that, an aggregate of distinctive intentions, goals, and values. What is true for the individual, moreover, is also true for the group; the United States today constantly struggles, as it has struggled throughout its history, with its pluralistic, diverse, often opposing purposes. Both as individuals and as societies, we cannot pursue all our purposes equally and simultaneously; our decisions are necessarily compromises. Personal and collective positionings on any given question, then, may mean the decision ultimately made may or may not fulfill a particular purpose, including—again, even for wild nature crusaders—natural landscape preservation.

The effort to join concern for wild nature with more general social goals, no less than insistence that protecting wild nature is mere sentimentality and thus deserves no support, denies the legitimacy of protected nature as a natural resource. The diverse meanings that people see in wild landscapes are in fact no less real than the meanings that humans attach to other types of landscapes—the small town, the neighborhood, the family farm, the city center, the graffiti-covered wall, the communal garden plot. The protectionist impulse in conservation is no less honest than the desire for wisdom in the use of resources or social equity in their allocation. The dedicated lands of park, wilderness, and refuge are no more peculiar than other human-created landscapes, those of urban arts centers and midwestern cropland, of logged forests and centers of civil government. All serve human needs, however those needs may differ. The issues that spark the debates over the uses and goals of protected nature raise questions as valid as any facing the richly pluralistic American society. To reduce these matters to either silly sentimentality or arrogant elitism is unworthy of enlightened citizens.

The acceptance of the wild landscape reserve as a valid natural resource necessarily implies that humans connect to the natural world through the creation and use of such reserves: the definition of any part of nature as a natural resource requires such connection. We have seen the relation between people and nature in the diverse meanings attached to wild landscapes; in the rich drama of the protectionist impulse, the elaborate systems of protected wild lands, the questions that continue to swirl around the appropriateness of outdoor recreation on reserved landscapes, the contestation over who properly speaks for wild nature, the perceptions of the scope of the natural world, the institutions established to protect nature in an increasingly complex world. All of this activity expresses connection between people and nature. To suggest that setting up wild landscape reserves severs the human world from the natural is naive, at best a dishonest or incomplete perspective, at worst a view that serves, whether or not intentionally, those for whom nature protection offers nothing worthwhile. People-nature connections born from the legitimacy of the wild landscape resource permeate the places we call Yellowstone and Linville Gorge, Yosemite and Wichita Mountains, Blue Mounds and Thousand Rocks Prairies.

The trail back from the top of North Dome wanders though a sampling of the nonalpine landscapes of Yosemite—cliff faces, rock shelves, gentle sandy ridges, densely forested uplands, lush pockets with quiet watery seeps, streams amid meadows, steep inclines with trees arching out and towering up into the sky. It has become one of my favorite walks. The route passes by reminders of the human activity involved in nature protection here—the boundary of the 1864 Yosemite Grant and a corner, on Indian Rock, of that memorable political act; a landscape protected not only as a national park but also as the Yosemite Wilderness; an abandoned campground, perhaps not noticed by most visitors but stored in the mind of a man now beyond sixty who recalls a warm summer afternoon when, as a teenager, he explored the surrounding forest and meadow with his mother; the Tioga Road, build by mining interests before the park was created, purchased for the park by the generous Stephen Mather, rebuilt as part of Mission 66 amid vituperative controversy over road standards, driven by countless Yosemite visitors—one of whom was my father, who traveled the old road in 1939, a happening that may have initiated the events that have led to my own love for this place. I hear the sounds of a few modern park visitors racing by on the new road as my wife and I trudge the final grade through the sunny red fir at trail's end. The personal and institutional intertwining of people and nature along the path remind me that stories of bonding of the human and natural worlds need not be told only about the common everyday landscapes of farm and village, suburb and city, but also about the typically grand landscapes of Yosemite. Such stories also structure the meanings of the immense views of rocks and plants, animals and soils, skies and water—meanings that reflect human connections to spectacular nature—from atop North Dome, high above the valley called Yosemite.

LITERATURE CITED

Abbey, E. 1977. *The Journey Home.* New York: Dutton.

———. 1979. "Introduction." Pp. xviii–xxiii in P. Wild, *Pioneer Conservationists of Western America.* Missoula, MT: Mountain Press.

Adams, A. 1962. *These We Inherit: The Parklands of America.* San Francisco: Sierra Club.

Adams, A., and N. Newhall. 1960. *This Is the American Earth.* San Francisco: Sierra Club.

Agee, J., and D. Johnson, eds. 1988. *Ecosystem Management for Parks and Wilderness.* Seattle: University of Washington Press.

Ahlgren, C., and I. Ahlgren. 1984. *Lob Trees in the Wilderness: The Human and Natural History of the Boundary Waters.* Minneapolis: University of Minnesota Press.

Alford, C. 1985. *Science and the Revenge of Nature.* Gainesville: University Presses of Florida.

Allen, T. 1987. *Guardian of the Wild: The Story of the National Wildlife Federtation, 1936–1986.* Bloomington: Indiana University Press.

Allin, C. 1982. *The Politics of Wilderness Preservation.* Westport, CT: Greenwood Press.

Alt, D., and D. Hyndman. 1984. *Roadside Geology of Montana.* Missoula, MT: Mountain Press.

Altherr, T. 1985. "The Pajarito of Cliff Dwellers' National Park Proposal, 1900–1920." *New Mexico Historical Review* 60:271–94.

Alverson, W., W. Kuhlmann, and D. Waller. 1994. *Wild Forests: Conservation Biology and Public Policy.* Washington, D.C.: Island Press.

Amory, C. 1974. *Man Kind? Our Incredible War on Wildlife.* New York: Harper & Row.

Anderson, E. 1956. "Man as a Maker of New Plants and New Plant Communities." Pp. 763–77 in W. Thomas, ed., *Man's Role in Changing the Face of the Earth.* Chicago: University of Chicago Press.

Anderson, J. 2000. *Wildlife Sanctuaries and the Audubon Society: Places to Hide and Seek.* Austin: University of Texas Press.

Anderson, K., and G. Nabhan. 1991. "Gardeners in Eden." *Wilderness* 55 (194): 27–30.

Applegate, D. 1997. "National Parks: Geology Matters." *Geotimes,* August, 15.

Atkinson, W. 1992. "Silvicultural Correctness: The Politicalization of Forest Science." *Western Wildlands* 17 (4): 8–12.

Avedon, R. 1985. *In the American West.* New York: Abrams.

Babbitt, B. 2000. "BLM Interactive Town Hall Meeting Remarks by Secretary Bruce Babbitt, Phoenix, Arizona, March 24, 2000." Washington, D.C.: Bureau of Land Management. Processed leaflet.

Backes, D. 1995. "The Land Beyond the Rim: Sigurd Olson's Wilderness Theology." *Forest and Conservation History* 39:56–65.

Bahro, R. 1984. *From Red to Green.* London: Verso.

Baird, R. 1992. "Indians Seek Protection from Religious Suppression." *High Country News* 24 (11): 3.

Baker, J. 1985. "Winning and Losing the West." *Wilderness* 70 (3): 56–60.

Baker, W. 1989. "Landscape Ecology and Nature Reserve Design in the Boundary Waters Canoe Area, Minnesota." *Ecology* 70:23–35.

Baker, W., J. Munroe, and A. Hessl. 1997. "The Effects of Elk on Aspen in the Winter Range in Rocky Mountain National Park." *Ecography* 20:155–65.

Baldwin, D. 1972. *The Quiet Revolution: Grass Roots of Today's Wilderness Preservation Movement.* Boulder, CO: Pruett.

Barnes, T., and D. Gregory. 1997. *Reading Human Geography: The Poetics and Politics of Inquiry.* London: Arnold.

Barrow, M. 1998. *A Passion for Birds: American Ornithology after Audubon.* Princeton: Princeton University Press.

Bartel, J. 2001. "Growing Listed Plants under Federal Law." *Fremontia* 29 (1): 24–25.

Baskin, Y. 1997. *The Work of Life: How the Diversity of Life Sustains Us.* Washington, D.C.: Island Press.

Bassin, N. 1985. "Dinosaur National Monument: The Evolution of a Federal Reserved Water Right." *Water Resources Bulletin* 21:145–49.

Bates, J. 1957. "Fulfilling American Democracy: The Conservation Movement, 1907–1921." *Mississippi Valley Historical Review* 44:29–57.

Bates, M. 1956. "Man as an Agent in the Spread of Organisms." Pp. 788–804 in W. Thomas, ed., *Man's Role in Changing the Face of the Earth.* Chicago: University of Chicago Press.

Beach, B. 2001. "A New Network of Wildlands." *Wilderness* 2001:48–49.

Bean, M., and M. Rowland. 1997. *The Evolution of National Wildlife Law.* 3rd ed. Westport, CT: Praeger.

Beasley, C. 1991. "Moore Takes On All." *Buzzworm* 3 (3): 38–43.

Behan, R. 2001. *Plundered Promise: Capitalism, Politics, and the Fate of the Federal Lands.* Washington, D.C.: Island Press.

Behlen, D. 1981. "Thirtieth Anniversary Issue: A History." Pts. I–III. *Nature Conservancy News* 31 (4): 4–18.

Beverdige, C. 1983. "A Park for the People." *Natural History* 92 (8): 29–38.

Bevis, W. 1986. "The Prairie: Cooper's Desert Ecology." *Environmental Review* 10 (1): 3–15.

Biehl, J. 1987. "Ecofeminism and Deep Ecology: Unresolvable Conflict?" *Our Generation* 19 (2): 19–31.

Biondo, B. 2000. "Stand By Our Land." *Nature Conservancy News* 50 (5): 26–33.

Blaikie, P., T. Cannon, I. Davis, and B. Wisner. 1994. *At Risk: Natural Hazards, People's Vulnerability, and Disasters*. London: Routledge.

Blair, W. 1986. "The Nature Conservancy: Conservation through Cooperation." *Journal of Forest History* 30 (1): 37–41.

———. 1991. "A Look Back." *Nature Conservancy News* 41 (6): 10–21.

Bonnicksen, T. 1989. "Fire Gods and Federal Policy." *American Forests* 95 (7–8): 14–16, 66–68.

Bonnickson, T., and E. Stone. 1981. "The Giant Sequoia–Mixed Conifer Forest Community Characterized through Pattern Analysis as a Mosaic of Aggregations." *Forest Ecology and Management* 3:307–28.

———. 1982. "Reconstruction of a Presettlement Giant Sequoia–Mixed Conifer Forest Community Using the Aggregation Approach." *Ecology* 63:1134–48.

Boorstein, M. 1992. "The Wonders and Origins of Four National Parks of the Southern United States." *Focus* 42 (4): 26–31.

Botkin, D. 1990. *Discordant Harmonies: A New Ecology for the Twenty-first Century*. New York: Oxford University Press.

———. 2000. *No Man's Garden: Thoreau and a New Vision for Civilization and Nature*. Washington, D.C.: Island Press.

———. 2004. *Our Natural History: The Lessons of Lewis and Clark*. New York: Oxford University Press.

Botti, S., and H. Nichols. 1995. "Availability of Fire Resources and Funding for Prescribed Natural Fire Programs in the National Park Service." Pp. 94–103 in J. Brown et al., eds., *Proceedings: Symposium on Fire in Wilderness and Park Management*. General Technical Report INT-GTR 320. Ogden, UT: U.S. Forest Service, Intermountain Research Station.

Bowden, M. 1992. "The Invention of American Tradition." *Journal of Historical Geography* 18:3–26.

Brandon, K. 1996. "Annex: Selected Ecotourism Cases." Pp. 41–56 in World Bank, *Ecotourism and Conservation: A Review of Key Issues*. Washington, D.C.

Briggs, J. 1996. "Need for Speed." *Wisconsin State Journal*, November 14.

Brower, B. 1982. "Policy and Power: The Forest Service and the Range Sheep Industry in the Wind River Mountains, Wyoming." M.A. thesis (Geography), University of California, Berkeley.

Brower, D. 1963. Foreword to E. Porter, ed., *The Place No One Knew: Glen Canyon on the Colorado*. San Francisco: Sierra Club.

———. 1990. *For Earth's Sake: The Life and Times of David Brower*. Salt Lake City: Peregrine Smith.

Brown, K. 1998. "The Great DOE Land Rush?" *Science* 282:616–17.

Brown, M., and J. May. 1991. *The Greenpeace Story: The Inside Story of the World's Most Dynamic Environmental Pressure Group*. New York: Dorling Kindersley.

Brown, T. 1991. "Water for Wilderness Areas: Instream Flow Needs, Protection, and Economic Value." *Rivers* 2 (4): 311–25.

Brown, W. 1988. "Beringia: A Common Border, Soviets and Americans Work to Create a Joint Park in the Bering Strait." *National Parks* 62 (11–12): 18–23.

Buchholtz, C. 1983. *Rocky Mountain National Park: A History.* Boulder: Colorado Associated University Press.

Bulte, E., and G. Van Kooten. 2000. "Economic Science, Endangered Species, and Biodiversity Loss." *Conservation Biology* 14:113–19.

Buol, S., F. Hole, and R. McCracken. 1997. *Soil Genesis and Classification.* 4th ed. Ames: Iowa State University Press.

Bureau of Land Management. 1993. "Interior Chief Calls Partnership Projects 'Model for the West.'" *Newsbeat,* July, 1, 4–5.

————. 1999. *Out of Ashes, an Opportunity.* Boise, ID.

Burnham, P. 2000. *Indian Country, God's Country: Native Americans and the National Parks.* Washington, D.C.: Island Press.

Butcher, D. 1955. *Seeing America's Wildlife in Our National Wildlife Refuges.* New York: Devin-Adair.

————. 1969. *Exploring Our National Parks and Monuments.* 6th ed. Boston: Houghton Mifflin.

Butcher, R. 2003. *America's National Wildlife Refuges.* Lanham, MD: Roberts Rinehart.

Butler, T. 2000. "The Wildlands Project: Mission, Vision, and Purpose." *Wild Earth* 10 (1): 4–5.

Byers, A. 2001. "25 Deals That Led the Way." *Nature Conservancy News* 51 (1): 18–29.

Cahn, R. 1981. "Evolving Together: Photography and the National Park Idea." Pp. 121–138 in R. Cahn, *American Photographers and the National Parks.* New York: Viking.

Cahn, R., and P. Cahn. 1992. "Parallel Parks." *National Parks* 66 (1–2): 24–29.

Callicott, J. 1989. "American Indian Land Wisdom? Sorting Out the Issues." *Journal of Forest History* 33:35–42.

Carson, R. 1947. *Parker River: A National Wildlife Refuge.* Conservation in Action, no. 2. Washington, D.C.: U.S. Fish and Wildlife Service.

————. 1955/1990. *The Edge of the Sea.* Boston: Houghton Mifflin.

Cartmill, M. 1983. "'Four Legs Good, Two Legs Bad.'" *Natural History* 92 (11): 65–79.

Castree, N. 2001. "Socializing Nature: Theory, Practice, and Politics." Pp. 1–21 in N. Castree and B. Braun, eds., *Social Nature: Theory, Practice, and Politics.* Oxford: Blackwell.

Cates, R. 1984. *Joshua Tree National Monument: A Visitor's Guide.* Chatsworth, CA: Live Oak Press.

Catton, T. 1997. *Inhabited Wilderness: Indians, Eskimos, and National Parks in Alaska.* Albuquerque: University of New Mexico Press.

————. 1999. "From Game Refuges to Ecosystem Assessments: Wildlife Management on the Western National Forests." *Journal of the West* 38 (4): 36–44.

Cecil, M. 1997. "Defenders Turns Fifty." *Defenders* 72 (2): 6–17.

Chadwick, D., and J. Sartore. 1995. *The Company We Keep: America's Endangered Species.* Washington, D.C.: National Geographic Society.

Chase, A. 1983. "The Last Bears of Yellowstone." *Atlantic* 252 (2): 63–73.

————. 1986. *Playing God in Yellowstone: The Destruction of America's First National Park.* Boston: Atlantic Monthly Press.

————. 1987. "How to Save Our National Parks." *Atlantic* 260 (1): 35–44.

————. 1988. "A Small Circle of Friends." *Outside* 8 (5): 49–53.

————. 1991. "French Show Not All Greens Are Red." *San Francisco Chronicle,* "This World," Dec. 8.

————. 1995. *In a Dark Wood: The Fight over Forests and the Rising Tyranny of Ecology.* Boston: Houghton Mifflin.

Chase, A., and D. Shore. 1992. "Our National Parks: An Uncommon Guide." *Outside* 16 (2): 52–98.

Chavez, D. 1993. *Mountain Biking: Issues and Actions for USDA Forest Service Managers.* Research Paper RP-226. Albany, CA: Pacific Southwest Research Station, U.S. Forest Service.

————. 1996. *Mountain Biking: Issues and Actions for USDA Forest Service Managers.* Research Paper PSW-RP-226. Albany, CA: Pacific Southwest Research Station, U.S. Forest Service.

Christensen, J. 2000. "Fire and Cheatgrass Conspire to Create a Weedy Wasteland." *High Country News* 32 (10): 8–11.

Christensen, N., et al. 1987. "Final Report: Review of Fire Management Program for Sequoia–Mixed Conifer Forests of Yosemite, Sequoia and Kings Canyon National Parks." San Francisco: National Park Service. Mimeo.

Chubb, M., and H. Chubb. 1981. *One Third of Our Time? An Introduction to Recreation Behavior and Resources.* New York: Wiley.

Clark, T., and A. Harvey. 1988. *Management of the Greater Yellowstone Ecosystem.* Jackson, WY: Northern Rockies Conservation Cooperative.

Clawson, M., and B. Held. 1957. *The Federal Lands: Their Use and Management.* Baltimore: Johns Hopkins University Press.

Clay, J. 1985. "Parks and People." *Cultural Survival Quarterly* 9 (1): 2–5.

————. 1991. "Cultural Survival and Conservation: Lessons from the Past Twenty Years." Pp. 248–73 in M. Oldfield et al., eds., *Biodiversity: Culture, Conservation, and Ecodevelopment.* Boulder, CO: Westview.

Clifford, H. 1997. "After the Fall." *National Parks* 71 (3–4): 34–37.

Coello, D. 1989. "Vicious Cycles?" *Sierra* 74 (3): 50–54.

Cohen, M. 1984. *The Pathless Way: John Muir and American Wilderness.* Madison: University of Wisconsin Press.

————. 1988. *The History of the Sierra Club, 1892–1970.* San Francisco: Sierra Club Books.

Colborn, T., D. Dumanoski, and J. Myers. 1996. "Hormonal Sabotage." *Natural History* 105 (3): 42–49.

Cole, D., A. Watson, and J. Roggenbuck. 1995. *Trends in Wilderness Visitors and Visits: Boundary Waters Canoe Area, Shining Rock, and Desolation Wildernesses.* Research Paper INT-RP-483. Ogden, UT: Intermountain Research Station, U.S. Forest Service.

Collins, B., and E. Russell. 1988. *Protecting the New Jersey Pinelands: A New Direction in Land-Use Management.* New Brunswick: Rutgers University Press.

Conniff, R. 1990. "Once the Secret Domain of Miners and Ranchers, the BLM Is Going Public." *Smithsonian* 21 (6): 30–47.

Conservation Directory. 2001. Washington, D.C.: National Wildlife Federation.

Conservation Foundation. 1985. *National Parks for a New Generation: Visions, Realities, Prospects.* Washington, D.C.

Corn, M., and J. Blodgett. 1988. *Arctic National Wildlife Refuge Controversy: An Overview.* Washington, D.C.: Congressional Research Service.

Cosgrove, D. 1984. *Social Formation and Symbolic Landscape.* London: Croom Helm.

Cosgrove, D., and S. Daniels, eds. 1988. *The Iconography of Landscape: Essays on the Symbolic Representation, Design, and Use of Past Environments.* Cambridge Studies in Historical Geography no. 9. New York: Cambridge University Press.

Costanza, R. 1997. *An Introduction to Ecological Economics.* Boca Raton, FL: St. Lucie Press.

Cox, T. 1983. "The 'Worthless Lands' Thesis: Another Perspective." *Journal of Forest History* 27:144–45.

———. 1988. *The Park Builders: A History of the State Parks in the Pacific Northwest.* Seattle: University of Washington Press.

Cronon, W. 1983. *Changes in the Land.* New York: Hill & Wang.

———. 1995a. "Toward a Conclusion." Pp. 447–59 in W. Cronon, ed., *Uncommon Ground: Toward Reinventing Nature.* New York: Norton.

———. 1995b. "The Trouble with Wilderness; or, Getting Back to the Wrong Nature." Pp. 69–90 in W. Cronon, ed., *Uncommon Ground: Toward Reinventing Nature.* New York: Norton.

Crumpacker, D., S. Hodge, D. Friedley, and W. Gregg. 1988. "A Preliminary Assessment of the Status of Major Terrestrial and Wetland Ecosystems on Federal and Indian Lands in the United States." *Conservation Biology* 2:103–15.

Cunningham, B. 1991. "The Wilderness Wars of the Northern Rockies: Time for a Truce?" *Western Wildlands* 17 (2): 22–28.

Cupper, D. 1993. *Our Priceless Heritage: Pennsylvania State Parks, 1893–1993.* Harrisburg: State of Pennsylvania.

Curry-Lindahl, K. 1974. *The Global Role of National Parks for the World of Tomorrow.* 14th H. M. Albright Conservation Lectureship. Berkeley: School of Forestry, University of California.

Curtin, C. 1993. "The Evolution of the U.S. National Wildlife Refuge System and the Doctrine of Compatibility." *Conservation Biology* 7:30–38.

Curtis, J. 1959. *The Vegetation of Wisconsin.* Madison: University of Wisconsin Press.

Daily, G., ed. 1997. *Nature's Services: Societal Dependence on Natural Ecosystems.* Washington, D.C.: Island Press.

Daley, J., and T. Sohn. 2003. "The O Files." *Outside* 28 (10): 57–72.

Daniel, J. 1990. "On the River of No Return." *Buzzworm* 2 (2): 82–91.

Darlington, D. 1989. "The Pastures of Class-L Heaven." *Sierra* 74 (5): 70–73, 110–13.

Dasmann, R. 1991. "The Importance of Cultural and Biological Diversity." Pp. 7–15 in M. Oldfield et al., eds., *Biodiversity: Culture, Conservation, and Ecodevelopment.* Boulder, CO: Westview.

Davis, J. 1993. "Hey! You! Get Offa My Ground!" *Outside,* October, 28.

Davis, S., J. Ogden, and W. Park, eds. 1994. *Everglades: The Ecosystem and Its Restoration.* Delray Beach, FL: St. Lucie Press.

Davis, T. 2003. "San Diego's Habitat Triage." *High Country News* 35 (21): 9–16.

DeBuys, W. 1985. *Enchantment and Exploitation: The Life and Hard Times of a New Mexico Mountain Range.* Albuquerque: University of New Mexico Press.

DellaSala, D., N. Staus, J. Strittholt, A. Hackman, and A. Iaoobelli. 2001. "An Updated Protected Areas Database for the United States and Canada." *Natural Areas Journal* 21:124–35.

Demars, S. 1991. *The Tourist in Yosemite, 1855–1985.* Salt Lake City: University of Utah Press.

Denevan, W. 1973. "Development and the Imminent Demise of the Amazon Rain Forest." *Professional Geographer* 25:130–35.

———. 1992. "The Pristine Myth: The Landscape of the Americas in 1492." *Annals of the Association of American Geographers* 82:369–85.

DeSimone, P., and D. Silver. 1995. "The Natural Community Conservation Plan: Can It Protect Coastal Sage Scrub?" *Fremontia* 23 (4): 32–36.

Despain, D., D. Houston, M. Meagher, and P. Schullery. 1986. *Wildlife in Transition: Man and Nature on Yellowstone's Northern Range.* Boulder, CO: Roberts Rinehart.

Devall, B., and G. Sessions. 1985. *Deep Ecology: Living as If Nature Mattered.* Salt Lake City: Peregrine Smith.

DeVoto, B. 1943. *The Year of Decision, 1846.* Boston: Little, Brown.

Diamond, J. 1992. "Must We Shoot Deer to Save Nature?" *Natural History* 101 (8): 2–8.

Dilsaver, L. 1987. "Taking Care of the Big Trees." *Focus* 37 (4): 1–8.

———. 1990. "Conservation Conflict and the Founding of Kings Canyon National Park." Pp. 111–19 in R. Orsi, A. Runte, and M. Smith-Baransini, eds., *Yosemite and Sequoia: A Century of California National Parks.* Berkeley: University of California Press.

———. 1992. "Stemming the Flow: The Evolution of Controls on Visitor Numbers and Impact in National Parks." Pp. 235–55 in L. Dilsaver and C. Colten, eds., *The American Environment: Interpretations of Past Geographies.* Lanham, MD: Rowman & Littlefield.

———. 2003. "National Significance: Representation of the West in the National Park System." Pp. 111–32 in G. Hausladen, ed., *Western Places, American Myths: How We Think about the West.* Reno: University of Nevada Press.

———. 2004. *Cumberland Island National Seashore: A History of Conservation Conflict.* Charlottesville: University of Virginia Press.

———, ed. 1994. *America's National Park System: The Critical Documents.* Lanham, MD: Rowman & Littlefield.

Dilsaver, L., and D. Strong. 1990. "Sequoia and Kings Canyon National Parks: One Hundred Years of Preservation and Resource Management." *California History* 69:98–117.

Dilsaver, L., and W. Tweed. 1990. *Challenge of the Big Trees: A Resource History of Sequoia and Kings Canyon National Parks.* Three Rivers, CA: Sequoia Natural History Association.

DiSilvestro, R. 1993. *Reclaiming the Last Wild Places: A New Agenda for Biodiversity.* New York: John Wiley.

Doherty, J. 1992. "When Folks Say 'Cutting Edge' at the Nez, They Don't Mean Saws." *Smithsonian* 23 (6): 32–45.

Doig, I. 1984. *English Creek.* New York: Atheneum.

Dolin, E. 2003. *Smithsonian Book of National Wildlife Refuges.* Washington, D.C.: Smithsonian Institution.

Dolton, G., et al. 1981. *Estimates of Undiscovered Recoverable Resources of Conventionally Producible Oil and Gas in the United States: A Summary.* Open-File Report 81–192. Washington, D.C.: U.S. Geological Survey.

Dombeck, M. 2003. *From Conquest to Conservation: Our Public Lands Legacy.* Washington, D.C.: Island Press.

Doughty, R. 1975. *Feather Fashions and Bird Preservation: A Study in Nature Protection.* Berkeley: University of California Press.

Douglas, M. 1947. *The Everglades: River of Grass.* New York: Rinehart.

Drabelle, D. 1983. "Going It Alone." *Wilderness* 47 (162): 12–15, 22–24.

———. 1994. "'Obey the Law and Tell the Truth': An Interview with Forest Service Chief Jack Ward Thomas." *Wilderness* 58 (206): 29–33.

Ducks Unlimited. N.d. *Birds Mean Business for America.* Memphis.

Duerr, H. 1985. *Dreamtime: Concerning the Boundary between Wilderness and Civilization.* New York: B. Blackwell.

Duncan, J., and N. Duncan. 2001. "The Aestheticization of the Politics of Landscape Preservation." *Annals of the Association of American Geographers* 91:387–409.

Dunlap, R., G. Gallup, and A. Gallup. 1993. *Health of the Planet: Results of a 1992 International Environmental Opinion Survey of Citizens in 24 Nations.* Princeton: George H. Gallup International Institute.

Durbin, K. 1997. "Restoring a Refuge: Cows Depart, but Can Antelope Recover?" *High Country News* 29 (22): 8–11.

———. 2003a. "A Revival on Hart Mountain." *High Country News* 35 (21): 4–5.

———. 2003b. "On a New National Monument, Has an Agency Been Cowed?" *High Country News* 35 (21): 5.

Dwyer, J. 1994. *Customer Diversity and the Future Demand for Outdoor Recreation.* General Technical Report RM-252. St. Paul, MN: Northcentral Forest Experiment Station, U.S. Forest Service.

Edwards, P., and C. Abivardi. 1999. "The Value of Biodiversity: Where Ecology and Economy Blend." *Biological Conservation* 83: 239–46.

Egan, D., and E. Howell. 2001. *The Historical Ecology Handbook: A Restorationist's Guide to Reference Ecosystems.* Washington, D.C.: Island Press.

Egler, F. 1954. "Vegetation Science Concepts. I. Initial Floristic Composition, a Factor in Old-Field Vegetation Development." *Vegetatio* 14:412–17.

Eilers, H. 1985. "Protected Areas and Indigenous Peoples." *Cultural Survival Quarterly* 9 (1): 6–9.

Eiseley, L. 1960. *The Firmament of Time.* New York: Atheneum.

Elliott, G. 1991a. "Whose Land Is It? The Battle for the Great Basin National Park, 1957–1967." *Nevada Historical Society Quarterly* 34:241–56.

————. 1991b. "Senator Alan Bible and the Expansion of the National Park System, 1954–1974." *Nevada Historical Society Quarterly* 34:488–502.

Engel, J. 1983. *Sacred Sands: The Struggle for Community in the Indiana Dunes.* Middletown, CT: Wesleyan University Press.

Evans, S. 1999. *The Green Republic: A Conservation History of Costa Rica.* Austin: University of Texas Press.

Evernden, N. 1985. *Natural Alien: Humankind and Environment.* Toronto: University of Toronto Press.

Fayter, P. 1990. "Senses of the Natural World: Recent Works in the Philosophy and History of Science." *Forest and Conservation History* 34:85–91.

Feld, S., and K. Basso, eds. 1996. *Senses of Place.* Santa Fe, NM: School of American Research Press.

Feldman, T., and A. Jonas. 2000. "Sage Scrub Revolution: Property Rights, Political Fragmentation, and Conservation Planning in Southern California under the Federal Endangered Species Act." *Annals of the Association of American Geographers* 90:256–92.

Ferguson, K. 1985. "A Geography of Environmentalism in the United States." Master's thesis (Geography and Environmental Studies), California State University at Hayward.

Fernside, P. 1989. "Extractive Reserves in Brazilian Amazonia." *Bioscience* 39:387–93.

Fiedler, C. 1992. "New Forestry: Concepts and Applications." *Western Wildlands* 17 (4): 2–7.

Fiedler, P., and S. Jain, eds. 1992. *Conservation Biology: The Theory and Practice of Nature Conservation, Preservation, and Management.* New York: Chapman & Hall.

Findlay, J., and J. White. 1999. *Power and Place in the North American West.* Seattle: University of Washington Press.

Fink, R. 1994. "The National Wildlife Refuges: Theory, Practice, and Prospect." *Harvard Environmental Law Review* 18:1–135.

Fischer, D. 2002. *Early Southwest Ornithologists.* Tucson: University of Arizona Press.

Fischer, H. 1985. "A New Problem in the Old West: Grazing on the Charles M. Russell Wildlife Refuge." *Western Wildlands* 11 (1): 8–11.

Fitzgerald, F. S. 1925/1995. *The Great Gatsby.* New York: Scribner.

Fitzsimmons, A. 1976. "National Parks: The Dilemma of Development." *Science* 191:440–44.

————. 1999. *Defending Illusions: Federal Protection of Ecosystems.* Lanham, MD: Rowman & Littlefield.

Ford, P. 1988. "Now Idaho Wants National Parks." *High Country News* 20 (20): 18–21.

Foreman, D. 2004. *Rewilding North America: A Bold, Hopeful Vision for Conservation in the 21st Century.* Washington, D.C.: Island Press.

Foreman, D., B. Budelby, J. Humphrey, B. Howard, and A. Holdsworth. 2000. "The Elements of a Wildlands Network Conservation Plan: An Example from the Sky Islands." *Wild Earth* 10 (1): 17–30.

Foresta, R. 1984. *American National Parks and Their Keepers.* Washington, D.C.: Resources for the Future.

Forman, R., ed. 2003. *Road Ecology: Science and Solutions.* Washington, D.C.: Island Press.

Foss, P. 1960. *Politics and Grass: The Administration of Grazing on the Public Domain.* Seattle: University of Washington Press.

Fox, S. 1981/1985. *The American Conservation Movement: John Muir and His Legacy.* Madison: University of Wisconsin Press.

———. 1984. "'We Want No Straddlers.'" *Wilderness* 48 (167): 4–19.

———. 2002. "Molded by Mountains." *Sierra* 87 (1): 28–31.

Franklin, J. 1989. "Toward a New Forestry." *American Forests* 95 (11–12): 37–44.

Freemuth, J. 1986. "A Democratic Parks Policy." *Denver Post,* Aug. 2.

———. 1991. *Islands under Siege: National Parks and the Politics of External Threats.* Lawrence: University of Kansas Press.

Frison, G. 1978/1991. *Prehistoric Hunters of the High Plains.* New York: Academic Press.

Frome, M. 1992. *Regreening the National Parks.* Tucson: University of Arizona Press.

Gabriel. T. 1994. "A Death in Navajo Country." *Outside* 18 (5): 78–84, 195–99.

Galtung, J. 1986. "The Green Movement: A Socio-Historical Exploration." *International Sociology* 1:75–90.

Gendlin, F. 1982. "A Talk with Mo Udall." *Sierra* 67 (4): 23–27.

General Accounting Office. 1989. *National Wildlife Refuges: Continuing Problems with Incompatible Uses Call for Bold Action.* Washington, D.C.

Gergely, K., J. Scott, and D. Goble. 2000. "A New Direction for the U.S. National Wildlife Refuges: The National Wildlife Refuge System Improvement Act of 1997." *Natural Areas Journal* 20:107–18.

Ghimire, K., and M. Pimbert, eds. 1997. *Social Change and Conservation.* Washington, D.C.: Island Press.

Gifford, B. 1995. "No, Uh, Cooperation in Defense of Mother Earth." *Outside* 19 (4): 25–26.

Gilbert, B. 1983. "Is This a Holy Place?" *Sports Illustrated,* May 30, 76–90.

———. 1986. "The Nature Conservancy Game." *Sports Illustrated,* October 20, 86–100.

Glover, J. 1986. *A Wilderness Original: The Life of Bob Marshall.* Seattle: Mountaineers.

Gmelch, G. 1990. "Caught in the Middle." *Natural History* 99 (9): 32–37.

Goetzmann, W. 1986. *The West of the Imagination.* New York: Norton.

Goldsmith, E. 1988. "Gaia: Some Implications for Theoretical Ecology." *Ecologist* 18: 64–74.

Gottlieb, R. 1993. *Forcing the Spring: The Transformation of the American Conservation Movement.* Washington, D.C.: Island Press.

Gould, S. 2002. "Baseball's Reliquary: The Oddly Possible Hybrid of Shrine and University." *Natural History* 111 (3): 56–60.

Graber, L. 1976. *Wilderness as Sacred Space.* Monograph Series no. 8. Washington, D.C.: Association of American Geographers.

Graf, W. 1990. *Wilderness Preservation and the Sagebrush Rebellions.* Savage, MD: Rowman & Littlefield.

Graham, F. 1990. *The Audubon Ark: A History of the National Audubon Society.* New York: Knopf.

————. 1991. "Beringia." *Audubon* 91 (7–8): 42–61.

————. 2003. "Where Wildlife Rules." *Audubon* 105 (2): 40–48.

Grayson, D., and D. Meltzer. 2002. "Clovis Hunting and Large Mammal Extinction: A Critical Review of the Evidence." *Journal of World Prehistory* 16:313–59.

————. 2003. "A Requiem for North American Overkill." *Journal of Archaeological Science* 30:585–93.

Greeno, R. 1990. "Who Controls the Bureau of Land Management?" *Journal of Energy, Natural Resources and Environmental Law* 11: 51–67.

Gregg, W. 1991. "MAB Biosphere Reserves and Conservation of Traditional Land Use Systems." Pp. 275–94 in M. Oldfield et al., eds., *Biodiversity: Culture, Conservation, and Ecodevelopment.* Boulder, CO: Westview.

Greider, W. 1987. "The Heart of Everything That Is." *Rolling Stone,* May 7, 37–38.

Griffin, D. 1992. "Land Use Conflict, Landscape Change, and Sustainability in the American West: A Case Study from the Chama Valley of New Mexico." Master's thesis (Geography), University of Wisconsin at Madison.

Grossener, G. 1979. "The Best of Our Land." *National Geographic* 156 (1): 1–2.

Grove, N. 1992. *Preserving Eden: The Nature Conservancy.* New York: Abrams.

Guha, R. 1989. "Radical American Environmentalism and Wilderness Preservation: A Third World Critique." *Environmental Ethics* 11:71–83.

————. 1997. "The Authoritarian Biologist and the Arrogance of Anti-Humanism." *Ecologist* 27:14–20.

Hall, J., et al. 1992. "Valuing the Health Benefits of Clean Air." *Science* 255:812–17.

Hamilton, B. 1989. "Unfinished Business." *Sierra* 74 (5): 48–51, 106–8.

————. 1994. "An Enduring Wilderness." *Sierra* 79 (5): 46–49.

Hammitt, W., and D. Cole. 1987. *Wildland Recreation: Ecology and Management.* New York: John Wiley.

Hampton, D. 1971. *How the U.S. Cavalry Saved Our National Parks.* Bloomington: Indiana University Press.

Hampton, H. 1981. "Opposition to National Parks." *Journal of Forest History* 25:36–45.

Harmon, D., ed. 1989. *Mirror of America: Literary Encounters with the National Parks.* Boulder, CO: Roberts Rinehart.

Harmon, D., and A. Putney, eds. 2003. *The Full Value of Parks: From the Economic to the Intangible.* Lanham, MD: Rowman & Littlefield.

Harrison, C., M. Limb, and J. Burgess. 1987. "Nature in the City—Popular Values for a Living World." *Journal of Environmental Management* 25:347–62.

Hawkes, H. 1960. "The Paradoxes of the Conservation Movement." *Bulletin of the University of Utah* 51:11.

Hays, S. 1959. *Conservation and the Gospel of Efficiency: The Progressive Conservation Movement.* Cambridge: Harvard University Press.

————. 1987. *Beauty, Health, and Permanence: Environmental Politics in the United States, 1955–1985.* New York: Cambridge University Press.

Heal, G. 2000. *Nature and the Marketplace: Capturing the Value of Ecosystem Services.* Washington, D.C.: Island Press.

Hearne, V. 1991. "What's Wrong with Animal Rights." *Harper's* 283 (1696): 59–64.

Hecht, S., and A. Cockburn. 1989. *The Fate of the Forest: Developers, Destroyers, and Defenders of the Amazon.* London: Verso.

Heiman, M. 1996. "Race, Waste, and Class: New Perspectives on Environmental Justice." *Antipode* 28:111–21.

Hendee, J. 1969. "Appreciative versus Consumptive Uses of Wildlife Refuges: Studies of Who Gets What and Trends in Use." *Transactions of the 34th American Wildlife and Natural Resources Conference* 34:252–64.

Hendee, J., et al. 1968. *Wilderness Users in the Pacific Northwest—Their Characteristics, Values, and Management Preferences.* Research Paper PNW-61. Portland, OR: Pacific Northwest Forest and Range Experiment Station, U.S. Forest Service.

Heritage Recreation and Conservation Service. 1979. *The Third Nationwide Outdoor Recreation Plan: The Assessment.* Washington, D.C.: U.S. Department of the Interior.

Herring, S. 2004. *Lines on the Land: Writers, Art, and the National Parks.* Charlottesville: University of Virginia Press.

Herscovici, A. 1985. *Second Nature: The Animal Rights Controversy.* Montreal: CBC Enterprises.

Hess, K. 1993. *Rocky Times in Rocky Mountain National Park: An Unnatural History.* Niwot: University Press of Colorado.

Higgs, E. 2003. *Nature by Design: People, Natural Process, and Ecological Restoration.* Cambridge: MIT Press.

Hinchman, S. 2000. See Marston 2000a.

Hirt, P. 1999. "Creating Wealth by Consuming Place: Timber Management on the Gifford Pinchot National Forest." Pp. 204–32 in J. Findlay and R. White, eds., *Power and Place in the North American West.* Seattle: University of Washington Press.

Hodges, C. 1995. "Mineral Resources, Environmental Issues, and Land Use." *Science* 268:1305–11.

Hoelscher, S. 1998. *Heritage on Stage: The Invention of Ethnic Place in America's Little Switzerland.* Madison: University of Wisconsin Press.

Holstine, C., and R. Bruce. 1991. "A Brief History of Turnbull National Wildlife Refuge." *Pacific Northwest Forum* 4 (2): 23–50.

Holt, H. 1988. "Madness in Yellowstone." *San Francisco Chronicle,* Sept. 17.

Hornsby, S. 1993. "The Gilded Age and the Making of Bar Harbor." *Geographical Review* 83:455–68.

Hummel, D. 1987. *Stealing the National Parks: The Destruction of Concessions and Park Access.* Bellevue, WA: Free Enterprise Press.

Hurley, A. 1995. *Environmental Inequalities: Class, Race, and Industrial Pollution in Gary, Indiana.* Chapel Hill: University of North Carolina Press.

Huth, H. 1948. "Yosemite: The Story of an Idea." *Sierra Club Bulletin* 33 (3): 47–78.

———. 1957. *Nature and the American: Three Centuries of Changing Attitudes.* Berkeley: University of California Press.

Hyde, P. 1957. "The Wilderness World of the Cascades." *Living Wilderness* 22 (60): 9–16.

Iltis, H. 1966/1997. "Whose Is the Fight for Nature?" *Wild Earth* 7 (2): 82–87.

International Crane Foundation. N.d. *Can These Ancient Birds Bring Unity to Man?* Baraboo, WI.

Ise, J. 1961. *Our National Park Policy: A Critical History.* Baltimore: Johns Hopkins University Press.

Iverson, J. 1956. "Forest Clearance in the Stone Age." *Scientific American* 194 (3): 36–41.

Jackson, D. 1987. "The Great Basin Is a Lonely Place for a National Park." *Smithsonian* 18 (8): 68–81.

Jacoby, K. 2001. *Crimes against Nature: Squatters, Poachers, Thieves, and the Hidden History of American Conservation.* Berkeley: University of California Press.

Jameson, J. 1996. *The Story of Big Bend National Park.* Austin: University of Texas Press.

Jansen, D. 2000. "Wildlands as Gardens." *National Parks* 74 (11–12): 50–51.

Jasper, J., and D. Nelkin. 1992. *The Animal Rights Crusade: The Growth of a Moral Protest.* New York: Free Press.

Jenkins, M. 2003. "The Wild Card." *High Country News* 35 (4): 1, 8–12.

———. 2004. "Two Decades of Hard Work, Plowed Under." *High Country News* 36 (1): 7–15.

Johnston, R. 1991. *A Question of Place: Exploring the Practice of Human Geography.* Oxford: Blackwell.

Jones, H. 1965. *John Muir and the Sierra Club.* San Francisco: Sierra Club.

Jones, L. 2000. "He's Worried about Weeds." *High Country News* 32 (10): 12–13.

Jordan, T., and L. Rowntree. 1986. *The Human Mosaic: A Thematic Introduction to Human Geography.* New York: Harper & Row.

Jordan, W. 2003. *The Sunflower Forest: Ecological Restoration and the New Communion with Nature.* Berkeley: University of California Press.

Jordan, W., M. Gilpin, and J. Aber. 1987. *Restoration Ecology: A Synthetic Approach to Ecological Research.* New York: Cambridge University Press.

Judd, R. 1997. *Common Lands, Common People: The Origins of Conservation in Northern New England.* Cambridge: Harvard University Press.

Kahler, K. 1986. "Loving Our Parks to Death." *American Way* (American Airlines magazine) 19 (8): 60–65.

Kane, B. 2000. "Attachment, Change, and Displacement among Winter Recreationists at Snoqualmie Pass." Pp. 65–70 in A. Watson, G. Aplet, and J. Hendee, eds., *Personal, Societal, and Ecological Values of Wilderness: Sixth World Wilderness Congress Proceedings on Research, Management, and Allocation,* vol. 2. Proceedings RMRS-P-14. Ogden, UT: Rocky Mountain Research Station, U.S. Forest Service.

Kareiva, P., and M. Marvier. 2003. "Conserving Biodiversity Hotspots." *American Scientist* 91:344–51.

Kastner, J. 1986. *A World of Watchers.* New York: Knopf.

Kaufman, P. 1996. *National Parks and the Woman's Voice: A History.* Albuquerque: University of New Mexico Press.

Kay, C. 1994. "Aboriginal Overkill: The Role of Native Americans in Structuring Western Ecosystems." *Human Nature* 5:359–98.

Kay, C., and R. Simmons. 2002. *Wilderness and Political Ecology: Aboriginal Influences and the Original State of Nature.* Salt Lake City: University of Utah Press.

Kay, J. 1985. "Native Americans in the Fur Trade and Wildlife Depletion." *Environmental Review* 9:118–27.

Keegan, P. 1996. "This Is Great! . . . : All Rise for Adam Werbach, the Sierra Club's New 23-Year-Old President." *Outside* 20 (9): 69–72, 156–57.

Keiter, R., and M. Boyce, eds. 1991. *The Greater Yellowstone Ecosystem: Redefining America's Wilderness Heritage.* New Haven: Yale University Press.

Keller, R., and M. Turek. 1998. *American Indians and National Parks.* Tucson: University of Arizona Press.

Kellert, S. 1976. "Perceptions of Animals in American Society." *Transactions 41st North American Wildlife Conference* 41:533–45.

———. 1980. "Americans' Attitudes and Knowledge of Animals." *Transactions 45th North American Wildlife and Natural Resources Conference* 45:111–24.

———. 1982a. *Activities of the American Public Relating to Animals: Phase II.* Washington, D.C.: U.S. Fish and Wildlife Service.

———. 1982b. *Public Attitudes toward Critical Wildlife and Natural Habitat Issues: Phase I.* Washington, D.C.: U.S. Fish and Wildlife Service.

———. 1985. "Historical Trends in Perceptions and Uses of Animals in 20th Century America." *Environmental Review* 9:19–33.

———. 1997. *Kinship to Mastery: Biophilia in Human Evolution and Development.* Washington, D.C.: Island Press.

Kellert, S., and J. Berry. 1980. *Knowledge, Affection and Basic Attitudes toward Animals in American Society: Phase III.* Washington, D.C.: U.S. Fish and Wildlife Service.

Kellert, S., and E. Wilson, eds. 1993. *The Biophilia Hypothesis.* Washington, D.C.: Island Press.

Kemmis, D. 2001. *This Sovereign Land: A New Vision for Governing the West.* Washington, D.C.: Island Press.

Kerr, A., and M. Salvo. 2000. "Livestock Grazing in the National Park and Wilderness Preservation Systems." *Wild Earth* 10 (2): 45–52.

Ketchum, R. 1981. "Curatorial Viewpoints and Observations." Pp. 139–44 in R. Cahn, *American Photographers and the National Parks.* New York: Viking.

Kilgore, B., and T. Nichols. 1995. "National Park Service Fire Policies and Programs." Pp. 24–29 in J. Brown et al., eds., *Proceedings: Symposium on Fire in Wilderness and Park Management,* General Technical Report INT-GTR-320. Ogden, UT: U.S. Forest Service, Intermountain Research Station.

Kirk, R. 1999. *Sunrise to Paradise: The Story of Mount Rainier National Park.* Seattle: University of Washington Press.

Kline, B. 2000. *First along the River: A Brief History of the U.S. Environmental Movement.* Lanham, MD: Rowman & Littlefield.

Kling, J. 1997. "Mixed Reviews for Habitat Plan." *Science* 275:749.

Klinkenborg, V. 1995. "Crossing Borders." *Audubon* 97 (5): 34–47.

Knight, R. 1997. "Field Report from the New American West." Pp. 181–200 in C. Meine, ed., *Wallace Stegner and the Continental Vision.* Washington, D.C.: Island Press.

Knox, J. 1995. "Fluvial Systems since 20,000 Years BP." Pp. 87–108 in K. Gregory, L. Starkel, and V. Bakers, eds., *Global Continental Palaeohydrology.* New York: John Wiley.

————. 2001. "Agricultural Influence on Landscape Sensitivity in the Upper Mississippi River Valley." *Catena* 42:193–224.

Knox, M. 1991. "The Rights Stuff." *Buzzworm* 3 (3): 31–37.

Komarek, E. 1971. "Herbert L. Stoddard, Sr." In *Proceedings of the Annual Tall Timber Fire Ecology Conference* 10: n.p.

Koppes, C. 1987. "Efficiency/Equality/Esthetics: Toward a Reinterpretation of American Conservation." *Environmental Review* 11:127–46.

Krakauer, J. 1995. "The Toll You Pay to Enter This Eden Is Sweat, Pain, and Fear." *Smithsonian* 26 (3): 60–71.

————. 1996. *Into the Wild.* New York: Villard.

————. 1997. *Into Thin Air: A Personal Account of the Mount Everest Disaster.* New York: Villard.

Kramer, T. 1991. "Great Basin National Park: Rationales, Concepts, and Conflicts." *Yearbook of the Association of Pacific Coast Geographers* 53:7–34.

Krist, J. 1993. "Reclamation." *Audubon* 95 (4): 66–68.

Kuchler, A. 1964. *Potential Natural Vegetation of the Conterminous United States.* New York: American Geographical Society.

Kusel, J., and E. Adler, eds. 2003. *Forest Communities, Community Forests: Struggles and Successes in Rebuilding Communities and Forests.* Lanham, MD: Rowman & Littlefield.

Kuzmiak, D. 1991. "The American Environmental Movement." *Geographical Journal* 157:265–78.

Ladd, E., and K. Bowman. 1996. "Public Opinion on the Environment." *Resources* (Resources for the Future), no. 124 (Summer), 5–7.

Lambert, D. 1989. *The Underlying Past of Shenandoah National Park.* Boulder, CO: Roberts Rinehart.

Landers, P., and S. Meyer. 1998. *National Wilderness Preservation System Database: Key Attributes and Trends, 1964 through 1998.* General Technical Report RMRS-GTR-18. Ogden, UT: Rocky Mountain Research Station, U.S. Forest Service.

Langston, N. 2003. *Where Land and Water Meet: A Western Landscape Transformed.* Seattle: University of Washington Press.

Larmer, P. 1999. "Is the Grand Staircase–Escalante a Model Monument?" *High Country News* 31 (22): 13–14.

————. 2001. "The Man in the Rubber Boots." *High Country News* 33 (15): 16.

Larson, E. 1999. *Isaac's Storm: A Man, a Time, and the Deadliest Hurricane in History.* New York: Crown.

Laughland, A., and J. Caudill. 1997. *Banking on Nature: The Economic Benefits to Local Communities of National Wildlife Refuge Visitation.* Washington, D.C.: U.S. Fish and Wildlife Service.

Laycock, G. 1965/1973. *The Sign of the Flying Goose: The Story of the National Wildlife Refuges.* Garden City, NY: Doubleday/Anchor.

Leopold, A. 1933. *Game Management.* New York: Scribner's.

————. 1949/1970. *A Sand County Almanac.* New York: Oxford University Press.

Leopold, A. S., et al. 1963. *Study of Wildlife Problems in National Parks: Report of the*

Advisory Board on Wildlife Management, Appointed by Interior Secretary Stewart L. Udall. Washington, D.C.: U.S. Department of the Interior. Reprinted in *Transactions of the North American Wildlife and Natural Resources Conference,* vol. 28. Washington, D.C.: Wildlife Management Institute.

————. 1968. *The National Wildlife Refuge System: Report of the Advisory Committee on Wildlife Management, Appointed by Interior Secretary Stewart L. Udall.* Washington, D.C.: U.S. Department of the Interior. Reprinted in *Transactions of the North American Wildlife and Natural Resources Conference,* vol. 33. Washington, D.C.: Wildlife Management Institute.

Lewis, M. 1992a. *Green Delusions: An Environmentalist Critique of Radical Environmentalism.* Durham: Duke University Press.

————. 1992b. "The Green Threat to Nature." *Harper's* 285 (1710): 26–32.

Ley, D., and J. Duncan. 1993. "Epilogue." Pp. 329–34 in J. Duncan and D. Ley, eds., *Place/Culture/Representation.* London: Routledge.

Lien, C. 1991. *Olympic Battleground: The Power Politics of Timber Preservation.* San Francisco: Sierra Club.

Limerick, P. 1987. *The Legacy of Conquest: The Unbroken Past of the American West.* New York: Norton.

Lindenmayer, D., and J. Franklin, eds. 2003. *Towards Forest Sustainability.* Washington, D.C.: Island Press.

Lipske, M. 1994. "The RARE Art of Promoting Nature by Stirring Pride." *Smithsonian* 25 (2): 84–92.

Little, J. 1998. "A Quiet Victory in Quincy." *High Country News* 30 (21): 4.

Long, B. 2001. "Yellowstone's Last Stampede." *High Country News* 33 (5): 16.

Lopez, B. 1977. *Giving Birth to Thunder, Sleeping with His Daughter: Coyote Builds North America.* Kansas City, KS: Sheed Andrews & McMeel.

————. 1995. "Caring for the Woods." *Audubon* 97 (2): 58–63.

Lovelock, J. 1988. *The Ages of Gaia: A Biography of Our Living Earth.* New York: Norton.

Lowenthal, D. 1959–60. "Nature and the American Creed of Virtue." *Landscape* 9 (2): 24–25.

————. 1962. "Not Every Prospect Pleases: What Is Our Criterion for Scenic Beauty?" *Landscape* 12 (2): 19–23.

————. 1968a. "The American Scene." *Geographical Review* 58:61–88.

————. 1968b. "Daniel Boone Is Dead." *Natural History* 77 (6): 6, 8–10.

————. 2000. *George Perkins Marsh.* Seattle: University of Washington Press.

Lubick, G. 1996. *Petrified Forest National Park: A Wilderness Bound in Time.* Tucson: University of Arizona Press.

Lucas, P. 1990. "A Glasnost-Era Park Is Born." *Natural History* 99 (6): 60–61.

Lucas, R. 1985. *Visitor Characteristics, Attitudes, and Use Patterns in the Bob Marshall Wilderness Complex, 1970–82.* Research Paper INT-345. Ogden, UT: Intermountain Research Station, U.S. Forest Service.

Luoma, J. 1998. "Habitat-Conservation Plans: Compromise or Capitulation?" *Audubon* 100 (1): 36–43.

Luten, D. 1986. *Progress against Growth: Daniel B. Luten on the American Landscape.* Ed. T. Vale. New York: Guilford.

Lyman, R. 1998. *White Goats, White Lies: The Misuse of Science in Olympic National Park.* Salt Lake City: University of Utah Press.

Macinko, G. 1968. "Conservation Trends and the Future American Environment." *Biologist* 50 (1–2): 1–19.

Mackintosh, B. 1985. "Harold L. Ickes and the National Park Service." *Journal of Forest History* 29:78–84.

Maffly, B. 2003. "Where the Antelope (and the Oil Companies) Play." *High Country News* 35 (15): 6–12.

Man and the Biosphere Program. 1990. *Bibliography on the International Network of Biosphere Reserves.* Washington, D.C.: National Technical Information Service.

Mann, C. 1991. "Lynn Margulis: Science's Unruly Earth Mother." *Science* 252:378–81.

Mann, C., and M. Plummer. 1997. "Qualified Thumbs Up for Habitat Plan Science." *Science* 278:2052–53.

Margolis, J. 1997. "With Solitude for All." *Audubon* 99 (4): 46–55, 114–17.

———. 2000a. "Remembering an Establishment Revolutionary." *High Country News* 32 (17): 16.

———. 2000b. "The U.S. Isn't Dead Yet." *High Country News* 32 (8): 16.

Marshall, R. 1956/1970. *Alaska Wilderness: Exploring the Central Brooks Range.* Berkeley: University of California Press.

Marston, E. 1988. "Coming into a New Land." *High Country News* 20 (19): 7–9, 11.

———. 1995. "How the West Won't Be Won." *Audubon* 97 (2): 140.

———. 1997. "The Timber Wars Evolve into a Divisive Attempt at Peace." *High Country News* 29 (18): 1, 8–12.

———. 1999. "A New Road for the Public Lands." *High Country News* 31 (21): 1.

———. 2000a. "Rural Green: A New Shade of Activism." *High Country News* 32 (14): 14–15.

———. 2000b. "Yes, We Need the Rural West." *High Country News* 32 (8): 17.

———. 2001a. "Interior View: Bruce Babbitt Took the Real West to Washington: A High Country News Interview." *High Country News* 33 (3): 8–11.

———. 2001b. "Restoring the Range of Light." *High Country News* 33 (16): 1, 8–14.

Martin, P., and H. Wright. 1967. *Pleistocene Extinctions: The Search for a Cause.* New Haven: Yale University Press.

Martinez, D. 1996. "First People, Firsthand Knowledge." *Sierra* 81 (6): 50–51, 70–71.

Maser, C. 1992. "New Forestry, New Questions: A New Future?" *Western Wildlands* 17 (4): 21–27.

Massey, D. 1994. *Space, Place, and Gender.* Minneapolis: University of Minnesota Press.

Matthews, M. 1997. "Forest Service Acts to Preserve 'The Front.'" *High Country News* 29 (19): 3.

———. 2003a. "Back on the Range?" *High Country News* 35 (13): 4.

———. 2003b. "Timber Companies Borrow a Tool from Environmentalists." *High Country News* 35 (18): 4.

Matthiessen, P. 1959. *Wildlife in America.* New York: Viking.

McArdle, R., and E. Maunder. 1975. "Wilderness Politics: Legislation and Forest Service Policy." *Journal of Forest History* 19:166–79.

McCann, J. 1999. "Before 1492: The Making of the Pre-Columbian Landscape." *Ecological Restoration* 17:15–30, 107–19.

McCool, S., and D. Cole. 1997. *Proceedings—Limits of Acceptable Change and Related Planning Processes: Progress and Future Directions.* General Technical Report INT-GTR-371. Ogden, UT: Intermountain Research Station, U.S. Forest Service.

McGhie, R., J. Scepan, and J. Estes. 1996. "A Comprehensive Managed Areas Spatial Database for the Conterminous United States." *Photogrammetric Engineering and Remote Sensing* 62:1303–6.

McGreevy, P. 1987. "Imagining the Future at Niagara Falls." *Annals of the Association of American Geographers* 77:48–62.

McKibben, B. 1989. *The End of Nature.* New York: Random House.

———. 1995. "An Explosion of Green." *Atlantic Monthly,* April, 61–64.

McKinsey, E. 1985. *Niagara Falls: Icon of the American Sublime.* New York: Cambridge University Press.

McNamee, T. 1992. "Yellowstone's Missing Wolves." *Defenders* 67 (6): 24–31.

McPhee, J. 1971. *Encounters with the Archdruid.* New York: Farrar, Straus & Giroux.

McQuillan, A. 1992. "New Perspectives: Forestry for a Post-Modern Age." *Western Wildlands* 17 (4): 21–27.

McRae, M. 1997. "Is 'Good Wood' Bad for Forests?" *Science* 275:1868–69.

Meagher, M., and D. Houston. 1998. *Yellowstone and the Biology of Time: Photographs across a Century.* Norman: University of Oklahoma Press.

Meine, C. 1988. *Aldo Leopold: His Life and Work.* Madison: University of Wisconsin Press.

Meinig, D. 1979. "The Beholding Eye: Ten Versions of the Same Scene." Pp. 33–48 in D. Meinig, ed., *The Interpretation of Ordinary Landscapes: Geographical Essays.* New York: Oxford University Press.

Melosi, M. 2000. "Environmental Justice, Political Agenda Setting, and the Myths of History." *Journal of Policy History* 12:43–71.

Merenlender, A., L. Huntsinger, G. Guthey, and S. Fairfax. 2004. "Land Trusts and Conservation Easements: Who Is Conserving What for Whom?" *Conservation Biology* 18:65–75.

Merriam, L. 1989. "The Irony of the Bob Marshall Wilderness." *Journal of Forest History* 33:80–87.

Meyer, J. 1996. *The Spirit of Yellowstone: The Cultural Evolution of a National Park.* Lanham, MD: Rowman & Littlefield.

Meyerson, H. 2001. *Nature's Army: When Soldiers Fought for Yosemite.* Lawrence: University of Kansas Press.

Miles, J. 1994. "A Mission to Educate." *National Parks* 68 (3–4): 39–41.

———. 1995. *Guardians of the Parks: A History of the National Parks and Conservation Association.* Washington, D.C.: Taylor & Francis.

Miller, B. 1983. *Estimates of the Portential Petroleum Resources in Wilderness Lands.* Circular 902-A. Washington, D.C.: U.S. Geological Survey.

Mitchell, J. 1977. "To Drill or Not to Drill." *Audubon* 79 (1): 78–85.

———. 1979–80. "Bitter Harvest: Hunting in America." *Audubon* 81 (3): 50–83; 81 (4): 64–81; 81 (5): 88–105; 81 (6): 104–29; 82 (1): 80–107.

———. 1980. "Friend vs. Friend." *Audubon* 82 (3): 36–53.

———. 1985. "In Wildness Was the Preservation of a Smile: An Evocation of Robert Marshall." *Wilderness* 48 (169): 10–21.

———. 2004. "Our Great Estate." *Sierra* 89 (2): 26–35.

Mitchell, R. 1983. *Mountain Experience: The Psychology and Sociology of Experience.* Chicago: University of Chicago Press.

Mitchell, T. 1983. "Behind the Waterfall: An Overview." *Wilderness* 47 (162): 4–11.

Mockler, K. 1999. "Counties Grab for Control of National Forests." *High Country News* 31 (24): 4.

Mohlenbrock, R. 1985. "Hercules Glade, Missouri." *Natural History* 94 (3): 82–85.

———. 1987a. "Dolly Sods, West Virginia." *Natural History* 96 (1): 76–79.

———. 1987b. "Sycamore Canyon, Arizona." *Natural History* 96 (9): 16–18.

———. 1991. "Otter Creek, West Virginia." *Natural History* 100 (5): 74–76.

Montaigne, F. 1998. "All Quiet on the Rocky Mountain Front." *Audubon* 100 (1): 74–76.

Moore, H. 2003. *Shenandoah: Views of Our National Park.* Charlottesville: University of Virginia Press.

Morehouse, B. 1996. *A Place Called Grand Canyon: Contested Geographies.* Tucson: University of Arizona Press.

Morrison, R. 2003a. "Invasion of the Rock Jocks." *High Country News* 35 (13): 10–15.

———. 2003b. "Riding the Middle Path." *High Country News* 35 (23): 6–11.

Muir, J. 1901. *Our National Parks.* Boston: Houghton Mifflin.

———. 1911/1987. *My First Summer in the Sierra.* New York: Penguin.

———. 1912/1962. *The Yosemite.* Garden City, NY: Doubleday/Anchor.

Murray, M. 1990. "Conservation of Tropical Rain Forests: Arguments, Beliefs, and Convictions." *Biological Conservation* 52:17–26.

Myers, N. 1984. *The Primary Source: Tropical Forests and Our Future.* New York: Norton.

———. 1995. "The World's Forests: Need for a Policy Appraisal." *Science* 268:823–24.

Myers, N., and R. Tucker. 1987. "Deforestation in Central America: Spanish Legacy and North American Consumers." *Environmental Review* 11:55–71.

Nabhan, G., and S. Trimble. 1994. *The Geography of Childhood: Why Children Need Wild Places.* Boston: Beacon.

Nash, R. 1967/2001. *Wilderness and the American Mind.* 4th ed. New Haven: Yale University Press.

———. 1989. *The Rights of Nature: A History of Environmental Ethics.* Madison: University of Wisconsin Press.

———, ed. 1968. *The American Environment: Readings in the History of Conservation.* Reading, MA: Addison-Wesley.

———, ed. 1970. *Call of the Wild, 1900–1916.* New York: G. Braziller.

National Association of State Park Directors. 1997. *The 1997 Annual Information Exchange.* Tucson, AZ.

National Atlas of the United States. 1970. Washington, D.C.: Government Printing Office.

National Park Service. 1961. *A Proposed Prairie National Park.* Washington, D.C.

———. 1964. *The Redwoods: A National Opportunity for Conservation and Alternatives for Action.* Washington, D.C.

———. 1972. *The National Park System Plan.* Washington, D.C.

———. 1977. *State Activities.* Vol. 2 of *Preserving Our Heritage.* Washington, D.C.

———. 1980. *State of the Parks.* Washington, D.C.

———. 1982. *Private, Academic, and Local Government Activities.* Vol. 3 of *Preserving Our National Heritage.* Washington, D.C.

———. 1986. *1982–1093 Nationwide Recreation Survey.* Washington, D.C.

———. 1990. *Natural History in the National Park System and on the National Registry of Natural Landmarks.* Washington, D.C.

National Parks Conservation Association. 1988a. "New Parks, New Promise: NPCA's Park Plan." *National Parks* 62 (7–8): 28–30.

———. 1988b. *Park Boundaries: Where We Draw the Line.* Washington, D.C.

———. 1996. *The Economic Importance of National Parks: Effects of the 1995–1996 Government Shutdowns on Selected Park-Dependent Businesses and Communities.* Washington, D.C.

Natural Resources Defense Council. 1995. *Twenty-five Years Defending the Environment.* New York.

Nature Conservancy. 2001. "50 Years of Saving Great Places." *Nature Conservancy* 51 (1): 1–74.

Naughton, J. 1989. "Disputed Land." *Scholastic Update* 121 (May 26): 8–10.

Nelson, R. 1983. *Make Prayers to the Raven: A Koyukon View of the Northern Forest.* Chicago: University of Chicago Press.

Neumann, R. 1998. *Imposing Wilderness: Struggles over Livelihood and Nature Preservation in Africa.* Berkeley: University of California Press.

"New Era in Indian Affairs." 1970. *Time,* Dec. 14, 49.

Nicolson, M. 1959. *Mountain Doom and Mountain Glory.* Ithaca: Cornell University Press.

Nietschmann, B. 1984. "Biosphere Reserves and Traditional Societies." Pp. 499–508 in *Conservation, Science, and Society.* Paris: UNESCO.

Nijhuis, M. 2003. "Change Comes Slowly to Escalante Country." *High Country News* 35 (7): 1, 8–12.

Noss, R., M. O'Connell, and D. Murphy. 1997. *The Science of Conservation Planning: Habitat Conservation under the Endangered Species Act.* Washington, D.C.: Island Press.

Nunes, P., and J. Van den Bergh. 2001. "Economic Valuation of Biodiversity: Sense or Nonsense?" *Ecological Economics* 39:203–22.

Nyerges, A. 1999. *In Praise of Nature: Ansel Adams and Photographers of the American West.* Dayton, OH: Dayton Art Institute.

O'Brien, B. 1999. *Our National Parks and the Search for Sustainability.* Austin: University of Texas Press.

Oelschlaeger, M. 1991. *The Idea of Wilderness: From Prehistory to the Age of Ecology.* New Haven: Yale University Press.

Office of Technology Assessment, U.S. Congress. 1990. *Forest Service Planning: Setting Strategic Direction under EPA.* Washington, D.C.: Government Printing Office.

———. 1992a. *Forest Service Planning: Accommodating Uses, Producing Outputs, and Sustaining Ecosystems.* Washington, D.C.: Government Printing Office.

———. 1992b. *Technologies to Sustain Tropical Forest Resources and Biological Diversity.* Washington, D.C.: Government Printing Office.

Olin, D. 1995. "Shake, Rattle, and Clank." *Outside* 19 (1): 15–16.

Olmsted, F. 1865/1990. *The Papers of Frederick Law Olmsted.* Ed. V. Ranney. Vol. 5, *The California Frontier, 1863–1865.* Baltimore: Johns Hopkins University Press.

Olson, W., and S. Cairns, eds. 1996. *The Sacred Place: Witnessing the Holy in the Physical World.* Salt Lake City: University of Utah Press.

Olwig, K. 1984. *Nature's Ideological Landscape.* London: George Allen & Unwin.

Olwig, K., and K. Olwig. 1979. "Underdevelopment and the Development of 'Natural' Park Ideology." *Antipode* 11 (2): 16–25.

Opie, J. 1987. "Renaissance Origins of the Environmental Crisis." *Environmental Review* 11 (1): 3–17.

O'Riordan, T. 1981. "Environmental Issues." *Progress in Human Geography* 5:393–407.

Orr, O. 1992. *Saving American Birds: T. Gilbert Pearson and the Founding of the Audubon Movement.* Gainesville: University Press of Florida.

Otto, R. 1925. *The Idea of the Holy.* London: Oxford University Press.

Outdoor Recreation Resources Review Commission. 1962a. *Outdoor Recreation for America.* Washington, D.C.

———. 1962b. *List of Public Outdoor Recreation Areas—1960.* Study Report no. 2. Washington, D.C.

———. 1962c. *Wilderness and Recreation—A Report on Resources, Values, and Problems.* Study Report no. 3. Washington, D.C.

Outside. 1994. "Inside the Environmental Groups, 1994." *Outside* 18 (3): 65–73.

———. 1999. "Near to the Ground" and "The Report Card." *Outside* 23 (4): 65–66, 72–80.

Page, J. 1992. "New Mexico's Gray Ranch: The Natural Preserve as Big as All Outdoors." *Smithsonian* 22:30–43.

Parsons, J. 1985. "On 'Bioregionalism' and 'Watershed Consciousness.'" *Professional Geographer* 37:1–6.

Peluso, N. 1993. "Coercing Conservation? The Politics of State Resource Control." *Global Environmental Change* 3 (2): 199–217.

Perrings, C., K. Maler, C. Folke, C. Holling, and B. Jansson, eds. 1995. *Biodiversity Loss: Economic and Ecological Issues.* New York: Cambridge University Press.

Pimentel, D., et al. 1995. "Environmental and Economic Costs of Soil Erosion and Conservation Benefits." *Science* 267:1117–23

Pisani, D. 1977. "Lost Parkland: Lumbering and Park Proposals in the Tahoe-Truckee Basin." *Journal of Forestry* 21:4–17.

Pollan, M. 1991. *Second Nature: A Gardener's Education.* New York: Dell.

Pollan, M., et al. 1990. "Only Man's Presence Can Save Nature." *Harper's* 280 (1679): 37–48.

Poole, D. 1971. "Salyer, John Clark, II." Pp. 281–82 in H. Clepper, ed., *Leaders of American Conservation.* New York: Ronald Press.

Porter, C. 1986. *Eagle's Nest: Natural History and American Ideas, 1812–1842.* University: University of Alabama Press.

Porter, E. 1962. *In Wildness Is the Preservation of the World.* San Francisco: Sierra Club.

————, ed. 1963. *The Place No One Knew: Glen Canyon on the Colorado.* San Francisco: Sierra Club.

Povilitis, T. 1993. "Applying the Biosphere Reserve Concept to a Greater Ecosystem: The San Juan Mountain Area of Colorado and New Mexico." *Natural Areas Journal* 13:18–28.

Price, J. 1995. "Looking for Nature at the Mall: A Field Guide to the Nature Company." Pp. 186–203 in W. Cronon, ed., *Uncommon Ground: Toward Reinventing Nature.* New York: Norton.

Pritchard, P. 1991. "'The Best Idea America Ever Had.'" *National Geographic* 180 (2): 36–59.

Proctor, J., and S. Pincetl. 1996. "Nature and the Reproduction of Endangered Space: The Spotted Owl in the Pacific Northwest and Southern California." *Environment and Planning D: Society and Space* 14:683–708.

Proescholdt, K., R. Rapson, and M. Heinselman. 1995. *Troubled Waters: The Fight for the Boundary Waters Canoe Area Wilderness.* St. Cloud, MN: North Star Press.

Public Land Law Review Commission. 1970. *One Third of the Nation's Land: A Report to the President and to the Congress.* Washington, D.C.: Government Printing Office.

Public Land Statistics. Various years, 1965–99. Washington, D.C.: Bureau of Land Management.

Pyne, S. 1982. *Fire in America: A Cultural History of Wildland and Rural Fire.* Princeton: Princeton University Press.

————. 1998. *How the Canyon Became Grand.* New York: Penguin.

Quammen, D. 1991. "Dirty Word, Clean Place." *Outside* 15 (8): 25–28.

————. 2003. "Saving Africa's Eden." *National Geographic* 204 (3): 50–77.

Quinn, D. 1999. "The Forest Service at a Crossroads." *Resources* (Resources for the Future), no. 137 (Fall), 12–13.

Ray, C. 2003. "Trouble over the Badlands." *High Country News* 35 (15): 4.

Redford, K. 1990. "The Ecologically Noble Savage." *Orion* 9 (3): 24–29.

Redford, K., and S. Sanderson. 2000. "Extracting Humans from Nature." *Conservation Biology* 14:1362–64.

Reed, N., and D. Drabelle. 1984. *The United States Fish and Wildlife Service.* Boulder, CO: Westview.

Reese, A. 2003. "National Preserve in Hot Water." *High Country News* 35 (24): 5.

Reffalt, W., and D. Barry, eds. 1992. "Special Session 8: The Dilemma of the National Wildlife Refuge System." *Transactions of the 57th North American Wildlife and Natural Resources Conference* 57:541–626.

Reiger, J. 1986/2001. *American Sportsmen and the Origins of Conservation.* 3rd ed. Corvallis: Oregon State University Press.

Rettie, D. 1995. *Our National Park System: Caring for America's Greatest Natural and Historic Treasures.* Urbana: University of Illinois Press.

Rice, L. 1987. "America's Unknown Wildlands." *Sierra* 72 (2): 44–53.

Rice, R. 1984. *The Petroleum Potential of Western Wilderness Lands.* Washington, D.C.: Wilderness Society.

Richter, D. 2001. *Facing East from Indian Country: A Native History of Early America.* Cambridge: Harvard University Press.

Ricketts, T., et al. 1999. *Terrestrial Ecoregions of North America: A Conservation Assessment.* Washington, D.C.: Island Press.

Ridenour, J. 1994. *The National Parks Compromised: Pork Barrel Politics and America's Treasures.* Merrillville, IN: ICS Books.

Riordan, P., and P. Bourget. 1985. *World Weather Extremes.* Fort Belvoir, VA: U.S. Army Corps of Engineers.

Robbins, J. 1984. "Do Not Feed the Bears?" *Natural History* 93 (1): 12–21.

Roberson, E. 2001. "Management of Rare Plants under State and Federal Endangered Species Laws: A CNPS Perspective." *Fremontia* 29 (3–4): 5–12.

Robertson, D. 1984. *West of Eden: A History of the Art and Literature of Yosemite.* Berekeley: Wilderness Press.

Robinson, G. 1975. *The Forest Service: A Study in Public Land Management.* Baltimore: Johns Hopkins University Press.

Roggenbuck, J., and R. Lucas. 1987. "Wilderness Use and User Characteristics: A State-of-Knowledge Review." Pp. 204–45 in R. Lucas, ed., *Proceedings—National Wilderness Research Conference: Issues, State-of-Knowledge, Future Directions.* General Technical Report INT-220. Ogden, UT: Intermountain Research Station, U.S. Forest Service.

Roholt, C. 1991. "The Wilderness Act of 1964: Testimony to Resilience." *Western Wildlands* 17 (2): 7–10.

Rolfe, A. 2001. "Understanding the Political Realities of Regional Conservation Planning." *Fremontia* 29 (3–4): 13–18.

Rosenzweig, R., and E. Blackmar. 1992. *The Park and the People: A History of Central Park.* Ithaca: Cornell University Press.

Roth, D. 1984. "The National Forests and the Campaign for Wilderness Legislation." *Journal of Forest History* 28:112–25.

———. 1988. *The Wilderness Movement and the National Forests.* College Station, TX: Intaglio Press.

Rothman, H. 1986. "Second-Class Sites: National Monuments and the Growth of the National Park System." *Environmental Review* 10:44–56.

———. 1989. *Preserving Different Pasts: The American National Monuments.* Urbana: University of Illinois Press.

———. 1992. "The End of Federal Hegemony: The Wilderness Act and Federal Land Management on the Pajarito Plateau, 1955–1980." *Environmental History Review* 16:41–59.

————. 1999. "Tourism as Colonial Economy: Power and Place in Western Tourism." Pp. 177–203 in J. Findlay and R. White, eds., *Power and Place in the North American West*. Seattle: University of Washington Press.

Rudner, R. 1994. "Sacred Geographies." *Wilderness* 58 (206): 10–26.

Runte, A. 1979. *National Parks: The American Experience*. Lincoln: University of Nebraska Press.

————. 1983. "Reply to Sellars." *Journal of Forest History* 27:135–41.

————. 1984. *Trains of Discovery: Western Railroads and the National Parks*. Flagstaff, AZ: Northland.

————. 1988. "The National Parks in Idealism and Reality." *Montana* 38 (3): 75–76.

————. 1991. *Public Lands, Public Heritage: The National Forest Idea*. Niwot, CO: Roberts Rhinehart.

Ryden, H. 1983. "Conflict and Compatibility." *Wilderness* 47 (Fall): 25–31.

Sack, R. 1986. *Human Territoriality: Its Theory and Practice*. New York: Cambridge University Press.

Sax, J. 1976. "America's National Parks: Their Principles, Purposes, and Prospects." *Natural History* 85 (10): 57–88.

————. 1980. *Mountains without Handrails: Reflections on the National Parks*. Ann Arbor: University of Michigan Press.

————. 1982a. "Free Enterprise in the Woods." *Natural History* 91 (6): 14–25.

————. 1982b. "In Search of Past Harmony." *Natural History* 91 (8): 42–51.

————. 1987. "Glacier National Park and Its Neighbors: A Study of Federal Interagency Relations." *Ecological Law Quarterly* 14:207–63.

Scarlett, L., and R. Watson. 2004. "Interior Supports Collaboration." *High Country News* 36 (1): 16.

Schell, O. 1991. "Dispatches from the Tibetan Plateau." *Natural History* 100 (1): 64–66.

Schmitt, P. 1969/1990. *Back to Nature: The Arcadian Myth in Urban America*. New York: Oxford University Press.

Schneider, P. 1997. *The Adirondacks: A History of America's First Wilderness*. New York: Henry Holt.

Schneider, S., and P. Boston, eds. 1991. *Scientists on Gaia*. Cambridge, MA: MIT Press.

Schoonmaker, P., B. Hagen, and E. Wolf, eds. 1997. *The Rain Forests of Home: Profile of a North American Bioregion*. Washington, D.C.: Island Press.

Schrepfer, S. 1976. "Perspectives on Conservation: Sierra Club Strategies in Mineral King." *Journal of Forest History* 20 (4): 176–90.

————. 1980. "Conflict in Preservation: The Sierra Club, Save-the-Redwoods League, and Redwood National Park." *Journal of Forest History* 24 (2): 60–77.

————. 1983. *The Fight to Save the Redwoods: A History of Environmental Reform, 1917–1978*. Madison: University of Wisconsin Press.

————. 1992. "The Nuclear Crucible: Diablo Canyon and the Transformation of the Sierra Club, 1965–1985." *California History* 61:212–37.

Schuh, J. 1966. "Hawaiian Land Tenure and the Proposed Kauai National Park." Master's thesis (Geography), University of California, Berkeley.

Schuler, J. 1989. *A Revelation Called the Badlands: Building a National Park, 1909–1939.* Interior, SD: Badlands Natural History Association.

Schullery, P. 1986. "Drawing the Lines in Yellowstone: The American Bison as Symbol and Scourge." *Orion* 5 (4): 33–45.

———. 1991. "The Service of the Parks." Pp. 1–21 in W. Sontag and L. Griffin, eds., *The National Park Service: A Seventy-fifth Anniversary Album.* Boulder, CO: Roberts Rinehart.

———. 1997. *Searching for Yellowstone: Ecology and Wonder in the Last Wilderness.* Boston: Houghton Mifflin.

Schwartzman, S., A. Moreira, and D. Nepstad. 2000. "Rethinking Tropical Forest Conservation: Perils in Parks." *Conservation Biology* 14:1351–57.

Scott, D. 1984. "The National Wilderness Preservation System: Its Place in Natural Area Protection." *Natural Areas Journal* 4:6–19.

Scott, J., et al. 1993. *Gap Analysis: A Geographic Approach to Protection of Biological Diversity.* Bethesda, MD: Wildlife Society.

Searle, R. 1978. "Autos or Canoes? Wilderness Controversy in the Superior National Forest." *Journal of Forest History* 22 (2): 68–77.

Sedjo, R., ed. 2000. *A Vision for the U.S. Forest Service: Goals for Its Next Century.* Baltimore: Resources for the Future.

Sellars, R. 1983. "National Parks: Worthless Lands or Competing Land Values." *Journal of Forest History* 27:130–34.

———. 1997. *Preserving Nature in the National Parks: A History.* New Haven: Yale University Press.

Shabecoff, P. 2000. *Earth Rising: American Environmentalism in the 21st Century.* Washington, D.C.: Island Press.

Shaver, D., and J. Wood. 2001. "Geology in the National Park Service." *Geotimes,* April, 14–15, 17.

Shelton, J. 1966. *Geology Illustrated.* San Francisco: W. H. Freeman.

Shelton, M. 1990. "Surface-Water Flow to Everglades National Park." *Geographical Review* 80:355–69.

Shepard, P. 1967. *Man in the Landscape: A Historic View of the Esthetics of Nature.* New York: Knopf.

Shore, D. 1994. "Badlands." *Outside* 18 (7): 56–71.

Short, J. 1991. *Imagined Country: Environment, Culture, and Society.* London: Routledge.

Shrake, E. 1970. "The Matter of Indian Giving." *Sports Illustrated,* May 17, 42–44.

Sides, H. 1996. "And the Bureaucrats Said: Let There Be High Water." *Outside* 20 (7): 38–43, 104–6.

Siebert, C. 1993. "The Artifice of the Natural: How TV's Nature Shows Make All the Earth a Stage." *Harper's* 286 (1713): 43–51.

Sierra Club. 1989. *The Sierra Club: A Guide.* San Francisco.

———. 1992. "A Centennial Celebration, 1892–1992." *Sierra* 77 (3): 52–73.

———. 1995. "Celebrate Earth Day." *Muir View* (newsletter of John Muir Chapter, Wisconsin) 33 (2): 5.

———. 1996. "Native Americans and the Environment." *Sierra* 81 (6).

———. 1997. "Four-Lakes Group Asks You to Oppose Measure on Population Change." *Four Lakes Sierran,* December, 4.

———. 1998. *Letter to Members on Immigration Policy in the United States.* San Francisco.

Simon, D. 1988. "New Parks: New Promise—NPCA's Park Plan." *National Parks* 62 (7–8): 28–30.

Simonian, L. 1995. *Defending the Land of the Jaguar: A History of Conservation in Mexico.* Austin: University of Texas Press.

Skow, J. 1999. "Scorching the Earth to Save It." *Outside* 23 (4): 66–71.

Smith, C. 1995. "What Happened Out Here?" *Outside* 19 (6): 27–28.

Smith, J. 1997. "Evangelical Christians Preach a Green Gospel." *High Country News* 29 (4): 1, 8–12.

Smith, M. 2001. *An Ethics of Place: Radical Ecology, Postmodernity, and Social Theory.* Albany: State University of New York Press.

Smythe, W. 1900/1969. *The Conquest of Arid America.* Seattle: University of Washington Press.

Soule, M., and G. Lease, eds. 1995. *Reinventing Nature? Responses to Postmodern Deconstruction.* Washington, D.C.: Island Press.

Soule, M., and G. Orians. 2001. *Conservation Biology: Research Priorities for the Next Decade.* Washington, D.C.: Island Press.

Soule, M., and B. Wilcox, eds. 1980. *Conservation Biology: An Evolutionary-Ecological Perspective.* Sunderland, MA: Sinauer Associates.

Spence, M. 1996. "Crown of the Continent, Backbone of the World: The American Wilderness Ideal and Blackfeet Exclusion from Glacier National Park." *Environmental History* 1(3): 29–49.

———. 2000. *Dispossessing the Wilderness: Indian Removal and the Making of the National Parks.* New York: Oxford University Press.

Spencer, R., et al. 1965. *The Native Americans.* New York: Harper & Row.

Speth, W. 1977. "Carl Ortwin Sauer on Destructive Exploitation." *Biological Conservation* 11:145–60.

Spurr, S. 1966. *Wilderness Management.* Horace M. Albright Conservation Lectureship 6. Berkeley: School of Forestry, University of California.

Stankey, G. 1973. *Visitor Perception of Wilderness Recreation Carrying Capacity.* Research Paper INT-142. Ogden, UT: Intermountain Forest and Range Experiment Station, U.S. Forest Service.

Starrs, P. 1994. "'Cattle Free by '93' and the Imperatives of Environmental Radicalism." *Ubique* (American Geographical Society) 14 (1): 1–4.

Statistical Abstract of the United States. Annual. Washington, D.C.: Government Printing Office.

Steely, J. 1999. *Parks for Texas: Enduring Landscapes of the New Deal.* Austin: University of Texas Press.

Stegner, W. 1955. *This Is Dinosaur: Echo Park Country and Its Magic Rivers.* New York: Knopf.

———. 1977. "Introduction." Pp. vii–xiii in C. Dutton, *Tertiary History of the Grand*

Canyon District. Santa Barbara, CA: Peregrine Smith. Reprint of 1882 monograph of U.S. Geological Survey.

————. 1983. "The Best Idea We Ever Had." *Wilderness* 46 (160): 4–13.

————. 1985. "Living on Our Principal." *Wilderness* 48 (168): 15–21.

————. 1990. "It All Began with Conservation." *Smithsonian* 21 (1) 35–43.

Steinbeck, J. 1962. *Travels with Charley: In Search of America*. New York: Viking.

Steinhart, P. 1988. "Place as Purpose: Muir's Sierra." *Orion* 7 (4): 43–49.

————. 1990. "Replanting the Forest." *Audubon* 92 (2): 26–29.

Stevens, S. 1997. *Conservation through Cultural Survival: Indigenous Peoples and Protected Areas*. Washington, D.C.: Island Press.

Stevens, W. 1992. "Novel Strategy Puts People at Heart of Texas Preserve." *New York Times*, Mar. 31, B5.

————. 1994. "Latest Threat to Yellowstone: Admirers Are Loving It to Death." *New York Times*, Sept. 13.

Stewart, G. 1951/1971. *Sheep Rock*. New York: Ballantine.

Stohlgren, T., and J. Quinn. 1992. "An Assessment of Biotic Inventories in Western U.S. National Parks." *Natural Areas Journal* 12:145–54.

Stone, E. 1965. "Preserving Vegetation in Parks and Wilderness." *Science* 150:1261–67.

Stottlemyer, J. 1981. "Evolution of Management Policy and Research in the National Parks." *Journal of Forestry* 79:16–20.

Strickland, D. 1981. "The Eskimo vs. the Walrus vs. the Government." *Natural History* 90 (2): 48–57.

Strong, D. 1984. *Tahoe: An Environmental History*. Lincoln: University of Nebraska Press.

Stubbendieck, J., and G. Willson. 1987. "Prairie Resources of National Park Units in the Great Plains." *Natural Areas Journal* 7:100–106.

Stuebner, S. 1999. "Go Tell It on the Mountain: Babbitt's Conservation Legacy Starts Here." *High Country News* 31 (22): 1, 8–12.

Sturgeon, N. 1997. Review of C. Merchant, *Earthcare: Women and the Environment*. *Environmental History* 2:366–67.

Sullivan, R. 1997. "Dark Behind It . . . " *Outside* 21 (7): 62–73, 141–43.

Sutter, P. 1998. "'A Blank Spot on the Map': Aldo Leopold, Wilderness, and U.S. Forest Service Recreation Policy, 1909–1924." *Western Historical Quarterly* 29:187–214.

————. 1999. "'A Retreat from Profit': Colonization, the Appalachian Trail, and the Social Roots of Benton MacKaye's Wilderness Advocacy." *Environmental History* 4:553–77.

————. 2002. *Driven Wild: How the Fight against the Automobile Launched the Modern Wilderness Movement*. Seattle: University of Washington Press.

Swanson, G., et al. 1969. *Fish and Wildlife Resources on the Public Lands*. Washington, D.C.: U.S. Department of Commerce, National Bureau of Standards.

Taylor, B. 1995. *Ecological Resistance Movements: The Global Emergence of Radical and Popular Environmentalism*. Albany: State University of New York Press.

Taylor, J. 1979. "Tree Worship." *Mankind Quarterly* 20:79–141.

Terborgh, J. 2000. "The Fate of Tropical Forests: A Matter of Stewardship." *Conservation Biology* 14:1358–61.

Terrie, P. 1997. *Contested Terrain: A New History of Nature and People in the Adirondacks.* Syracuse: Syracuse University Press.

Thompson, T. 1994. "Give Me Your Birders, Your Paddlers, Your Huddled Masses . . . " *Outside* 18 (9): 68–77, 148–49.

Thorsell, J. 1990. "Through Hot and Cold Wars, Parks Endure." *Natural History* 99 (6): 54–59.

Tilden, F. 1951. *The National Parks: What They Mean to You and Me.* New York: Knopf.

Tober, J. 1981. *Who Owns the Wildlife: The Political Economy of Conservation in Nineteenth-Century America.* Westport, CT: Greenwood Press.

Tobin, M. 2003. "Management Presents a Management Morass." *High Country News* 35 (7): 11.

Trefethen, J. 1966. "Wildlife Regulation and Restoration." Pp. 16–37 in H. Clepper, ed., *Origins of American Conservation.* New York: Ronald Press.

———. 1975. *An American Crusade for Wildlife.* New York: Winchester Press.

Trimble, S. 1989. *The Sagebrush Ocean: A Natural History of the Great Basin.* Reno: University of Nevada Press.

Truettner, W. 1991. *The West as America: Reinterpreting Images of the Frontier, 1820–1920.* Washington, D.C.: Smithsonian Institution.

Tuan, Y.-F. 1970. "Our Treatment of Environment in Ideal and Actuality." *American Scientist* 58:244–49.

———. 1971. "Man and Nature." Resource Paper no. 10. Washington, D.C.: Association of American Geographers.

———. 1974. *Topophilia.* Englewood Cliffs, NJ: Prentice-Hall.

———. 1977. *Space and Place: The Perspective of Experience.* Minneapolis: University of Minnesota Press.

———. 1979. "Space and Place: Humanistic Perspective." Pp. 387–427 in S. Gale and G. Olsson, eds., *Philosophy in Geography.* Boston: D. Reidel.

Tucker, W. 1982. *Progress and Privilege: America in the Age of Environmentalism.* Garden City, NY: Doubleday/Anchor.

Turner, F. 1985. "Cultivating the American Garden." *Harper's* 271 (1623): 45–52.

Turner, F., and S. Gregory. 1990. "Forum: Only Man's Presence Can Save Nature." *Harper's* 280 (1679): 37–48.

———. 1997a. "No Surrender." *Outside* 21 (8): 49–54, 118–20.

———. 1997b. "Oh, Wilderness." *Outside* 21 (4): 64–70, 152–57.

Turner, F. J. 1920. *The Frontier in American History.* New York: Henry Holt.

Turner, N. 1997. "Traditional Ecological Knowledge." Pp. 275–98 in P. Schoonmaker et al., eds., *The Rain Forests of Home: Profile of a North American Bioregion.* Washington, D.C.: Island Press.

Turner, T. 1990. "Who Speaks for the Future?" *Sierra* 75 (4): 30–39, 67–72.

Tweit, S. 2000. "The (Next) Spotted Owl." *Audubon* 102 (6): 64–70.

Twight, B. 1983. *Organizational Values and Political Power: The Forest Service versus the Olympic National Park.* University Park: Pennyslvania State University Press.

U.S. Fish and Wildlife Service. N.d. *Seney National Wildlife Refuge.* Washington, D.C.: Government Printing Office.

———. 1979. *Final Recommendations on the Management of the National Wildlife Refuge System.* Washington, D.C.

———. 1998. *National and State Economic Impacts of Wildlife Watching.* Arlington, VA.

U.S. Forest Service. 1978. *RARE II: Draft Environmental Statement, Roadless Area Review and Evaluation.* Washington, D.C.

Utley, R. 1983. "Commentary on the 'Worthless Lands' Thesis." *Journal of Forest History* 27:142.

Vale, T. 1970. "Objectivity, Values, and the Redwoods." *Landscape* 19 (1): 30–33.

———. 1974a. "Conservation Strategies in the Redwoods." *Yearbook of the Association of Pacific Coast Geographers* 36:103–12.

———. 1974b. "Sagebrush Conversion Projects: An Element of Contemporary Environmental Change in the Western United States." *Biological Conservation* 6:274–84.

———. 1977. "Forest Changes in the Warner Mountain, California." *Annals of the Association of American Geographers* 67:28–45.

———. 1979a. "New Landscape Reserves in Alaska." *Environmental Conservation* 6:147–48.

———. 1979b. "Use of Public Rangelands in the American West." *Environmental Conservation* 6:53–62.

———. 1982. *Plants and People: Vegetation Change in North America.* Washington, D.C.: Association of American Geographers.

———. 1987. "Vegetation Change and Park Purposes in the High Elevations of Yosemite National Park, California." *Annals of the Association of American Geographers* 77:1–18.

———. 1988. "No Romantic Landscapes for Our National Parks?" *Natural Areas Journal* 8:115–17.

———. 1995. "Mountains and Moisture in the West." Pp. 141–65 in W. Wyckoff and L. Dilsaver, eds., *The Mountainous West: Explorations in Historical Geography.* Lincoln: University of Nebraska Press.

———. 1997. "Nature and People in the American West: Guidance from Wallace Stegner's Sense of Place." Pp. 163–79 in C. Meine, ed., *Wallace Stegner and the Continental Vision: Critical Essays and Commentary.* Washington, D.C.: Island Press.

———. 1998. "John Muir, Aldo Leopold, Wallace Stegner: Three Wisconsinites, Three Connected Lives." *Wisconsin Academy Review* 44 (4): 18–21.

———. 2002. "From Frederick Clements and William Morris Davis to Stephen Jay Gould and Daniel Botkin: Ideals of Progress in Physical Geography." In R. Sack, ed., *Progress: Geographical Essays.* Baltimore: Johns Hopkins University Press.

———, ed. 2002. *Fire, Native Peoples, and the Natural Landscape.* Washington, D.C.: Island Press.

Vale, T., and G. Vale. 1984. *U.S. 40 Today: Thirty Years of Landscape Change in America.* Madison: University of Wisconsin Press.

———. 1989. *Western Images, Western Landscapes: Travels along U.S. 89.* Tucson: University of Arizona Press.

———. 1994. *Time and the Tuolumne Landscape: Continuity and Change in the Yosemite High Country.* Salt Lake City: University of Utah Press.

———. 1998. *Walking with Muir across Yosemite.* Madison: University of Wisconsin Press.

Vest, J. 1985. "Will-of-the-Land: Wilderness among Primal Indo-Europeans." *Environmental Review* 9:323–29.

Vogel, G. 1997. "The Pentagon Steps Up the Battle to Save Biodiversity." *Science* 275:20.

Vollmann, W., C. Bowden, and C. Vetter. 1993. "Postcards from over the Edge." *Outside* 17 (3): 71–81, 168.

Voynick, S. 1987. "Shale Shock on the Western Slope." *Sierra* 72 (3): 29–31.

Walker, R. 1989. "Geography from the Left." Pp. 619–50 in G. Gaile and C. Willmott, eds., *Geography in America.* Columbus, OH: Merrill.

Walker, R., and M. Heiman. 1981. "Quiet Revolution for Whom?" *Annals of the Association of American Geographers* 71:67–83.

Wallace, D. 1992. *The Quetzal and the Macaw.* San Francisco: Sierra Club.

Wallach, B. 1988. "Taking Heart from Upper East Tennessee." *Focus* 38 (4): 22–27.

———. 1991. *At Odds with Progress: Americans and Conservation.* Tucson: University of Arizona Press.

Waller, D. 1998. "Getting Back to the Right Nature: A Reply to Cronon's 'The Trouble with Wilderness.'" Pp. 540–567 in J. Callicott and M. Nelson, eds., *The Great New Wilderness Debate.* Athens: University of Georgia Press.

Walter, J. 1983. "'You'll Love the Rockies.'" *Landscape* 27 (2): 43–47.

Warren, L. 1997. *The Hunter's Game: Poachers and Conservationists in Twentieth-Century America.* New Haven: Yale University Press.

Watkins, T. 1983. "Islands of Life." *Wilderness* 47 (162): 3.

———. 1994a. "The Hundred-Million-Acre Understanding." *Audubon* 96 (5): 36–38, 106.

———. 1994b. "Sustainable Ideas." *Wilderness* 58 (207): 9.

———. 1997. "National Parks, National Paradox." *Audubon* 99 (4): 40–45.

Watson, A., M. Niccolucci, and D. Williams. 1993. *Hikers and Recreational Stock Users: Predicting and Managing Recreation Conflicts in Three Wildernesses.* Research Paper INT-468. Ogden, UT: Intermountain Research Station, U.S. Forest Service.

Watson, T. 2000. "New Mining Rules Protect Federal Lands." *U.S. Today,* Nov. 22, 17A.

Watts, M. 1983. *Silent Violence: Food, Famine, and Peasantry in Northern Nigeria.* Berkeley: University of California Press.

Weisman, A. 1993. "Paradise Sold." Pp. 8–10 in "This World," *San Francisco Chronicle,* May 9.

Wellner, A. 1997. *Americans at Play: Demographics of Outdoor Recreation and Travel: Report from the 1994–95 National Survey on Recreation and the Environment.* Washington, D.C.: U.S. Forest Service.

West, R. 1989. "Gaia: She's Alive: A Conversation with James Lovelock." *Orion* 8 (1): 58–64.

Western, D., and M. Pearl, eds. 1989. *Conservation for the Twenty-first Century.* New York: Oxford University Press.

Western, D., and R. Wright, eds. 1994. *Natural Connections: Perspectives in Community-Based Conservation.* Washington, D.C.: Island Press.

Westmann, W., and R. Gifford. 1973. "Environmental Impact: Controlling the Overall Level." *Science* 181:819–25.

Wheelright, J. 1995. "Atomic Overreaction." *Atlantic* 275 (4): 26–38.

White, P., and S. Bratton. 1980. "After Preservation: Philosophical and Practical Problems of Change." *Biological Conservation* 18:241–55.

White, R. 1985. "Introduction: American Indians and the Environment." *Environmental Review* 9:101–3.

———. 1991. *The Middle Ground: Indians, Empires, and Republics in the Great Lakes Region.* New York: Cambridge University Press.

———. 1995. "'Are You an Environmentalist or Do You Work for a Living?': Work and Nature." Pp. 171–85 in W. Cronon, ed., *Uncommon Ground: Toward Reinventing Nature.* New York: Norton.

Whitson, P. 1974. *The Impact of Human Use upon the Chisos Basin and Adjacent Lands.* National Park Service Scientific Monographic no. 4. Washington, D.C.: National Park Service.

Whittlesey, L. 1995. *Death in Yellowstone: Accidents and Foolheardiness in the First National Park.* Boulder, CO: Roberts Rinehart.

Wilcove, D. 1999. *The Condor's Shadow: The Loss and Recovery of Wildlife in America.* New York: W. H. Freeman.

Wilderness Society. N.d. *Celebrating the American Earth: A Tribute to Ansel Adams.* Washington, D.C.

———. 1935. "A Summons to Save the Wilderness." *Living Wilderness* 1 (1): 1.

———. 1954. "Three Sisters Wilderness." *Living Wilderness* 19 (50): 42–45.

———. 1983. "Toward the Twenty-first Century: A Wilderness Society Agenda for the Wildlife Refuges." *Wilderness* 47 (162): 32–38.

———. 1984. "Toward the Twenty-first Century." *Wilderness* 48 (165): 34–39.

———. 1989a. *America's Imperiled Coastal Parks.* Washington, D.C.

———. 1989b. "Special Report—Wilderness America: A Vision for the Future of the Nation's Wildlands." *Wilderness* 52 (184) 1–65.

———. 1997. "Special Places for Wildlife." *Wilderness America* 2 (2): 1–2.

Wilkinson, C. 1992. *Crossing the Next Meridian: Land, Water, and the Future of the West.* Washington, D.C.: Island Press.

Wilkinson, T. 1993. "Ancestral Lands." *National Parks* 67 (7–8): 30–35.

———. 1998. "Forest Service Seeks a New (Roadless) Road to the Future." *High Country News* 30 (8): 8–11, 14–16.

Williams, F. 1994. "On the Borderline: A Bleak, Flat, Grim, Hot, Gritty and Wondrous Desert." *High Country News* 26 (5): 1, 10–13.

Williams, T. 1991. "The Dirty Dozens." *Fly Rod and Reel,* April, 56–60.

———. 1996a. "A Bedrock Democracy." *Audubon* 98 (3): 120.

———. 1996b. "Seeking Refuge." *Audubon* 98 (3): 34–45, 90–94.

———. 2000. "Clinton's Last Stand." *Audubon* 102 (3): 46–49, 90–97.

Wilson, E. 1984. *Biophilia.* Cambridge: Harvard University Press.

———. 1994. *Naturalist*. Washington, D.C.: Island Press.

Winks, R. 1983. "Upon Reading Sellars and Runte." *Journal of Forest History* 27:142–43.

———. 1995. "Debating Significance." *National Parks* 69 (3–4): 24–25.

———. 1996. "Dispelling the Myth." *National Parks* 70 (7–8): 52–53.

Wirth, C. 1980. "Working with Conservationists: Reflections of a National Park Service Director." *Journal of Forest History* 24 (3): 152–55.

Wolf, T. 1990. "The New Historians Attack the Frontier." *High Country News* 22 (1): 14.

Wolkomir, R. 1994. "Hot on the Trail of Toxic Dumpers and Other Eco-Outlaws." *Smithsonian* 25 (5): 26–32.

World Resources Institute. 1994. *World Resources: 1994–95*. Washington, D.C.

———. 1998. *World Resources: 1998–99*. Washington, D.C.

Worster, D. 1986. *Rivers of Empire: Water, Aridity, and the Growth of the American West*. New York: Pantheon.

———. 1987. "The Vulnerable Earth: Toward a Planetary History." *Environmental History* 11:87–103.

———. 1992. *Under Western Skies: Nature and History in the American West*. New York: Oxford University Press.

———. 1994. *An Unsettled Country: Changing Landscapes of the American West*. Albuquerque: University of New Mexico Press.

———. 1997. "The Wilderness of History." *Wild Earth* 7 (3): 9–13.

Wright, J. 1993. *Rocky Mountain Divide: Selling and Saving the West*. Austin: University of Texas Press.

———. 1997. "Hispano Forestry: Land Grants and the U.S. Forest Service in Northern New Mexico." *Focus* 44 (1): 10–14.

Wuerthner, G. 1990a. "Managing the 'Bob.'" *Wilderness* 53 (188): 44–51.

———. 1990b. "The Price Is Wrong." *Sierra* 75 (5): 38–43.

———. 1991. "How the West Was Eaten." *Wilderness* 54 (192): 28–37.

Yapa, L. 1996. "Improved Seeds and Constructed Society." Pp. 69–85 in R. Peet and M. Watts, eds., *Liberation Ecologies: Environment, Development, Social Movements*. London: Routledge.

Yochim, M. 2001a. "The Recent Winter Use History of Yellowstone National Park: How Should the National Park Service Envision Its Dual Mission?" *Annals of Wyoming* 73:33–46.

———. 2001b. "Aboriginal Overkill Overstated: Errors in Charles Kay's Hypothesis." *Human Nature* 12:141–67.

———. 2003a. "Beauty and the Beet: The Dam Battles of Yellowstone National Park." *Montana* 53:14–27.

———. 2003b. "Snow Machines in the Gardens: The History of Snowmobiles in Glacier and Yellowstone National Parks." *Montana* 54:2–14.

Young, J. 1989. *State Parks of Utah: A Guide and History*. Salt Lake City: University of Utah Press.

Young, R. 1985. *Darwin's Metaphor: Nature's Place in Victorian Culture*. New York: Cambridge University Press.

Zapf, C. 1995. "Celebrate Earth Day." *Muir View* (Sierra Club, Wisconsin Chapter) 33 (2): 5.

Zaslowsky, D. 1983. "The 'Black Cavalry of Commerce.'" *Wilderness* 46:25–32.

Zaslowsky, D., and T. Watkins. 1994. *These American Lands.* 2nd ed. Washington, D.C.: Wilderness Society.

Zbicz, D., and M. Green. 1997. "Status of the World's Transfrontier Protected Areas." *Parks* 7 (3): 5–10.

Zerner, C., ed. 2000. *People, Plants, and Justice: The Politics of Nature Conservation.* New York: Columbia University Press.

Zielenziger, M. 1987. "Wilderness Drilling Battle Looms." *Wisconsin State Journal,* Sept. 6, 1987.

Zimmerer, K. 2000. "The Reworking of Conservation Geographies: Nonequilbrium Landscapes and Nature-Society Hybrids." *Annals of the Association of American Geographers* 90:356–69.

Zimmerer, K., R. Gall, and M. Buck. Forthcoming. "The Worldwide Coverage of Protected Areas (1980–2000) and Globalization Trends: An Overall Assessment."

INDEX